the delegat...
for a short period...
rather surprised at his...
a Press man', with the Press...
a Press man' into this state or mid...
his himself into John Nicoll, tha...
en, such as John Nicoll.
e says, at his inadequacies.
and even lazy tho' he may
judge of many situations.
I got home in time to see a few.
splendid but just — as ponderous and b...
think I would have stayed the whole co...
down to the station to meet Anne and Jane o...
had been in Stepney to hear Ben singing in...
well, and I came on looking very busi...

18 December, Friday
Went to the surgery at 9 as my neck sho...
long wait for Kirkham as other patients o...
room at high speed on their way to lis...
the same complaint, and had been fo...
for an appointment at the Orthopaedi...
much hope of a quick cure.
A contingent from PA came in a...
substance to discuss, in fact. Earl...
High Wycombe plant and asked...
machine minutes. I suggested th...
with GBT as to his estimate t...
of the reduction we had t...
To the Randolph after lun...
next Tuesday's managem...
the new web offset p...

at
y
all.
speak,
things.
forment.
rious moment
e of its purity.
is not now

contemporary of
exactly the
and

DIARY OF A MASTER PRINTER

Vivian Ridler as Printer to the University in his office at the Walton Street premises of the Press; he holds the Coronation Bible which he had designed. See also plate 4.

Vivian Ridler

DIARY OF A MASTER PRINTER

*A Year in the Life of the
Printer to the University, Oxford*

EDITED AND INTRODUCED BY
Colin Ridler

THE PERPETUA PRESS
OXFORD

EDITOR'S NOTE

I wish to thank Oxford University Press for its
assistance in the creation of this book. I am most grateful to
Penny Hutchings of the OUP Archive for her considerable help
in typing up the extensive handwritten original of this diary, and
to the Press Archivist, Martin Maw, for his support in very many
ways – not least reading and checking the complete typescript, as
well as tracking down photographs in the OUP Archive. Mrs Tracey
Salt also assisted greatly in preparing the final version of the whole
typescript. My old friend Edward Wates, who now has charge of
the Perpetua Press imprint, has been kind enough to allow me to
use it for this publication, and has given me the benefit of his long
production experience. Advice and practical assistance from
Susanna Ingram, Sebastian Carter and Nic Jones are also
greatly appreciated. Hilary Bird expertly produced
the index. The book's designer, Karin Fremer,
has been a joy to work with.

A CIP catalogue record for this book is available from the British Library

ISBN 978-1-870882-23-1

Further copies of this book may be obtained by contacting
Ben Ridler: b.ridler@talktalk.net or
Colin Ridler: colin.ridler@gmail.com

Designed and typeset in Adobe Caslon and Gill Sans by Karin Fremer
Printed in Great Britain by Gomer Press Ltd, Llandysul, Ceredigion, Wales

CONTENTS

JOHN FELL

THE UNIVERSITY PRESS AND
THE 'FELL' TYPES

The Punches and Matrices designed for Printing in the Greek,
Latin, English, and Oriental Languages bequeathed in 1686 to the
University of Oxford by JOHN FELL, D.D., Delegate of the
Press, Dean of Christ Church, Vice-Chancellor of the University
and Bishop of Oxford

BY STANLEY MORISON

WITH THE ASSISTANCE OF HARRY CARTER

This book, on which Dr. Morison, doyen of British typographers, has been
engaged for many years, was composed entirely by hand in type cast at
the Press in matrices bequeathed to the University by John Fell. Dr. Fell
(1625–86), was Dean of Christ Church, Bishop of Oxford, and a great benefactor to the University's Press. Many of the matrices were brought from
Holland, some being the work of famous French engravers of the sixteenth
century, while others were made at Oxford by Fell's typefounder.

The types, Greek, Black Letter, Roman, Italic, exotic, and flowers, are
shown in synopses displaying every character and in re-settings of pages
from Fell's press 'in the Theater' at Oxford. Notes on their condition and
history give a good deal of new information. Dr. Morison introduces the
types with a review of learned printing up to Fell's time, a biography of the
Bishop, and an account of the evolution of the letter-forms in manuscripts
and early printing. The Appendixes include Bibliographies by J. S. G.
Simmons of Fell's published works and of early Oxford-type specimens.

The Fell types and others acquired by the University before 1700 (described in an Appendix) make the collection at the Press one of the main
sources of typographical history.

Edition limited to 1,000 *copies*
Crown folio, 296 *pp., frontispiece in colour,* 22 *plates,* 12 *text-figures,* £25 *net*

PLEASE ORDER FROM YOUR BOOKSELLER

OXFORD UNIVERSITY PRESS

ELY HOUSE, 37 DOVER STREET, LONDON, W.1

Printed in England 10/67

A leaflet produced to advertise the publication in 1967 of what would prove to be the
grandest and most lavish volume ever issued by the Press: Stanley Morison's John Fell, a
folio of 278 pages (not 296 as advertised here), entirely set by hand using the so-called
Fell types. It was the high point of printing at Oxford. See plates 29 and 30.

FOREWORD
by John Randle

VIVIAN & WHITTINGTON

I became interested in printing at school when I was about 14, and my grandparents' neighbours on Boar's Hill suggested I went to see their acquaintance Vivian Ridler. I was ushered into his large wood-panelled, book-lined office in Walton Street where he showed me some Roxburghe Club and no doubt other examples of fine printing from the University Press. He was welcoming to a rather nervous schoolboy, and may even have suggested I applied for a place at the London School of Printing and Graphic Arts, which indeed I in due course did. He then introduced me to Mr Carter, who showed me round the museum he was in the process of setting up elsewhere in the building, which included the enormous cupboards that contained the Holy Grail: the moulds, punches and matrices for the 17th-century type purchased for the Press by Bishop Fell. Little did I imagine that some 40 years later I would see to the repair of one of the matrices and the re-casting of some of the type (by Theo Rehak in New Jersey) so that the Whittington Press[1] could complete the printing in 1995 of the magnificent quarto *The Book of Common Prayer* begun at the University Press in 1913.[2] I did also happen to see a notice set in 24-point Caslon (or was it Double Pica Fell?) advising that 'any man confusing Caslon with Fell will be liable to dismissal' – or words to that effect. This seemed to me a little harsh at the time, but underscored the standards then prevalent at the Press.

1 Which I had started at Whittington in 1971 as a weekend diversion from working in publishing in London. It became a full-time activity with my wife Rose in 1974.
2 The story is told by Peter Foden, then Archivist at Oxford University Press, in *The Fell Imperial Quarto Book of Common Prayer* (Whittington Press 1998).

I think I went to see Vivian again when job hunting after leaving the London College of Printing (as it had become), but he was too perceptive to offer employment in a 900-strong multi-skilled printing establishment to a young man with his head in the clouds of Albion presses and hand-made paper. But strangely enough, as the years went by, our links with OUP became stronger, as we were able to continue at Whittington with some of the craft skills that were no longer viable in a modern printing works. We took on some of their redundant machinery (including a large Western proof press[3] on which we completed the 1913 *Book of Common Prayer*), their precious stock of some 20,000 sheets of hand-made paper,[4] and most especially the Monotype matrices and ancillary equipment.

I realize now that Vivian and I both had similar backgrounds in that our final education had been through printing. He had been a trainee at the mighty E S & A Robinson in Bristol after leaving Bristol Grammar School, which had spawned whole generations of bright Bristolian boys (one of whom had taught me Classics at school), just as I had gone on to the London School of Printing after leaving school. Ruari McLean, Vivian's close friend and contemporary, had followed the same path by going to work for Basil Blackwell's Shakespeare Head Press after failing to achieve the necessary Classical scholarship to Oxford. But printing turned out to be a sort of university in itself, as is borne out by this Diary. Vivian met Prime Ministers, Vice-Chancellors, Ministers of the Crown, Captains of Industry, Professors of Physics, Union Bosses, Playhouse Directors, Fellows of All Souls, and took them all in his stride as though encountering them in the High on a sunny May morning; yet at the same time he was quite pithy and even amusing in his assessments that he allows us to share here. I am not surprised he shut the Diary away in a drawer after recording this eventful year. He was the last person to wish to give offence, and by so doing he could be

---

3 Which I saw standing forlornly on the pavement in Great Clarendon Street, and which Richard Russell of OUP persuaded me to take home.

4 Meticulously described, with a sample of each paper, by John Bidwell in his *Fine Papers at the Oxford University Press* (Whittington Press 1999).

perfectly truthful and straightforward in recording his reactions to the people and events the Diary records.

Vivian was among the first to subscribe to our annual *Matrix* in 1981, and wrote an informative and perceptive review of it for *Antiquarian Book Monthly Review* in May 1982. I happened upon this shortly before the publication of *Matrix 36*, the last of the series, and included a copy of it with the edition. Vivian's innate modesty made him a reluctant contributor, but I did eventually get him to write a few paragraphs about the *Monotype Newsletter* in *Matrix 19*. He wrote to me on 3 January 2001: 'Another magnificent number [*Matrix 20*] – what an achievement. So glad that you included a piece by Harold Dotterill. He was the mainstay of our caster room in my time and a great character, as you will have found.' Harold Dotterill, the last Monotype supervisor at the Press, had written about his time in the printing industry in *Matrix 20*, including the following:

> During my time – 17 October 1940 to 28 February 1983 – I worked under three very different bosses who were officially known as 'Printers to Oxford University': John Johnson, Charles Batey and Vivian Ridler. Before Mr Johnson was appointed Printer, he had done some distinguished work as an archaeologist in Egypt. It was he who engaged me. He was remote from his staff, with whom he had little personal contact. His successor as Printer, Mr Batey, had been personal assistant to Mr Johnson, and was an efficient boss who did more 'managing' than Mr Johnson had done. He was succeeded as Printer by a man with 'hands-on' printing experience, Mr Ridler, who had learned his craft with E S & A Robinson of Bristol. Mr Ridler would come round the printing works and the bindery once or twice a week and have a friendly chat with members of the staff. He was a fantastic lover of print. Not surprisingly, the staff did not mind him telling them what to do. Two proofs were pulled of every galley and I would check

for technical errors and Mr Ridler would check for other errors. The final stage of proof-reading was done from page proofs when the job had been made up.

As previously mentioned, we had taken the Monotype equipment from the Press when it was about to be discarded at the closure of the Press in 1989. This was thanks to the intervention of Richard Russell, who recognized the importance of preserving this unique heritage of Monotype matrices, and I suspect with the tacit approval of Vivian enabled it all to be moved to Whittington, where it has enlarged the scope of the Whittington Press to an unprecedented degree. It was a most satisfying moment when Harold visited it in its new home 40 miles west of Oxford and gave it his seal of approval.

So we had a most enjoyable and productive relationship with the University Press, and several major publications are the result of this. Vivian's kindly presence hovered in the background, and I used to enjoy my visits to Stanley Road and meeting Anne and the rest of the family, and hearing Vivian's vivid tales of his printing contemporaries, many of whom I knew of as senior figures when I worked in printing and publishing in London in the 1960s. Although Vivian never offered me a job, I felt I had become an honorary member of that unique institution, which he personified at its very best. His Diary will become a classic of printers' lore, on a par with Frank Sidgwick's of working at the Shakespeare Head Press in 1904,[5] and Charles Manby-Smith's *The Working Man's Way in the World*[6] of 1851.

---

5 *Frank Sidgwick's Diary*, published by Basil Blackwell under his Shakespeare Head Press imprint, attractively designed by Ruari McLean, and printed at the Alden Press in 1975.
6 Edited and introduced by Ellic Howe, Printing Historical Society 1967.

PREFACE

The Diary that forms the centrepiece of this book was written by my father, Vivian Ridler, over the course of a year, from 29 June 1970 to 30 June 1971 (with a coda for his final year as Printer in 1977-78). Quite why he wrote it at that time is not explicitly stated, but in the Introduction I speculate on the most likely reason. In any case, it forms an invaluable record of life in a world-famous printing plant, at the world's oldest and largest university press, during a period of great change both in book publishing and in technology and industrial relations more generally.

A man of great rigour and self-discipline, my father would sit down each evening – often after an exhausting day both in and outside the Press – to draft an entry in his beautiful (I use the word advisedly) italic script, with a fountain pen, on foolscap paper. Indeed, when it came to estimating the number of words in the Diary, the regularity of the script made it possible to produce a quick and rough word count that, once the entries had been typed, proved to be out by less than a thousand words.

It is one of the mysteries of my father's life that, having drafted the Diary with great diligence and effort, he did nothing with it – not even depositing a photocopy at Oxford University Press for its Archive. His wife Anne Ridler's poem, 'Lines to a Retiring Printer', reprinted here at the end of the Diary, gives a sense of the huge relief he felt on leaving the Press, after over thirty years of unremitting labour, managing the disparate demands of the print unions and his publishing colleagues. The Introduction recounts how, after 1978, he could return in his retirement to the creative life of a craftsman-typographer which he had been required largely to relinquish as Printer. Indeed, always keen to pursue his wider interests, in 1980 he was free to sign on as an extra in Mike Cimino's *Heaven's Gate*, parts of which were filmed in Oxford (bizarrely standing in for Harvard in 1870). My father even drafted another vivid and amusing handwritten account of that experience, complete with a printed title page that read Heaven's Gate: The Diary of an Extra, 'The Greatest Disaster in Film History' (it is said to have lost over $100 million). In this and in so many ways during his later years he was busy and contented. He felt no need to dwell on the past. The Diary was forgotten about, and remained buried in a drawer at the family home till his death in 2009.

In editing the Diary I have made four kinds of intervention: first, attempting by and large to standardize use of capital letters (e.g. for departments of the Press) and abbreviations for names; second, correcting obvious errors of fact (of which there were very few, e.g. Apollo 14 instead of Apollo 13); third, omitting in a few places remarks my father himself, were he alive, would agree were today inappropriate; and fourth, adding footnotes to explain the identities of many people he meets (he knows, but we may not) – just occasionally interpolating an italicized explanation in the text itself, where a full footnote seems unnecessary. The footnotes are extensive but not exhaustive: some identities elude clarification half a century on from the Diary's composition, or are for readers to elucidate for themselves.

Some thought was given to the question of whether quite a lengthy Diary might with benefit be shortened. But what to omit? Occasional longueurs in the daily routine or pattern of events? Non-OUP or family matters? In the end it was felt that, apart from the small cuts mentioned above, the Diary should stand as written, drafted as it was 'in the heat of battle'. It is precisely the insights this gives on the stresses and strains experienced by a senior figure in the book business – and the ways in which his broader interests across the industry and outside it allowed him a deeper perspective on everyday affairs – that enhance the picture created. Nor is this a dry discussion of business practice.

You as a reader can gradually form your own opinion of the leading figures as they emerge in the narrative, from Colin Roberts the rather enigmatic chief executive, and John Brown ('Bruno') the often exasperating OUP London Publisher, to Gerry Fulton the tiresome Printing House union man who surprises his boss by going to see a Shakespeare play at Stratford. Above all, the Diary in its entirety gives us a rich and satisfying insight into the character of the man writing it, and how he views the momentous changes going on around him as well as his part in those transformations.

The Introduction gives a brief overview of his career and time at the Press both before and after the period of the Diary – while simultaneously trying to explain to the uninitiated reader some of the complex yet fascinating history of the Press itself. On occasion that story reads more like a C P Snow novel of donnish intrigue and manoeuvring than an account of a sober institution renowned throughout the world for its scholarly output. To help me in this sketch I have drawn on the volumes listed in the Further Reading, especially the Waldock Report, Volume III of *The History of Oxford University Press*, and the wonderful *On the Press* by Mick Belson, which gives a flavour of shop-floor life at the Printing Works during the 20th century. Anne Ridler's *Memoirs* adds a more personal dimension to the story. (Appropriately for a family memoir it was published by Vivian Ridler's reincarnated Perpetua Press – see the Introduction – and typeset by my sister Jane Scott's husband, Neil Scott.)

Several former OUP employees have kindly read through and commented on (or edited!) my remarks: I extend my thanks to Hugo Brunner, Jonathan Crowther, Genevieve Hawkins, Andrew Schuller and Frances Whistler. Other friends and family members have likewise improved the Introduction and saved me from errors – though no doubt some remain. As for checking the details in the Diary itself, it was a boost when I might be flagging to have my brother Ben Ridler's critical input and encouragement to persevere. And my late brother-in-law, Richard Wilson, carried the torch for my father in so many ways, not least carefully archiving – with the help of my sister Kate Wilson – much of the material that makes up the contents of this volume. I have drawn extensively on Richard's catalogue booklet he produced for the exhibition he organized of my father's work, held to mark his 80th birthday, at the Ruskin School of Drawing and Fine Art in Oxford (1993) and the Brynmor Jones Library in Hull (1994).

I am immensely grateful to Richard Russell, former Assistant Printer, for recording a long and most useful interview with my father in 1998 which now resides in the OUP Archive. Richard has likewise carried the torch for him over many years, and wrote his obituary in *The Times*. He also wrote a reminiscence of his own apprenticeship and subsequent career at the Press, extracts from which appear with permission at the back of this book to help provide more context and greater depth to the account in the Diary. John Randle, who published that reminiscence in his magnificent bibliophile's journal *Matrix*, has been kind enough to contribute the Foreword to this volume, with his recollections of encountering my father during his time as Printer and subsequently.

Finally, I also wanted to supplement the Diary with a short, vivid letter from New York during the Press Quincentenary celebrations there, and four other examples of my father's prose that provide further evidence of his wit and perspicacity as a judge of his fellow man. These shed additional light too on figures who feature in the Diary: John Ryder (Appendix 1), John Hall (Appendix 2), Brooke Crutchley (Appendix 3), and Hugh Williamson (Appendix 4). Together with the Diary, they convey something of my father's warmth and humanity that those of us who were lucky enough to be close to him experienced when he was a living presence.

The Life & Times of a Master Printer

ivian Ridler, Printer to the University, Oxford, from 1958 to 1978, stood almost at the end of a long line of holders of that distinguished office stretching back centuries to 1585. His predecessor as Printer, Charles Batey, had in 1948 persuaded him to give up his enjoyable London life as a freelance book designer and part-time lecturer in typography at the Royal College of Art to return to Oxford as Works Manager and later, from 1949, Assistant Printer. I say 'return', because my father (or, as I shall on occasion call him, VR) had previously worked at the Press in Walton Street in 1937. The then Printer, John Johnson, had spotted the talent of this energetic young type enthusiast, at that time employed by the packaging printer E S & A Robinson in Bristol as a management trainee. The two had corresponded, sharing a keen interest in the history of printing and typography, and Johnson convinced VR to relinquish his promising career in Bristol and move to Oxford.

However, as my mother, Anne Ridler, later remarked, working for Johnson was 'like life in a monastery without the consolations of religion'. An obsessive, he 'drove the Printing House to a new pitch of excellence' in the words of the OUP Archivist, Martin Maw, but at the cost of his own and his staff's health, 'driving one or two to an early death' according to his secretary. Johnson would say to his deputy, 'I'm not taking a holiday this year, Batey, are you?' Famously, during World War II – when it is true the Printing House became a vital part of the war effort, producing top-secret documents and codes – Johnson slept on a bed in his office. But by that time he had peremptorily sacked my father, for a reason that he was no doubt too shame-faced ever to reveal. Only later did the true explanation emerge.

To understand what motivated Johnson, we need to delve into OUP's history between the wars and consider the principal actors. As Printer from 1925, Johnson felt almost fanatically that he had to guard the independence of the Printing House in Oxford. OUP (or 'the Press' in shorthand) was by this stage essentially a three-headed hydra (four-headed if one includes the less important Paper Mill, see below): the Clarendon Press (the old Learned Press) based in Oxford, which published academic titles and was overseen directly by R W Chapman, the Secretary to the Delegates (overall head of OUP); the London Business (formerly the London Bible Warehouse), which had outgrown its original function as a bible distributor to become a major publisher of more general and popular books under its dynamic head Humphrey Milford, known as the Publisher; and finally the Printing House in Oxford run by Johnson, tasked with producing books for the two publishing wings. Johnson's predecessor as Printer had suffered, and he and all his successors – including my father – would suffer, from the shift in power from Printer to London Publisher instituted in 1905. In that year, control over paper orders and Bible printing was moved to London.

Humphrey Milford, as Publisher from 1913, proceeded with vigour over the next three decades greatly to expand the scale and scope of the London office, and to build up the international business that underpins OUP's success today. Crucially, he was given the liberty to choose outside suppliers if their quotes were lower than those of the Oxford Printer. Chapman and Milford worked well together, but Johnson felt he was being excluded from the senior management of OUP and 'treated as an "inferior"'. Matters came to a head in 1937 in a fracas known as the 'rumpus', when Johnson joined forces with Hugh Last, a distinguished but cantankerous academic and Press Delegate who was highly critical of the secrecy and lack of accountability on the publishing side, and advocated sweeping reform (presaging many of the changes that eventually took place in the 1970s – see below). Both men wrote letters to members of the University, Johnson accusing Chapman of being shifty, even deceptive, while Milford, he claimed, had 'his own patriarchal or squirearchical form of government' that had 'not allowed...other dominant people near his throne' (a jibe with some force, since the Publisher was known to his admiring staff as 'Caesar'). Milford was furious, suffering sleepless nights. He hinted that the Printer overcharged and was protected from the Depression, and thus economic realities, unlike the Publisher. The rumpus rumbled on into 1938.

It so happened that Milford's niece was one Anne Bradby, a young poet who had started work at Faber & Faber in London and was now T S Eliot's assistant there. The production manager at the time was David Bland, a childhood friend of VR from Bristol days – together they had run a little private press called the Perpetua Press, one of whose books was chosen by the First Editions Club as among the Fifty Best Books of the Year in 1935. Bland introduced my father to Miss Bradby, and it was not long before they fell in love and got engaged. It was this act of betrayal, as Johnson saw it – of in effect 'consorting with the enemy' that provoked him to sack my father in the autumn of 1937 (as Uncle Humphrey at the time suspected was the reason, but was only confirmed after the war). Johnson explained his decision by telling VR he was a selfish young man who put outside interests before those of the Printing House, yet in a display of his vacillating behaviour could write to my father in June 1939: 'I am thrilled by...your appointment as a teacher at the Royal College of Art. For that is the kind of post about which I have always dreamed for you. The level routine of factory life would never allow opportunity enough for the magnanimity of your art, which as you know I have always extolled.'

And Johnson likewise supplied a glowing testimonial to my father's next employer, the bibliographer Theodore Besterman, who wished to establish a small press in London that VR would run. This Bunhill Press, in Bunhill Row near Old Street tube station, now became the focus for my father's energies, after he and my mother had married. The first production, a morocco-bound edition and translation of Magna Carta, set in 16pt Bembo – a favourite typeface of my father's – was called 'a treasure for the lover of fine books' by a reviewer. It had handsome head and tailpiece designs by the immigré from Nazi Europe Berthold Wolpe (see Diary, 29 July 1970), whose now famous Albertus typeface was used for the title page and part titles. I have on my wall at home an attractive watercolour painting my father did of Bunhill Cemetery (where Bunyan and Blake are buried), demonstrating his mastery of line and form. And his artistic skills as well as his wit were in evidence in two delightful pocket ABCs he drew and produced for Faber, featuring offbeat words like Nosegay, illustrated whimsically with two sailors handing a posy to a lady at a window.

Yet this creative London life came quite literally under threat with the Blitz, and one night in January 1941 the Press took a direct hit, scattering along Bunhill Row the magenta jackets (designed by VR) of my mother's *Poems* (her first poetry collection, issued by OUP). Ten days later my father joined the RAF, serving in Orkney and Nigeria, and later as an intelligence officer in Germany (see his *War Diary of an Airman* (The Perpetua Press 2022)). Once demobilized in June 1946, he took up the life of a freelance designer, working for Lund Humphries and with the young George Weidenfeld on his magazine *Contact*, sharing his office as art editor. ('I sat in one corner and George in another', my father once told me. It was a small world. *Contact* had its office in the same building as Poetry London run by Tambimuttu, publisher of my mother's second poetry book.) Supplementing this income, VR took up a part-time appointment as the first Lecturer in Typography at the Royal College of Art.

OXFORD-BOUND AGAIN

In the autumn of 1947 came the invitation from Batey to rejoin the Printing House, initially as Works Manager, but with the prospect of becoming Assistant Printer and later Printer. What a dilemma this posed. It was not just the unpleasant memories that would have to be overcome. The relative freedom of a freelance life would now give way to the restrictions and stresses of working in a factory again. Yet with a growing family to support, the financial security had a considerable appeal. And, as T S Eliot remarked to my mother, 'Vivian will be in a position to influence all the printing in England' (which did indeed prove to be the case). Batey pressed VR for a response, or, as my father recorded, 'rather put me into a corner', and ultimately got his man. In April 1948 my father started again at the Printing House on an annual salary of £1250 (see the Diary entry for 30 June 1970 for comparative salaries by that date). As my father said, 'It was a bit like jumping into a cold bath, having been my own boss.' And this was no exaggeration. The initial problem was an employee and former army major called Peakman, who believed that he should be Works Manager and made my father's life hell. After six months of this VR told Batey he intended to leave, at which Batey acted decisively, telling Peakman to go away and write out a letter of resignation at once, which he did. 'One Friday night Peakman wasn't there.'

However, an enduring and much greater long-term challenge was the need to manage and control over 900 unionized men, particularly in the early years after the war, when workers were far less inclined than in the depressed 1930s to fall in with their employers' requirements. Indeed, it will become apparent to anyone reading the year-long Diary in the Life of a Printer that follows, that an inordinate amount of my father's time in 1970-71 was still spent in dealing with the unions and their demands – financial demands in particular that, at a time of rampant inflation, were to make the task of maintaining the profitability of the Printing Works extraordinarily difficult. As my father once remarked, 'Half my time is spent arguing with unions and the other half negotiating the purchase of machinery with banks.' Richard Russell, Works Manager from 1961 and later Assistant Printer, tells the story of one such union negotiation:

We had the leading people from the Typographical Association arguing about agreements one Monday morning and we broke for lunch so both sides could think things over. The Press Sports Day had been on the Saturday, so Vivian borrowed the starting pistol and, when we got going again, he put this on the table with his TA card from his Bristol days and said: 'If you dislike me as much as you suggest, here is a pistol so you can shoot a former member.' We won the argument.

Yet there is so much else that the Diary reveals, both about working life in a manufacturing plant half a century ago – before the Thatcherite revolution swept away a large part of Britain's manufacturing capability (the Printing House itself would close for good in 1989), a loss we are only now fully coming to appreciate and regret – and about the creative aspects of making fine books and maintaining the high standards for which Oxford books were world-renowned. And I find impressive the sheer empathy and humanity the Diary reveals in the way my father went about running the business, particularly in the constant references to hospital or home visits he made to sick or retired employees. As Mick Belson writes in his book, *On the Press* (2003), about the craftspeople at the Works, 'He really cared for his staff, and all of the employees ... had deep respect for what he stood for and his unquestionable knowledge of the gentle art of printing.'

In this task of management, VR relied heavily on the support of another sympathetic figure – who features frequently in the Diary – John Hall, the Personnel Manager. Hall was so devoted to his staff that he would personally take pay packets round to employees if they were off sick at home. It was thus a great shock and a painful loss to my father when one day in November 1974 he came to work, only to find Hall prostrate on the ground at the Press entrance after a heart attack, from which he never recovered. (See Appendix 2 for VR's Address at Hall's funeral.)

There are happily lighter moments too in the Diary, when VR's sense for the humorous or ridiculous shines through. On 28 August, for instance, Percy Best comes to take his leave on retirement and expresses his 'joy' at saying goodbye, which causes my father to call to mind the episode when he had found Best lolling on a pile of precious proofs and had 'bawled him out'. And in the very final paragraph of the last entry for the 1978 coda, my father discovers he is pinioned to his chair by his gown at the grand Quincentenary Dinner held in the Codrington Library at All Souls, and is forced to remain seated while everyone else stands to hear the Loyal Toast given by Harold Macmillan. As the bibliophile Nicolas Barker – who himself features occasionally in the Diary, not always in a favourable light – wrote in his generous obituary of VR in the *Independent*, 'There was always a glint of humour behind his spectacles, and he had a vivid turn of speech....He made the University Press a happy place to work.'

But why, you may ask, did my father start the Diary in the first place? I suspect the thought must have struck him, after reading the highly influential and critical Waldock Report on the whole workings of OUP, published just one month before the Diary's first entry, that change was afoot at the Press, and that as a central figure in the enterprise he should for posterity make some record of events that were unfolding. He could also record his broader experience of the printing industry generally, having been President of the British Federation of Master Printers, the employers' body, in 1968-69. (The Diary makes numerous references to his visits to Bedford Row in London, the headquarters of the BFMP, and its Southwestern Alliance branch in Bristol.)

THE PRESS BEFORE WALDOCK

OUP was a peculiar institution. A branch of the University, which was liable for its debts, for much of the 20th century up to the 1970s it oper-ated at arm's length, with little oversight from the University as a whole. There were, it is true, ten Delegates appointed from among the dons, but the canny Secretary to the Delegates (ie the chief executive), Charles Cannan (in office 1898-1919), had neutered their executive powers and turned the fortnightly Delegates' meetings into 'a sort of literary seminar', primarily for the approval of new titles for the Clarendon Press, the academic imprint. (The ever-growing number of titles commissioned by the London Business and the international branches largely escaped Delegate scrutiny until after World War II.) More significant was the Finance Committee (which features regularly in the Diary), made up of five Delegates plus the Vice-Chancellor and Secretary. Yet even here most power lay with the Secretary, who drew up the agenda and wrote the minutes. Cannan and his successors did their utmost, moreover, to retain profits within OUP rather than give funds to the University or colleges, and hence maintained secrecy around Press accounts.

Nor did OUP operate like most commercial publishers, with the prime objective of making money on each title. As a later Secretary, Thomas Norrington, wrote in 1954, 'The essence of the Press is that it is not a business... It needs to be run in a business-like way, but it is not business considerations that should dominate.' Or, as his successor Colin Roberts (mentioned frequently in the Diary) expressed it, the Press would publish any book it chose to, whether or not it might make a loss. Roberts's Assistant Secretary, Dan Davin (also a regular in the Diary), was editor-in-chief – ebullient, beer-drinking and gregarious, unlike the Secretary, whose somewhat cold and aloof demeanour was accompanied by a disconcertingly direct stare. Davin, according to one of his admirers, the OUP editor Jon Stallworthy, was 'the greatest academic publisher of his time' and himself an accomplished novelist. Tireless in his devotion to editorial quality in Clarendon Press books, he would conduct 'Morning Prayers' where all the mail of the day was gone through meticulously with his editors and frank judgements were meted out. Yet, like that other consummate OUP list-builder Humphrey Milford, Davin preferred intuition and guesswork to management systems in such matters as deciding print runs. He also had an almost pathological aversion to the introduction of computers – even for the London warehouse at Neasden – which he thought would be the ruin of the Press (Neasden did get its first computer in 1965).

This was all very well, but OUP was by now a huge organization, publishing over 800 titles a year by the late 1960s (as opposed to 200 in the 1930s), with 17,000 titles in stock in 1970. Moreover, because of the relative autonomy of the London Business and the overseas branches in North America, India, Australia and elsewhere, there was no clear strategy as to who would publish what, and difficulties in establishing uniform levels of scholarly and production quality across the list – needed for what was by now an international 'brand'. The haphazard way of operating is exemplified by the belated birth of the Oxford paperback list. The success of Allen Lane's Penguin Books, and its main paperback rival Pan Books, meant that there was a danger OUP would get left behind as the market changed postwar. In the end it was left to the New York branch to take the first step in 1956, with the creation of Galaxy Books (referred to briefly in the Diary). Their success prompted the gradual development in the early 1960s of Oxford Paperbacks back in Britain.

To be fair to Roberts, he was aware of many of the problems, not least of which was his poor relationship with the Publisher in London, John Brown or 'Bruno' – another prominent Diary figure – who had been in post since 1956 (two years after Roberts became Secretary). Brown came from a sales, not academic, background with wide contacts in the London publishing scene, to the extent that the outside world viewed him, not Roberts, as OUP's figurehead. (It is a curious fact that it was he, not Roberts, who was eventually knighted in 1974; Roberts was made CBE in 1973 – for papyrology, not publishing! - and VR, CBE in 1971.) Brown's outside interests culminated in his serving as President of the Publishers Association (1963-65), which led him to delegate heavily at OUP in London. By 1967 Roberts could write, 'London is badly run down, with no guidance and few clear objectives.'

Brown, it should be said however, was responsible for overseeing the international branches (except New York), which expanded so much that by 1970 they accounted for 46% of OUP's sales (but not profits), if New York is included. A good deal of this growth could be attributed to two of the most entrepreneurial figures in OUP's history:

Eric Parnwell, who built and massively enlarged the crucial Overseas Education Department (later the ELT Department, with sales of £80 million by 1995), and Raymond Brammah, dynamic head of OUP in East Asia. But Brown gave free rein to these men, and had himself in the 1940s spotted the potential of what became known as Hornby's *Advanced Learner's Dictionary of Current English*, one of OUP's most successful titles ever, its second edition going through 19 impressions in the 1960s. Nevertheless the editors in London felt that the captain was absent from the bridge, and the ship was drifting and leaking, as the chief editor John Bell (also in the Diary) told the Publisher to his face in the late 1960s. (Bell was to write an amusing set of verses called *Mutiny on the Bembo*, using the same maritime metaphor, which VR published at his revived Perpetua Press in his retirement.)

Roberts was concerned by the heavy losses now being incurred by the London Business on bibles – once such a milchcow for OUP – and by increased competition. He foresaw the need to rationalize the structure of the Press and, in 1966, put forward a plan to transfer many of the functions of the London Business to Oxford. He also took modest steps to boost the output of science books – a weak link in the overall list – and in 1965 entered college textbook publishing as a direct response to the vast expansion of universities in that decade. It was this expansion that prompted the setting up of a commission led by Lord Franks to investigate the University of Oxford. His report came out in 1966 and led directly to the creation of another inquiry, chaired by the international lawyer Sir Humphrey Waldock, which spent the years 1967-70 looking into all aspects of OUP and its relationship with the University.

One focus for the inquiry was two aspects of the business for which Roberts, as Secretary, also had ultimate responsibility – the Printing House and the Paper Mill at Wolvercote on the edge of Oxford. Each accounted in the 1960s for about 10% of OUP's revenue, but the Printing House was vastly more profitable. Indeed, the Mill, acquired in 1855 and invaluable during World War II at a time of paper shortages and quotas for publishers, was by now a white elephant. Using a vast Fourdrinier machine the length of a railway platform, it sucked in 100,000 gallons of water for every one ton of paper produced. Moreover it committed OUP to staggering capital expenditure for maintenance and upgrades. In the period 1948-67 it absorbed £1.17 million for a total profit of £58,000, the comparable figures for the Printing House being £156,000 capital expenditure as against £2.55 million in profit. And the paper produced was often inappropriate for the Printing House's needs. No wonder Roderick Henderson, Controller of the Mill from 1948, took to drink and was forced to retire in 1971 (he too features in the Diary). Scrutiny by the Waldock Committee propelled the inevitable frank appraisal by the Press that the Mill should be sold off, which it was in 1978. Paper production there ceased all together in 1997 and the Mill was demolished seven years later.

The Printing House was an entirely different matter.

CHALLENGES FOR THE PRINTING HOUSE

The Printing House underpinned the very existence and history of the Press going back to 1585. The quality and typographic elegance of its productions were world-renowned. The Queen had sworn her solemn oath at Westminster Abbey in 1953 on the Coronation Bible (designed by VR), while the prestigious and highly profitable *New English Bible* was produced jointly at the Oxford and Cambridge printing houses (the Cambridge Printer being Brooke Crutchley, a good friend of my father's who appears in the Diary). In designing the smaller, popular edition of the *NEB* to be printed at Oxford, VR had carefully chosen the typeface Goudy Catalogue for its combination of legibility and economy. (It might be noted that my mother, Anne Ridler, was the only female member of the Literary Panel tasked with assessing the quality of the Old Testament translation, and alone represented her sex in the procession, again at Westminster Abbey, during the service to dedicate the *NEB* in 1970.)

In the 1960s, too, the Printing House was renowned for its team of about 15 graduate readers, expert in numerous languages, and so-called craftsmen readers without a degree, employed to check and query authorial proofs – a service found invaluable by scholars and academics published by the Clarendon Press. (Readers, it should be said, were not allowed to be in direct touch with authors, part of the archaic working practices at the Press – nor indeed were they allowed to set foot in the publishing offices, as the former graduate reader Genevieve Hawkins told me; she was not even supposed to mix with craftsmen readers.) Nevertheless, this high-quality service provided by the readers brought with it a heavy overhead cost that inevitably had to be included in the prices the Printer could offer on Clarendon Press work.

Another service with costs attached arose from the craft skills in hot-metal typesetting that the Printing House had built up over decades, in fact centuries. The Walton Street Works held a range of special sorts and typefaces, such as a font for hieroglyphic setting, that meant it could undertake work for such learned societies as the Egypt Exploration Society. In the days before computerized typesetting, such expertise was unmatched elsewhere. The culminating manifestation of these skills came with the production of the great typographer Stanley Morison's *John Fell* in 1967 – a large 278-page folio describing how the Press had acquired and employed the magnificent so-called Fell types during the 17th century. The book had been commissioned in 1925 and eventually completed by the Press archivist Harry Carter (appointed by Batey in 1954 and held in high regard by my father). Set entirely by hand in the Fell types, newly recast from 17th-century matrices, and designed by VR, the John Fell volume was, in the words of the official *History of Oxford University Press* (Vol. III, page 812), 'a masterpiece of printing of outstanding beauty... set in the very materials that formed its subject matter'. No other printer in the world could have produced such a landmark volume. And yet the date of its publication, 1967, is significant, in that it coincided with the appointment of the Waldock Inquiry which would lead ultimately to the demise of the Printing House itself.

My father had rejoined the Printing Business in the early postwar

years, when work was plentiful. He later remarked, 'It was staggering...
a list of about 600 reprint titles.' Batey and VR – the latter effectively
in charge from 1952 when Batey fell ill – introduced new technology to remain competitive and keep up with demand. Offset litho
and web-letterpress machines came in the '50s, web-offset litho and
automatic plate-making in the '60s. Inevitably these changes involved
alterations in staffing, for instance as letterpress printing declined and
litho took over. This in turn involved negotiations with the unions –
possible if immensely time-consuming and difficult at a plant level: the
so-called Father of the Chapel, in the arcane terminology of the print
unions, was Gerry Fulton in 1970 when VR began his Diary, and is a
leading character in it. However, sometimes it was a national dispute
that brought the Printing House unions out on strike. This happened
soon after my father became Printer. He had to deal with months of
disruption from June 1959, including a total shutdown of the Works for
part of that time. Naturally this in its turn badly disrupted the London
and Oxford publishing businesses, and did not endear the Printer to
the Secretary, Colin Roberts. (I remember my father having a certain
grim satisfaction when Roberts came to see him – Diary, 24 August
1970 – about the NGA union's first-ever move into the publishing
offices. At last, he felt, publishing would get a taste of what he had had
to cope with for decades.)

The Printing House joined in the boom of the early 1960s. But
ominous clouds were on the horizon. Although it was an innovatory
move in 1960 to introduce filmsetting for type composition, using
Monophoto, as my father later remarked it was ultimately one of the
things that sounded the death knell of the Printing House. Now film
could be sent 'in a jiffy bag anywhere in the world' to a cheaper printer.
Moreover the rapid expansion of OUP's output meant that the Printing
Works – which was in any case, according to the Waldock Report, kept
as a matter of Delegate policy at a capacity well below home publishing
requirements – simply could not meet demand. In 1965 Roberts wrote a
critical memo to VR about an inability to keep to schedules, and static

production at the Works. This was hardly surprising given the restricted nature of the Walton Street premises, dating back to 1832. VR, with the Delegates' blessing, instituted a radical plan to demolish the shanty town of sheds that had sprung up to the west of the Printing House, and erect a new extension of 100,000 square feet designed by the architect John Fryman. It opened in 1968 and housed, in VR's words, 'a group of departments arranged on a rational plan and capable of adaptation to changing needs'. (My father, as a designer himself, hugely enjoyed the collaboration with Fryman – who became a lifelong friend – and I remember chose flooring that he had admired at an airport.)

Nevertheless, satisfying the rapidly evolving and expanding needs of the publishing business would prove an almost impossible task for the Printer, as became evident in the wake of the Waldock Inquiry.

THE WALDOCK REPORT AND ITS AFTERMATH

Apart from the lawyer Waldock himself, the four other Inquiry Committee members were a merchant banker, a former head of Cambridge University Press (the only member with publishing experience), a don representing the humanities, and Rex Richards, an Oxford scientist. Richards was highly critical of OUP's low number of science titles (20 out of a total Clarendon Press output of 300 titles). And where were the science journals? Two out of every five Oxford dons were scientists, Richards pointed out. The Secretary, Colin Roberts, responded by saying that he should have to 'cut loose' from the Printer in order to achieve rapid publication of science journals. (Richard Russell later claimed that Roberts was exculpating himself, and denied that the Printer couldn't handle journals.)

The main thrust of the Inquiry and the Report was that OUP had outgrown the capabilities of its governance and its financial management. There was a tension between its scholarly and commercial activities. Jon Stallworthy, in his submission to the Committee from his then position as an editor at the London Business, described 'a condition of inherited schizophrenia from which the Press is at present suffering'. By implication in the Report, the Delegates had divested themselves of their responsibility for oversight. Their number should be increased from 10 to 15, to broaden the range of expertise, and none of the Delegates should serve 'in perpetuity', as had been the case for 5 of them. Roberts readily agreed to these changes, as they chimed with his desire for reform. For the first time, too, the Press agreed to provide detailed accounts. It brought to an end what Waldock himself repeatedly emphasized as excessive secrecy. But, in a vindication of a policy going back to Charles Cannan, the Committee concluded that OUP should not be required to pay a regular dividend to the University, and should instead plough profits back into the business. (From the 1990s, once substantial profits were being made, OUP did begin transferring large sums to its owner, for example £60 million in 1999 alone.)

In 1970, however, OUP certainly needed reform, as Roberts had been planning. His good relationship with Waldock meant that he could engineer the recommendation that he would no longer be required to manage the Clarendon Press as well as OUP as a whole, but could concentrate solely on the latter, with Davin as Academic Publisher of the CP. Davin himself came in for veiled criticism by the Committee, as being too rigid and taking on far too much editorial work: he should delegate 70% of manuscripts to his editors, of whom there were too few (16 in 1970, up from 12 in 1967). Furthermore, CP editors were too passive, failing actively enough to cultivate prospective authors among the dons. For Davin, though he went along loyally with the changes proposed by Roberts, both the Franks and the Waldock Reports were 'symptoms of a penitential navel-gazing, hair-shirt, apologetic, prostrate defeatism that was rife in Oxford'. (This makes the Diary entry for 17 December 1970, where Davin unburdens himself to VR, seem less surprising.)

As for the London Business, the Committee believed it should remain in its current location, as the centre of a worldwide enterprise – not a view endorsed by Roberts. John Brown testified to the Committee that the LB was the 'principal moneymaker'. Although strictly true for the period 1964-68, when the LB contributed 38% to group profits, the CP 19% and the Printing House 17%, by 1969-70 London was struggling. Moreover the implication that it subsidized the supposedly unprofitable Clarendon Press was an untruth that infuriated Roberts. He was not to be deflected from his steely resolve to bring both parts of OUP together in Oxford, which was duly begun in 1973 – a consolidation made all the more urgent by the 75% collapse in OUP profits in 1971, as a perfect storm of skyrocketing inflation, slashed educational budgets and general unrest in the country buffeted the firm. (The Press historian Peter Sutcliffe records that the Chief Rabbi announced it to be the worst crisis since the Flood.)

And what verdict did Waldock pronounce on the Printing House? In fact the Report devoted only 4 of its 184 pages to the Walton Street Works. It failed adequately to address the scale of the problems facing the manufacturing business. In 1967 only 40% of its work came from the Clarendon Press and 10-15% from the London Business, the rest being made up of 22.5% for exam papers, 7.5% direct work for the University and 10-15% 'general orders'. In other words, the Printer had to seek outside work to remain profitable, an arrangement increasing his exposure in the event of a recession. In a reflection of policies going back to Milford half a century before, the London Publisher had the upper hand and could and did place work elsewhere if quotes were lower than from the Printing House. The same increasingly now applied to the Clarendon Press, as its output grew.

What, then, was the purpose of owning a tied printer if it no longer fulfilled much more than half the publishing needs? The Printing House – and with it OUP as a whole – had a world-wide reputation for the highest standards of typography and craftsmanship: in his remarks, on formally retiring as a perpetual Delegate, the eminent scholar Maurice Bowra spoke from the heart in referring to 'the uniqueness of the Press and the excellence of its printing' (Diary, 17 December 1970). Yet now Walton Street was being asked to provide the kind of cheap, quick printing offered by rival firms, often to a lower standard. In a sign of things to come, on 8 June 1970 – a few days before VR began his Diary – the Delegate and economist Sir John Hicks expressed the view, in a confidential memo to Colin Roberts, that the management of the Press would eventually have to consider 'the dispensability of the Printing Works'.

My father, generally an optimist and 'doer' in life, eager to look forward rather than back, was not given to introspection. But, in an unusually self-reflective passage in the Diary (1 October 1970), we catch a glimpse of the toll on him of the challenges he was experiencing. After exactly 12 years as Printer, he no longer feels 'quite the same zest for the job' that he used to. He regrets that while 'OUP as a whole has expanded rapidly, this business, in spite of the new buildings, has remained static in size', its prestige and importance 'somehow diminished'. Could he 'have done more to stem the tide' if he had been 'a more political animal'? Surely the answer is 'no', once one takes into account the economic forces and resistance to change on the part of the unions that together were devastating British manufacturing as a whole at this period. In any case, as we see in the Diary, VR has to turn back to matters in hand, introducing changes where he can, investing in new machinery and dealing with whatever the publishing side throws at him.

Soon enough Dan Davin – himself as we have seen the subject of criticism by the Waldock Committee for overly painstaking work – writes to VR on 26 October 1970. The time has come, he maintains, to make a resolute effort to do something about 'our reputation for slowness'. Clarendon sluggishness has 'severely damaged our science list'. This fills VR with 'some gloom' when he receives it (Diary, 29 October). 'Several of the points he makes are difficult to answer, but to my mind the root cause of these continuing problems – in the main, Composing and Reading Room problems – lies in the large number of titles we are handling for *one* customer. As I don't really want to reduce that number because our raison d'être is primarily to serve the CP, I have this dilemma, and finding a solution, or partial solution, is not easy.' The day-by-day account in the Diary about how the saga unfolds is one of the many great values of this important record – unfortunately unavailable to the authors of the 876-page official *History of Oxford University Press*, Vol. III: 1896-1970, published by the firm in 2013, which therefore sometimes shows a bias towards the publishing perspective for the later years.

Ultimately, as my father reflected in an interview in 1998 with his faithful and longstanding colleague Richard Russell, 'No publisher should ever own a printing house....A publisher should be free to go to any printer he wants.' But this verdict was from the tranquil vantage point of a rewarding and creative retirement, during which my father revived the Perpetua Press with his friend and one-time OUP publisher Hugo Brunner, issuing some outstanding fine press volumes, many with Anne Ridler as author or editor. He revelled in his freedom from the burden of responsibility for a workforce of hundreds of men and women, and the travails of dealing with often difficult colleagues and their sometimes contradictory or impossible demands.

In the Diary, by contrast, we see him battling, often successfully, to maintain standards and morale, while endeavouring to increase output and improve profitability in order to justify the Printing House's existence – all in the midst of a hurricane: a major financial crisis and unprecedented technological change, coupled with accelerating transformation across the printing and publishing industries. By the time he wrote the short coda to the Diary for the year 1978, he could be proud of what had been achieved – as celebrated in a major exhibition of OUP productions at the Pierpont Morgan Library in New York to mark the Press Quincentenary that year – and yet glad to pass on the baton to his successor Eric Buckley. Buckley and his own successor David Stanford would fight a losing struggle to keep the Printing House afloat, and it eventually sank in 1989, with the loss of over 200 jobs and after five centuries of tradition and craftsmanship.

I think it is fitting to conclude this introduction to the Diary – a Diary, after all, of a working life in a factory as well as beyond – by giving the perspective from the shop floor. Martin Slade (who after the closure of the Printing House helped resurrect from its ashes a jobbing printer called Oxuniprint) wrote this deeply felt tribute to my father after VR's death in 2009:

> The office of Printer to the University is a great and ancient one and Vivian Ridler filled it with distinction as perhaps the last great printer....He was a real inspirational man who cared for his craft and the people working for him. I was one of his lads, apprenticed to him in the early 1960s – for five years and nine months....He was held in great respect and even when he was tough on us, and he knew how to be, he was held in great affection. An old-style boss, in another age, who knew how to manage and get the best out of his staff.
>
> He did so much for the industry he served, ensuring not only his people but those in other companies had first-class apprenticeships and management training.
>
> Mr Ridler also had time for his staff in their recreational times and supported so many of the Press societies and organisations.
>
> I know from personal experience that he might be head of the business but he had time for us youngsters, especially on Press outings. He would always choose one of us to spend time with him and I remember Mr Ridler taking me on my first visit to the National Portrait Gallery in London and afterwards tea and ice cream. A man of great talent and humility and his contribution to my life will never be forgotten.

CHIEF PROTAGONISTS IN THE DIARY

FAMILY
Vivian Ridler (VR)
Anne Ridler (A or AR), poet, editor, librettist and literary critic
Their children
Jane (married at the time of the Diary to Rolf Länge,
their children
Karin and Juliette)
Kate (married at the time of the Diary to Tim Wilson)
Ben
Colin

OXFORD UNIVERSITY PRESS
Colin Roberts (CHR), Secretary to the Delegates

THE CLARENDON PRESS
Dan Davin (DMD), Assistant Secretary
Tim Chester, Production Manager
Peter Spicer (PJS), Head of Schools and Further Education
Department
John K Cordy, Classics Editor
Peter Sutcliffe, History Editor
Geoffrey Hunt, Religious Editor
John Nicoll, Art and Archaeology Editor

THE LONDON BUSINESS
John Brown (Bruno), Publisher
Philip Chester, Deputy Publisher
K S Thompson (KST), Production Manager
John Bell, Chief Editor
Simon Nugent, ELT Manager

John Ashton, Personnel Manager
John Lord, Publicity Manager
Jimmy Huws-Davies, Neasden Warehouse Manager (later President
of OUP New York, 1972-76)

THE PRINTING HOUSE
Vivian Ridler (VR), Printer to the University
Pat Cox, Printer's Secretary
Sid Church ('Church'), Printer's Chauffeur
Richard Russell (RR), Assistant Printer
John Hall (JH), Personnel Manager (deputy, Mrs Salmon)
Gerard Frost (GF), Finance Director
Gerry Fulton, Father of the Chapel (FOC) (succeeded as FOC in
1971 by Philip Walker)
Harry Carter (HGC), Press Archivist
Mrs Clothier, Library
Graham Halsey, Forwarding Manager
Ken Butler, Forwarding Department
Cyril Cox, Reading Room Supervisor
Ken Stewart, Head of Layout Department
Gordon Taylor (GBT), Production Manager
Ron Harris, Composing Room Manager
Ken Walker, Mono Composing Room
Ken Beckley, Filmsetting Supervisor
Ken Scroggs, Stereotype Department Manager
Max Kibbey, Stereotype Supervisor
Norman Mansfield, Letterpress Machine Room Manager
Jim Coles, Lithographic Machine Room Manager
Jack Sinclair, Lithographic Machine Room Supervisor
Colin Webb, Lithographic Machine Room
Percy Boswell, Paper Office Manager
Reg Chalmers, Bindery Manager

Alec Fortescue, Bindery Supervisor
Aubrey Beesley, Bindery Forwarding and Fire Brigade
Herbert Ashby, Chief Engineer
Norman Reeves, Engineer and deviser of Press pantomimes
Mrs Kath Fulton, Sewing Supervisor
Victor Sugden, Exam paper printing and Editor of *The Clarendonian*
Muriel Morris, Exam Despatch Supervisor

THE WOLVERCOTE PAPER MILL
Roderick Henderson, Controller

OUP NEW YORK
John Brett-Smith, President
Byron Hollinshead, Vice-President (later President, 1976-82)
Fon Boardman, Vice-President and Publicity Manager
Ella Oelrich, Head of Bible publishing

OUP DELEGATES
Jack Thompson, Chairman of the Finance Committee (FC)
Alan Bullock, Vice-Chancellor of Oxford University (V-C)
Maurice Bowra (retired as Delegate December 1970) (Classics)
Helen Gardner (English literature)
J R Hicks (Economics)
Herbert Hart (Law)
Kenneth Wheare (retired as Delegate December 1970)
(Constitutional expert)
Henry Chadwick (Theology)
George Richardson (from March 1971) (Economics)
Robert Blake (from March 1971) (History)
Rex Richards (from April 1971) (Science)

THE DIARY

29 JUNE 1970 – 30 JUNE 1971

June 1970

❦

29 June, Monday

iss Cox (*VR's secretary*) back from the Lakes – a great relief. Dan Davin[7] (*Assistant Secretary to the Delegates*) only at Clarendon Press meeting, with Chester (*Tim Chester, Clarendon Press Production Manager*). Discussed new English-Arabic dictionary project. Davin wants to consider conventional setting. Calligraphers on Arabic-English take far too long. I am giving him a cost comparison. Further talk about *OED* (*Oxford English Dictionary*) and *SOED* (*Shorter Oxford English Dictionary*) schedules, which are worrying all of us.

To BFMP (*British Federation of Master Printers*) council meeting on lunch train for special meeting on the latest development over nat. agreements with NGA (*National Graphical Association, for compositors and machine minders*). Burfield seems to want a settlement and not a fight. We agreed his latest proposal for another 5/- on the second stage payment to come on 1 Aug 1971. He also wants an escape clause, mentioning VAT and the Common Market as reasons for an approach before the expiry of the agreement. No one wanted specific mention of VAT etc, in spite of what has been done in Scotland. Left to negotiators to draft something suitably vague. Only Yorkshire wanted the whole agreement referred back for further discussion.

---

7 Dan Davin (1913-1990), Assistant Secretary to the Delegates 1948-70, and Deputy Secretary 1970-78, was a New Zealander who had a distinguished war record – fighting in Greece, Crete and Italy – and wrote seven novels and other prose works in addition to his role as chief editor at the Clarendon Press.

Travelled back with John Alden (*of Alden Press, Oxford*). He is thinking of extending into security printing. Not getting a proper return on capital from bookwork, he says. Took Anne some carnations and an avocado, to soften the nasty fall she had yesterday. Reading Maude's *Life of Tolstoy*. Ben singing upstairs.

❧

30 June, Tuesday

Puzzled and rather disturbed by press reports of national negotiations. They say that NGA has rejected employers' offer and may strike after meeting on Thursday. Difficult to believe after yesterday but rang Santilano at Alliance Office (*BFMP branch in Southwest*) and he says that Bedford Row are indeed worried and puzzled by the NGA tactics.

Preparing for Finance Committee this afternoon. Profit for month better, but on far too narrow a basis of highly profitable jobs. Gerard Frost (*Printing House Finance Director*) presented his cost & profit analysis of exam paperwork. Plenty of scope for axing many of the smaller bodies and some of the larger ones as well.

Had a long and fairly cheerful talk with Gerry Fulton (*Father of the Chapel at the Printing House*).[8] He is hoping for a straight £3 increase 'and forget all about next year'. I told him to prepare for some disappointment. He still hankers after plant bargaining even tho' I tell him that no such bargain could bring the chaps very much. I also said again that we would not be bargaining on equal terms, as he would refer everything back to the NGA for vetting.

A thinly-attended FC. Roderick Henderson (*Controller of the Wolvercote Paper Mill*) was there, slowly explaining the Mill accounts and its troubles. Also put in a paper arguing that his tax losses should be put to the benefit of the business. Chairman & other delegates unreceptive. I gave my estimate of the effect of the proposed wage

---

8 Fulton was the head shop steward ('Imperial Father') and, according to Anne Ridler, a 'power-hungry man who caused endless trouble', as she recorded in her *Memoirs*. She found it appropriate that at the annual Press pantomime 'he used to play the part of the Demon King'.

increase on the Printing Business – £100,000 a year now and another £55,000 next year, or nearly 25% overall. FC suitably dismayed. Also gave an account of the strike and its consequences. Meeting adjourned so that the salaries sub-committee could meet to decide the new salary scales for senior officers. When FC reconvened, chairman announced all salaries, the first time we have known what each of us is getting or will get from 1 July. Secretary to the Delegates (Colin Roberts[9]) is top man at £8500, Publisher (John Brown[10]) £7500, Davin and myself £6500, and Henderson £6000. In view of assets we each control I thought this reasonable. At least we shall now have room to do more for our subordinates.

Earlier in day also discussed with John Hall (*Printing House Personnel Manager*) new proposals for our pensioners and the staffing of our Production Control Section now that we plan to move O'Reilly to Personnel.

Richard Russell (*Assistant Printer*) produced a draft letter from Schaefer of PA (*Personnel Administration, outside consultants*) destined for the City Architect and intended to argue in favour of the proposed 50ft-high warehousing at Jordan Hill (*Press Warehouse in North Oxford*). Drafting v. poor. I left it with Secretary for him to brood over. It will be interesting to see what line Murray takes with it.

July 1970

§

1 July, Wednesday

Took Ben to Bristol with me on my way to a special Alliance meeting

---

9 Colin Roberts (1909-1990), Secretary to the Delegates 1954-74, made his name in the early part of his career as a papyrologist, and also worked in intelligence at Bletchley Park during World War II.

10 Sir John Brown (1916-2003), OUP Publisher 1956-80, began his career in 1937 at OUP's Bombay branch, but during World War II was captured by the Japanese and held as a prisoner of war. He rejoined the Press in London in 1946, becoming Sales Manager in 1949. On his retirement from OUP in 1980 he took up a post at Blackwell Publishing Group, becoming Vice-President in 1987.

at the Grand Hotel. Amused that he should be turned away from the GH dining room because he wasn't wearing a jacket. Went to Berni Inn, where we saw on TV Roger Taylor almost beating Clark Graebner at Wimbledon. He did succeed in the end but I couldn't stay to see the result.

Meeting fairly well attended. Most people resigned to the size of the proposed wage increases, and most also felt that the clauses in the agreement now being resisted by Burfield were negotiable, tho' they should be there in some form. Left just after 4pm to find Ben and Sid Church (*VR's Press chauffeur*) waiting for me outside. Home by 6.15.

❦

2 July, Thursday

Ivor Robinson, the leather binder, came in to see me. He has asked me to produce the catalogue for an exhibition of British fine binding to be held at the Pierpont Morgan and Newbury Libraries in the autumn of next year. We discussed formats and time-tables, and he went away happy. Later I had lunch with John Simmons, who takes office as Librarian at All Souls on 1 October. We discussed arrangements for handling the library work here when he is no longer available to help.

Visited Fred Allen and Bill Sutton in their respective wards at the Radcliffe. Allen, who has cancer, was hazy but cheerful, saying he 'felt like a new man'. But he looked very weak and ill, and I doubt whether we shall see him on a folding machine again. Sutton also was in good spirits, with his wife sitting alongside him. He hopes to be home again early next week. Both said how well they were being looked after by the staff.

❦

3 July, Friday

Spent some time discussing possibility of increasing pensions for our old age pensioners with J Hall; and the various warehousing projects we have in hand with RR. The consultants propose a 50ft high building at Jordan Hill. A letter has now gone to the City Architect's office putting the case for such a building. I'm very doubtful whether it will go through, and I'm not sure it ought to. Just before lunch I made a staff presentation to Mrs Lucas in the Library. They gave her a cheque and a large greeting card with their names inscribed inside. Mrs L is not looking forward to retirement although she is going at her own wish. She has been running the Sewing Section of the Bindery very well and I am sorry to lose her.

At 4 o'clock RR and I left for our weekend ICL course at Hedsor House, near Bourne End. The house was built in the 19th c. and stands in pleasant surroundings on a hill above the Thames. There are 16 people in the course, which is intended to give directors some idea of what computers can now do for them. Food good, and we were able to see some of the tennis in colour on TV. Not impressed.

☙

6 July, Monday

Main event of the day a visit from Sir Frank Lee and Dick David, of CUP.[11] Rather surprised that Lee, sitting in one of my leather armchairs, should suddenly cock his leg over one of the arms. David gave him a hard look but he remained oblivious. We had a long talk on profitability, and on the present unprofitability of the Cambridge bindery and their slowness in getting into lithography. Lee said he was very impressed with our new Litho and Bindery, but that may have been politeness. CHR (Colin Roberts) and RR joined us for tea in my room. We discussed the question of rising costs, the new wage agreement, and printing abroad, particularly in Hong Kong. Also warehousing, and our plans for Jordan Hill. They left soon after 4.30.

☙

7 July, Tuesday

Comparatively quiet day. JH & RR both went to London on different

---

11 Sir Frank Lee (1904-1971) and Richard David (1912-1993) were Chairman and Secretary to the Syndics respectively of Cambridge University Press. David was Secretary 1963-70.

errands. Saw Frost again on the difficult questions arising from our costing and charging system. I want to avoid 'across-the-board' increases, but it is going to be difficult to do that and to restore the Bindery to something like its former profitability. Wrote to Brooke Crutchley[12] about his article on learned presses for *Scholarly Publishing*, the Canadian journal. I added a note on *his* note about the enlarged *NEB* page for the proposed desk Bible, which the Joint Board is anxious to have on the market by Christmas. He has a point about the length of line, which is certainly not ideal, but his other criticisms carry less force. I am sure the publishers will go ahead, and if Brooke doesn't want to put his imprint to it (as he says), then I am quite ready to print it for them. Also received and answered John Simmons' official letter of resignation.

Stratford with A and Kirstie[13] in the evening. *Measure for Measure.* Ian Richardson of course splendid as Angelo. The others are rather a mixed bag: having another company in London has diluted the quality.

❦

8 July, Wednesday

Publishers' sales conference at New College. Slight pessimism of Secretary and Publisher's report on present and future sales not modified by the coming increase in labour costs I announced. Travellers were most critical of sudden heavy price increases on prices shown in the spring and autumn lists, and on lack of stock before Christmas of the most saleable Oxford books. Some 'before-and-after' jacket designs were produced. I was delighted to find that most of those present thought and hoped that the 'before' (which had been designed in my Layout Dept) were the 'after'. Laughter all round, but I doubt whether the lesson will have sunk in. The present design policy must be costing a fortune.

Harold Osborne, editor of the *Companion to Art*, was billed to speak

---

12 Brooke Crutchley (1907-2003) was University Printer 1946-74 at Cambridge University Press, and a good friend of VR. Together they had printed the *New English Bible* (see Introduction). See Appendix 3.
13 Kirstie Milford was the widow of AR's cousin, the composer Robin Milford (1903-1959), who was the son of Sir Humphrey Milford (1877-1952), OUP London Publisher 1913-45 (see Introduction).

about it before lunch but failed to turn up. Apparently he has a reputation for losing his way. He didn't turn up at the lunch either.

When I got home I was rather dismayed to find that Valerie Eliot (*TS Eliot's widow*), who had been coming to make a few alterations to *The Waste Land* manuscript, was still there.[14] I now have grimmest forebodings as to what will happen to the proofs when she gets them. I suggested that she should bring the corrected ms to the Press in the morning, when the redoubtable Ken Butler can take care of her.

❦

9 July, Thursday

Spent a good deal of time in the Works. Mrs Fulton, successor to Mrs Lucas, seems to be making a good start in the Sewing Section, and the other Bindery supervisors are well pleased with the amount of work now going through the department. A great contrast to this time last year, when we were very low indeed, at least in some sections.

A sample volume of the Hazell printing of *NEB* has at last reached me. Some pages are badly out of position, so much so that the verse numbers on the foredge have been chopped off. My part of the joint imprint is also incorrect, and altogether I feel their impressions are a bad letdown from the high standard we set ourselves.

Signed the indentures of one comp. apprentice and one electrician. The latter very bright, the other slow and pudding-like, tho' JH thinks we shall make something of him. I hope so.

Drafted a brief note on examination papers for Finance Committee. I am anxious to have their full support if I begin turning long-established customers away. The pressure of CP work continues to grow, and I must do something about it.

Wives' night for the Management Club. At Brasenose, with Lord

---

14 Faber & Faber, TS Eliot's publisher, had asked the Printing House to undertake the complex task of producing the facsimile edition of Eliot's *The Waste Land* (with its annotations by Ezra Pound and Eliot's first wife, Vivienne), being edited by Valerie Eliot.

Goodman[15] as guest speaker. He put up an astounding performance on the subject of 'The changing role of the professional adviser'. No notes, marvellous fluency, controversial, interesting stuff. He got a lively response from one of the largest attendances the Club has had for some time. My proposal to enlarge the number of members had its 'first reading', so to speak, and went through unopposed.

☙

10 July, Friday

Long discussion with JH on salary increases that will arise out of new agreement with the unions. It looks as tho' nothing less than 12½% will be adequate to keep supervisors reasonably well ahead of the men.

In the afternoon, Cummings of the OLE Board brought in a draft of his report to his Delegates. He wanted me to see it because it contains several references to the Press, some of them mildly critical. I had no objection to them because on the whole it showed understanding of our difficulties (mainly of staffing), and, as he says, it is important from his point of view to have 'close and amicable relations' with us. After he had gone I discussed with RR (who had been present at the meeting) plans for extending the Reading Room into the old Drawing Office.

☙

13 July, Monday

(On Sat. we joined Philip Wright (*Southwestern Alliance printing colleague*) and his wife in celebrating their silver wedding by a trip up the Thames to Abingdon in the *Mary Stuart*, hired by Philip for the occasion. Packed with relatives. Pleased to have Sam, Philippa and the baby Mark Wright for company, as well as the Brookhouse Richards's. Bernard BR told me that altho' virtually retired he was looking after the rebuilding of Marden International's office block opposite Temple Meads station, and had just been given the biggest increase in salary he'd ever had. Whole

---

15 Arnold Goodman (1913-1995), famous lawyer, adviser to Harold Wilson and Chairman of the Arts Council 1965-72.

trip too long, but lovely weather and very peaceful. The next morning I was on the river again, watching 'our lads' do their annual river swim, and giving out the prizes at the Isis Hotel afterwards. Again very lucky with the weather, tho' v. little current to help the swimmers.)

At our usual meeting this morning the Secretary mentioned how much faster and cheaper Clowes were with the setting of *SOED*. This worries me a good deal because, as I suspected, they are making use of their patent enlarged Monotype die-case, which eliminates much of the handwork that we have to do. There is nothing I can do about it just now, not until we install a filmsetter capable of doing this work; and there are other problems with that.

At managers' meeting the serious shortage of bookbinders & girls was again reported. JH does his best but it is very difficult these days to match work flow and labour force. We are also in trouble in the Letterpress Machine Room, where the staff, partly because of holidays, is now too small for the handling of urgent work, whatever may be said of the long-term load. The Litho Department is also facing a bleak second half of the year, with v. little long-run work for the big machines. The two bright spots are the Composing Rooms, as usual, and the Bindery. The Bindery load is in striking contrast to last year's, when we were searching around for work.

Further discussion with Frost on forthcoming wage increases and our charging policy.

Also had meeting – the AGM – of the Ex-Servicemen's Association. Good financial state (£38 balance!), and annual dinner now fixed for 9 Dec.

❦

14 July, Tuesday

The shortest Finance Committee I can remember. It was held after a full Delegates meeting which began at 2 or 2.15, so that no one was in the mood for a prolonged meeting. Several matters deferred, including that of shedding some exam paperwork. Agreed that all John Fryman's (*Press architect*) recommendations on stonework restoration should be accepted, which is sensible tho' expensive. Further talk on the future of the Mill. It is a great problem. Apparently some Canadians, introduced by Rothschilds, are faintly interested, not in buying but in either some form of trading agreement or renting. After FC Bruno came down to my room for a talk. He feels that we are not publishing a sufficient number of the right books. Even the *Companions*, as he says, are based on an idea now 40 years old, and we should be exploiting our strength in reference books more, instead of living on it. Rather pessimistic in fact, and alarmed by the number of mergers and take-overs made over the last few years. Also imparted the useful information that London is already allowing for a 15% increase in manufacturing costs from next month. In view of my talks with Frost about possible increases this was timely. But SOGAT (*Society of Graphical and Allied Trades, for bindery workers*) has not yet agreed to ballot its members so it may be well into August before wages are actually raised.

Inquired of Mick Foster's brother Tim, how Mick was doing after his sudden collapse in the Litho Dept yesterday morning. Still unconscious and may not last the day. The surgeon can do nothing until he comes round. A nice man, and someone we shall very much miss if he doesn't survive. Only 36, with 2 young children.

Lord Leicester came in to see me at the end of the day, with Bill Hassall (*of the Bodleian*). Very pleased and grateful with all that we are doing on his Roxburghe book.[16] I told him we might have copies ready by the end of the year, which quietened both of them.

Dined at the Eltons.[17] A long time since we have done so. Both of them as delightful as ever.

☙

15 July, Wednesday

---

16 Founded in 1812, the Roxburghe Club is the oldest society of bibliophiles in the world. The Club has 40 members and it was a prestigious matter that my father took pride in to produce a special volume for the Club.
17 Charles Elton (1900-1991) was a pioneer of the study of animal ecology, conducting a 20-year animal survey in Oxford's Wytham Woods. His wife, E. J. Scovell (1907-1999), was a distinguished poet and translator.

Just heard that Foster died at 5 o'clock this morning. It will be a great blow to his father, who is still very active here, altho' he thinks of retiring.

To the head offices of Benn Bros in Bouverie Street for a meeting of the Newspaper Design Award committee. My fellow-judges, John Dreyfus[18] and Edwin Taylor, were there, also the managing director of BB and two of his colleagues. Colley, editor of *Printing World*, chaired the discussion after lunch. Allen Hutt[19] also present, and voluble – but then, so was I. Slipped round to the new museum at St Bride's after the meeting. Very well displayed. Items included an Ingles stop cylinder that James Mosley[20] had rescued from a firm in the north. He appeared, to tell me all about it and other pieces on show. James Moran[21] also came in later, with two visitors from Yale. The room is dual-purpose: various cases can be pushed back and space made for seats when lectures are given. Money for the museum put up by City of London.

While Church is on holiday, Brown drives me to and from the station. This morning he described how his little sister, aged 3, had been burned to death while she was ill in bed. He was 14 at the time. He smelt the smoke and rushed up to her room, but she was enveloped in flames and there was nothing he could do to save her. She had been playing with cigarette cards, got out of bed to pick some of them up and must have caught her nightdress on the fire. What an experience for a young boy.

☙

16 July, Thursday

Letters and talks with several managers this morning. Thrashed out charging policy to put to Sec & Publisher with Frost and RR. SOGAT has not yet agreed to ballot its members on the increases but I assume

---

18 John Dreyfus (1918-2002) was a book designer and printing historian who worked for CUP and the Monotype Corporation.
19 Allen Hutt (1901-1973), a journalist and political activist, wrote *Newspaper Design* (1967) and *The Changing Newspaper* (1973), both standard works on the subject.
20 James Mosley was Librarian of St Bride Printing Library 1958-2000, and collected much disused hot metal printing equipment for the Library.
21 James Moran is a typographer and historian of printing, whose books include *Stanley Morison: His Typographic Achievement* (1971) and *The Double Crown Club* (1970).

they will soon do so. My increases will average 12½% in cost, the largest ever made, if they are accepted. As Bruno told me that he was already allowing for another 15%, I don't expect much argument except perhaps over binding, where I want 20% on runs of 1-1000.

Instructed Fryman to put stonework repairs on the main frontage in hand.

The Pensioner Party took place in the afternoon. We now have about 165 pensioners in all, and 65 accepted the invitation – much the same figure as in previous years. The oldest on the scene was Young, 85, and Joe Ayres, 84. It is delightful to hear from them how much they enjoy going around the Works and meeting their old friends. This time we had a good gathering of ladies, including Miss Wheeler and Miss Osler, neither of whom had been before. At tea I pointed out that the pond in the quad was now stocked with goldfish and water lilies, and told them of the new Keyboard Room being built in the Mono annexe, the *NEB*, and the *Companion to Art*. The clever and irredeemably snobbish Fanny Williams was also present, and looking as though she would have liked more attention; but I felt I had to spread my favours rather thinly. The sun was shining when we went into the quad for the traditional photograph, taken this year by Jim Coles in baggy trousers. Afterwards I had Joe Ayres and Cecil Holt in my room for a drink and a gossip. Chagrined to hear that Joe had sold his magnificent green bike to a publican for £5.

❦

17 July, Friday

Long lunchtime meeting with Oates and Roberts (of the BM) on Bibliographical Society business. Main item: the new Short Title Catalogue and the schedule for producing proofs. The copy is good and nearly ready. I suggested we might show a new specimen in which the notes are set in the same size as the main entries. This would save an enormous amount of handwork when we come to make up into pages. This was agreed, but it may not satisfy the editor or other members of the BS Council.

To a Playhouse meeting at 5.[22] Usual deficit, but Hauser as spry as ever, tho' blenching at the fact that he is to produce Alan Badel as both Kean (Sartre) and Othello. I can't see Badel as Othello, clever actor tho' he is.

In the evening went with Philippa[23] to S Hinksey Church, to see Arthur's granite gravestone in position. The setting, with a dark yew tree in the background, is just right, and the bronze plaque fits neatly on to the broken surface of the stone.

᳓

18 July, Saturday

Mick Foster's funeral at the Crematorium. Largest attendance I have ever seen. The dreary vicar of Beckley ploughed through the service, not much help, I thought, to the poor widow who was sobbing her heart away under his nose.

᳓

20 July, Monday

Discussed proposed increase in my charges with CHR. His only comment was that the production department will tend to shop around more to get competitive prices, more work may go to Hong Kong, fewer reprints would be put in hand, but new book composition would go on as before. All these things may indeed happen, and I must be prepared, and must prepare the men, for possible cold winds later in the year.

Rather wasted the afternoon by going to Bedford Row for a finance meeting. It started at 2.30 and ended at 3.10, and no business of vital importance was discussed. At least I managed to catch the 4.15 back and continued reading Maude's *Life of Tolstoy* (vol.2) both coming and going. What a fascinating and fantastic story, and what a man.

---

22 VR was a director of the Meadow Players, the resident theatre company at the Oxford Playhouse run by Frank Hauser.

23 Philippa Kingsbury (1913-2014), close friend and school contemporary of Anne Ridler, was the widow of the Oxford geologist Arthur Kingsbury (1906-1968). Their son Martin became a director of Faber Music.

Two long letters from Colin (*Ridler*) awaited me.

❦

21 July, Tuesday

To BFMP Council meeting in London. Presented the Legislation Committee report and left shortly after to get the mid-day train back to Oxford. Finance Committee at 2.30. New York's vice-president Byron Hollinshead reported on the state of the Branch. Laconic delivery. Optimistic in spite of fairly dismal figures. My proposed increases were received quietly. The chairman made the agreeable point that the Ptg Business could if necessary make less profit so that the Publishing Business could make more. I said that I would certainly remember this, but warned the Delegates that my budgeted net profit for this financial year assumed some increase in sales. From all I had heard and observed I now thought it doubtful that sales would be greater than last year's, even allowing for inflation, so that profits could in any case fall quite drastically. At the end of the main meeting we had another of the chairman, one Delegate (Hart) and the officers, to discuss senior salaries in the various businesses. The new grades should allow for substantial increases for RR, JH, and GF.

Exam paper printing also discussed. FC agreed that I should as necessary reduce the amount I now do. CHR assured the meeting that if I turned away some of this profitable work there would be no diminution in the flow of new CP composition. This is most important to me.

❦

22 July, Wednesday

Taken up with meetings. After the 10 o'clock, a managers' meeting to discuss their departmental joint committee reports before the Works Advisory Cttee later in the day. That meeting, held at 3.15, went fairly smoothly, tho' I am always faintly depressed that so few members take part in the discussions. Fulton and I do most of the talking, and by the end of the meeting I usually feel pretty worn. Still, this time there was no serious discussion, in fact most of the talk was amiable and cool. I left to catch the 5.30 for my Wynkyn de Worde dinner in London. The purpose was to honour the next day's guest speaker, a Belgian by the name of Michel Olyff. I knew the name only because I had printed the menu at home. I can't say that I found him particularly attractive, but the time passed agreeably enough as I was sitting next to Roy Fullick's wife whom I found pleasant to talk to. RF is not bad but he will show off: the way he criticized the white wine, using snob-language, I found very tiresome. Another person I like and talked to is Basil Harley, now managing director of the Curwen Press.[24] Allen Hutt presided. I left soon after eleven for Whitehall Court, which is now being spivved up with gilt and red paint. Read *Tolstoy* for an hour before turning out the light.

☙

23 July, Thursday

Looked in on KS Thompson at Ely House (*OUP London HQ, where Thompson was Production Manager*). Glad I did because he had our Nigerian manager, Chief Solam, with him. Solam was looking for help in getting some of his school books printed. Many are done in Lagos but others are done by Butler and Tanner, Clowes, and Hazells over here. I was exasperated to hear him say, when I said that of course I could print for him if he only asked, that he had always been told that the 'Clarendon Press' was far too busy to be approached. This is the sort of thing that gets said without any consultation with me and I find it very tiresome. So now I am expecting to receive from Ibadan specimens of the sort of titles he wants done.

The W de Worde lunch passed off well. As I expected, many people wanted to know what a 'smooter' was (I had used it for my imprint

---

24 The Curwen Press became famous from the 1920s onwards for its collaboration with artist-printmakers such as Paul Nash, Graham Sutherland, Edward Bawden, Eric Ravilious, Barnett Freedman, John Piper, Henry Moore and many others. It was led by Harold Curwen, Oliver and Herbert Simon, and latterly Basil Harley.

on the menu)[25] and both James Moran and I were asked to enlighten them. Olyff's piece, which he translated from French into English as he went along, was not interesting or well delivered; in consequence the discussion afterwards more or less faded after a few minutes and I was able to leave in good time to catch the 3.15 back to Oxford. Stationers' Hall is a fine place but the acoustics are very poor. Herbert Newman (*of CUP*) was there. He had printed the previous speaker's talk, so the printed contributions were in one sense Oxbridge, as Hutt remarked.

In the evening with A and Philippa to see the new Fry play, *A Yard of Sun*. Magnificent set, acting good to middling, play ditto. Not a bad audience for Oxford in July. Earlier I had picked up the printed copies of A's opera libretto *The Jesse Tree*[26] from Mr Parchment in Hurst Street. He had done it very well, and quickly. His premises are much smarter than I had expected – much smarter than he is, in appearance I mean, for he is bright enough in running his little business.

24 July, Friday

A long discussion with Frost, Walker, and RR on making further use of the Neasden computer. Walker, as yet still v. inexperienced, thinks I'm an old fuddy-duddy because I won't at once forge ahead with his various schemes. The one he is now pressing is for production control. I don't want to discourage him: our present system does need improvement but his scheme sounds impossibly ambitious and rigid. I have told him to go away and put his plan on paper, showing the stages needed to bring it into force. He looked rather downcast at this, but I'm sure the experience will be good for him.

---

25 At both the Wynkyn de Worde and the Double Crown Club dining clubs for printers and book designers, it is a tradition that members will each, in rotation, design and print the menu. Here VR had styled himself 'Smooter to the University', a 'smooter' being a casual worker in a printing house.

26 Elizabeth Maconchy (1907-1994) was the composer of *The Jesse Tree*. She and AR had collaborated before on another opera, *The Departure* (1969). Influenced by Bartók, who taught her briefly, and one of the finest composers of the 20th century, she produced over 200 works, including 13 string quartets.

To the Manor House, Little Gaddesden, in the evening, for Ben's concert. He played to a 'packed house' in the upper drawing room and received many compliments afterwards. (*VR and AR had been married in the local church in 1938.*)

🦟

27 July, Monday

Two complaints to be dealt with: proofs of Surtees's *Rossetti*[27] plates criticized again, and a letter of complaint from Schmoller[28] about the folding and trim of the Penguin *NEB* New Testament. These things always arrive on a Monday, or seem to. CHR also produced Garland's offering for the Almanack: a watercolour of Keble in impressionist-atmospheric style, and an earlier Lynton Lamb[29] of the same subject. The second would be much easier to reproduce and I prefer it to the rather weak construction of the Garland. No decision reached, but I expect we will be reproducing the watercolour.

To Help the Aged Meeting[30] after lunch, followed by a Stated Meeting at Teddy Hall (*where VR was a professorial fellow*). Dined in the new senior common room – very noisy at the moment without either carpets or curtains, but the fine wood panels make an agreeable background.

🦟

28 July, Tuesday

Main meeting to discuss with Sugden[31] and RR the reduction in the number of universities and other examining bodies we print for and the possible complications that might arise when I write to give them notice. I

---

27 Published in 1971 by OUP as *The Paintings and Drawings of Dante Gabriel Rossetti: A Catalogue Raisonné* (Vol. 1) by Virginia Surtees.
28 Hans Schmoller (1916-1985) was Typographer and later Head of Production at Penguin Books 1949-77.
29 Lynton Lamb (1907-1977), a member of the 'Euston Road' school of artists, designed many book jackets for OUP, and was a friend of A and V from the 1930s. Colin Ridler was his godson.
30 VR was an outside adviser to Help the Aged, and later, in his retirement, joined the board of its sheltered housing offshoot, Anchor Housing.
31 Victor Sugden was in charge of the printing of exam papers at the Printing House, and the editor of the in-house magazine *The Clarendonian*.

want this year to get the total number of individual papers handled down from 8600 to nearer 6000. Sugden saw no difficulties tho' he thought his section might be underemployed in the second half of the year.

Message from JH that Arthur Gray, who has run a machine in the Bindery for more than 40 years, died suddenly from angina over the weekend. He had a steadying influence in the room and we shall miss him, particularly just now, when we are short of men.

Frost also came to see me, partly to give me the period accounts for June (better than we expected after the strike: total cost about £10,000), and partly to tell me of his housing troubles. He is moving from the new house he bought in Charlbury about two years ago because the builders have never finished the site and are now going bankrupt. But before he made a move he wanted to be sure that I was satisfied with his services! Characteristic that he should even ask.

I had Peter Stone in at 4.30 to give him the engraving of fish that I had framed for him. He was delighted, almost speechless, but I felt I owed him something in return for the two books he had given me.

A party (pre-birthday) at home for AR, with Philippa, Peter Pelz (*Ben's artist friend*), Ben & me. Singing and playing after a turkey supper and two bottles of '52 claret most generously brought by Philippa. Ben gave A Bartók's *Bluebeard's Castle*, a great treat, and P some shells from the Mediterranean in a glass bowl. I am keeping my two presents for Thursday, but Ben and Peter are going off to Wales tomorrow morning. Reading Tolstoy's 'The Tree Felling', an early story.

❦

29 July, Wednesday

Longish talk with Walker on what I want him to do over improving our production control system. Explained that I always preferred taking one step at a time rather than a spectacular leap, and that he might concentrate first on the Bindery, which he had criticized very strongly. This seemed to cheer him up after our earlier meeting, and he went off happily.

At the end of the morning I had Thompson, Production Manager at Ely House, in for a talk with RR and myself over a glass of sherry. He is in a dreadfully nervous and highly strung state. It is painful to listen to and I had to keep pushing him back to the main source of contention just now, the printing and binding of *Hornby*[32] in Hong Kong. A difficult situation, and one I am not at all happy about, altho' we are doing all we can to retain the work here. KST is very indiscreet, deliberately, given his present state, but what he discloses is useful.

In the afternoon I had the Proctors and Assessor in to tour the works. They seemed impressed and not too weary at the end of it, and we talked about the problem of exam paper printing and other University work over a cup of tea. Stockton, the Senior Proctor, whom I had not taken to in FC, was rather more friendly than I had expected. But my first assessment of him as a probably bad-tempered man on his home ground still remains.

Berthold Wolpe[33] rang up soon after they left. I took him home to supper and to the station afterwards. After David's[34] death, he said, Brian Rooney had been made production manager, and someone else given a new title. He asked Dick de la Mare (*Faber director*) 'what about me, what am I supposed to be'. 'Well, you know we all love you', said D (obviously embarrassed). The next day, after a board meeting, D called him in and told him he was to be called 'Design and typographic consultant' to the firm. No increase in salary but B seemed happy at the news. He is now 65, and cannot afford to retire, he says, while his youngest child, Toby, is still at school.

With Ben and Peter gone the house seemed very quiet and empty.

---

32 AS Hornby's *Advanced Learner's Dictionary of Current English*, first published by OUP in 1948, had become a huge Press bestseller worldwide (see Introduction).

33 Berthold Wolpe (1905-1989), a student of Rudolf Koch in Germany before the war, worked for Faber & Faber 1941-75, designing over 1,500 book jackets and covers for the firm, often using his own typeface Albertus. He also designed the typefaces Hyperion, Pegasus and Tempest among others.

34 David Bland (1911-1970), VR's oldest friend, was Production Manager and then Production Director at Faber & Faber until his death in January 1970. As an RAF bomber navigator during the war, he had been shot down over Germany, and spent two harrowing years in Stalag Luft III prisoner-of-war camp, which affected his health. See also Introduction.

❦

30 July, Thursday

At 9.30 I saw Brian Hardy, one of our Composing Room apprentices, to commend his work and the meticulous notebook he has been keeping at the school. I wondered while I was speaking to him whether he might one day make a supervisor. He is quiet and diffident now, as often happens, and that makes it hard to guess how he will turn out.

Soon after 11, to the Crematorium for Gray's funeral. A fair number there, including Beal, the SOGAT Branch Secretary, and his father. The priest, whom I didn't know, was an improvement on the last, and spoke the words clearly and without affectation.

Wrote to a correspondent who wanted to know why the verse of *NEB* is indented as it is. Shades of Driver.[35] I did my best, after looking up the early memoranda that had passed between me and CHR. Also wrote a difficult letter to Schmoller in reply to his complaint of the Penguin *NEB* NT printing.

A's birthday today. Home for lunch, just in time to see Tim (*Wilson, VR's son-in-law*), who had been scouring Wales in a search for *hermits*. He is writing on the subject for *New Society* and had called in to breakfast. A's new binoculars received with joy and gladness.

Toured some of the departments after lunch. Said goodbye to Hughes, a good Press reader now suffering from cataracts. He doesn't want to go and I am sorry to lose him, but the strain on his eyes is too great.

RR reported to me the result of Mansfield's visit to Pettys of Leeds to see their automatic binder. Favourable. Cost high but we should reduce our cost rate on the letterpress rotary by 10%. I said go ahead at once. Also discussed R's draft reply to Chester's[36] (Ely House) testy letter on the Hornby dictionary for the English Language Books series. I think it too long and must now have a go myself.

---

35 GR Driver (1892-1975), Professor of Semitic Philology at Oxford, chaired the panel overseeing the new translation of the Old and New Testaments for the *New English Bible*, published in 1970 by OUP and CUP (see Introduction).
36 Philip Chester was Deputy Publisher at OUP in London.

❦

31 July, Friday

Three more retirements today, a young woman graduate reader who is getting married and moving to Dublin; Clements, who has been in charge of our Monotype matrix section for many years; and Morse, one of our better compositors. All of them will be a loss to us, and the two men assured me that the young men now coming up have a different attitude and think of nothing but the money. One of those generalizations with a grain of truth in it.

A long meeting with RR and the litho experts on the *Rossetti* plate proofs. Some of them are not as good as they should be, but most of the criticism goes well beyond the limits of the process. I shall have to try to get this over at our meeting with the CP people on Monday.

The first fifteen pages of *The Waste Land* transcript went to Valerie Eliot and to Faber this evening. A fine job so far and I hope she approves. The remainder is well in hand. Another fine litho job appeared on my desk this morning: the first volume of the Beethoven notebook facsimile. The two volumes will sell at £25 and should be worth it.

August 1970

❦

3 August, Monday

At the Secretary's meeting we had an amicable discussion on the *Rossetti* illustrations. We are to go on, making what improvements we can in light of their criticisms. I am not really very happy with parts of what we have done: we should have done better but I am not certain whether the fault lies in the materials, process or men. But we haven't time for prolonged experiment. Also talked about the much reduced output of CP books from the Bindery. We are short of men, as I said, but we have been producing some large orders for other customers, and on this point we remained silent.

After lunch I went over to the Radcliffe to see poor Busby, who has now had another piece of his leg off, up to the knee. His wife, a cheerful-looking soul, was in the ward with him. He looks grey and drawn, but seems determined to make the best of things.

A Housing Society meeting at 5. Mainly matters of repairs and maintenance. CHR has taken on a property manager, Ayres, who seems to me an excellent man who could save the business some money by good management and a close watch on maintenance. The other main item was the question of putting up fences for some of the tenants at the Wolvercote estate. No one seemed keen – I certainly wasn't – and in the end we agreed to a small section to act as a screen from the path alongside.

The new Rover 2000 was ready for me at the end of the day. It runs very smoothly and easily and I think it will suit us. Church is excited, tho' he is said to not like the dark green colour which I find quite pleasant. CHR tells me he is changing his Volvo for a Triumph.

☙

4 August, Tuesday

Mainly correspondence until it was time to go for the London train. I lunched with John Bell (*chief editor at the London Business*) and Philip Chester at Ely House. Afterwards JB, Audrey Bayley, and I called upon Blanche Henrey at her very luxurious flat at Hyde Park Gate, overlooking the Park. She has been working since 1946 on a history and bibliography of gardening.[37] We were there to look through the vast mass of material she has collected together from which illustrations are to be chosen. The whole work will make three volumes and by the time it is finished should sell at about £30 a set. After an hour and a half I began to feel quite dazed by Xerox and photostat prints of flowers, flower books and title pages. There must be well over 300 and cutting them down to a practical number will be a formidable job for someone. At 5 we had an

---

37 Published in 1975 as *British Botanical and Horticultural Literature Before 1800* by Blanche Henrey.

elegant tea, watching the cars sail by below, and at 5.30 I took my leave. I now wait on JB for the next move.

❧

5 August, Wednesday

While I was in London yesterday Richard de la Mare phoned to fix an appointment. He came in this morning at 11.15. We went over plans for *The Waste Land*, the limited edition in particular, and he is now anxious to have my estimates as soon as possible. The limited edition is to be 530 copies, bound in full buckram and printed on the rather pleasant paper supplied by Grunfeld for the BM *Beethoven*. Valerie Eliot has still not sent me the remaining material, but Dick assured me it should be here before the end of the week. I wonder.

He confessed that the real purpose of his visit was to ask my advice on the problem of their production department. David's death left them unprepared, and although they felt they had to give Brian Rooney, the next young man in line, a chance, it had not been successful. He wondered whether I could recommend anyone. I gave him three names: Leonard Chance, Peter Guy,[38] and Hugh Williamson.[39] He knows HW slightly, and we agreed that he is a bit of a bore tho' very able. He is now going to consult the office discreetly to see what they think about the prospect of HW, who could be his best bet. I said I would approach him informally if he wanted me to.

He gave me a glowing account of the Rover 2000. He has had one for 5½ years and says it is the most comfortable and finest car he has ever had. I certainly find the new one comfortable, and very easy to drive in traffic.

Immediately after he had left I had Sir Douglas Veale waiting to see me. I was a bit nervous at the prospect, knowing his power of persuasion,

---

38 Peter Guy (1938-2000) was a gregarious typographer and book designer with a penchant for flamboyant hats who worked at Chatto and Windus, the Folio Society, and Gordon Fraser, and was Secretary of the Wynkyn de Worde Society.

39 Hugh Williamson (1918-1992) was a book designer whose *Methods of Book Design: The Practice of an Industrial Craft*, first published by OUP in 1956, became a standard work on the subject. See Appendix 4.

but he only wanted help over the production of an appeal leaflet for St Luke's Home (*a nursing home in Oxford*), which gave me no problem.

After lunch I went through some of the departments. In the Litho I had another talk with Sinclair and Bradley (Coles is still away) on the problem of the *Rossetti* plates and how we should tackle them. I am most anxious to give the CP a fine job but I'm afraid young John Nicoll[40] is asking for, and expecting, too much. I think we can do better than we have done, at least in some cases, but not very much.

At 4.30 the PA consultant, Stiefel, came in with Richard to put me up to date with the plans for warehouse reorganization at Jordan Hill. He had a mass of detail to impart and as he also has rather a soporific voice I became rather restless after half an hour or so, and ended the meeting. Not that the subject isn't of great importance, but this was only information, not a request for decisions.

Afterwards, when the office had gone, I managed to read a few more chapters of Harry's history of OUP.[41] All, or almost all, first-source stuff, and fascinating.

❦

6 August, Thursday

John Hall rang me this morning with the exasperating news from the Alliance office that the union ballots are through and so the Federation has agreed that the wage increases will apply from yesterday – mid-week! This will cause a great deal of work here and even more for those firms that have their wages records on computer. It may even pay us to pay the increase for the whole week.

I spent some time studying the sub-committee report on computer-assisted composition for OUP. I am strongly in favour of its proposal that we should commit ourselves to a pilot experiment at a cost of about

---

40 Clarendon Press editor who left OUP in 1973, frustrated by the lack of interest in expanding the art list. He went on to run Yale University Press in London, establishing it as a major force in art book publishing.

41 Harry Carter (1901-1982), OUP Archivist from 1954, in the end completed only the first volume (to 1780) of his *History of the Oxford University Press* (1975).

£6000. I wrote to CHR to say so. No one can yet assess the advantages in monetary terms or even whether there will be any, but the potential is so great that we should take moderate risks to find out.

Continued reading HGC's draft chapters of Press history. More impressed than ever at the breadth of his learning. I only hope he can complete it while he is still in good health.

Handed over the indenture of a litho retoucher, Justice by name. Unusual in being an RC convert to the Salvation Army. We nearly lost him to the Army but some difference of opinion kept him with us. An amiable, conscientious, slow-witted boy.

Skelly came to see me later in the afternoon. He wants to apply for the position of Clerk to the Schools that falls vacant next year. I doubt whether he will get it, tho' I wished him well. As a liaison man with Ely House he is too heavy-handed to be persona grata, but he is a good watch-dog of our interests, and in some respects I should be sorry to lose him, tho' in that post I am sure we could find someone better. He has another 15 years to go here and feels that this is his last chance of promotion.

Dick de la Mare rang up. I told him I had been having second thoughts about Williamson because he might be too much of a bore in spite of his competence. I suggested Ruari McLean[42] as another possible. Dick is going to get in touch with him and with Peter Guy.

Bruno wants me to give him a cut price for the Ruby Bible in order to compete with Collins in the Scottish market. He claims they are subsidizing their edition for political and religious reasons. I haven't much scope for cutting as we already lose money on the folding; but I must try to do something to help.

Just sent off a quotation to Kuwait for reprinting the Quran from material to be supplied. I suspect we are being used as a test figure and I shall be surprised (agreeably – the job is worth £15,000) if I hear any more.

---

42 Ruari McLean (1917-2006) was VR's contemporary, friend, and fellow book designer, who wrote extensively on the subject and became Typographic Adviser to HMSO 1966-90. He had also designed the famous children's comics *Eagle* and *Girl* in the 1950s.

A few polite and sorrowful replies in from examining bodies which have been turned away. It will be interesting to see how many do reply.

☙

7 August, Friday

Meetings... Late in the morning I took CHR and Ashton up on to the fire escape of the south wing to show how it would be possible to build office extensions for the CP over the Letterpress Machine Rooms. I said that it was partly dependent upon going ahead with Phase II of the Printing Business extensions because it would be an expensive as well as difficult job working over the machine room while the department was still running. CHR is enthusiastic enough to want Fryman to look at the problem. The site area must be extremely valuable and could be put to better use than it is now. Immediately after lunch to Vera Smith's funeral at Botley Cemetery. A sad affair. The parents so overcome that our presence seemed an intrusion. Yet it may have helped.

Finished Harry's draft chapters of the *History*. He confirms in it what I had always doubted: that the Clarendon Building was *not* built from the proceeds of the *Rebellion*.[43] Even at 18th-cent. costs it seemed impossible, and the book contributed only a few hundred pounds.

☙

10 August, Monday

Christopher[44] with us over the weekend. Took him to *Kes* at the ABC last night, which we all enjoyed. Karin's birthday on Saturday: usual excitement and bustle. Some tennis before her tea party.

RR on holiday for three weeks from today. Now raining, in spite of a favourable forecast; it looks like staying for the rest of the day. No, soon after lunch the sun was shining.

---

43 Edward Hyde, 1st Earl of Clarendon (1609-1674), was Lord Chancellor to Charles II before falling from favour in 1667 and going into exile in France. Here he wrote his *History of the Rebellion and Civil Wars in England*, which OUP published in 1702-1704.

44 Christopher Bradby (1905-1983) was Anne Ridler's elder brother, and had worked in publishing for the first part of his career, including at an OUP branch office in India. He also worked for the publisher George Bell in the 1930s and the pioneer book packager Adprint in the 1940s.

Usual meetings. Coles back from holiday. Mansfield complaining of lack of staff and of a good forward load at the same time – as usual. I asked whether it was true that we now had about 26,000 pages of new bookwork ready for machine. He thought this might be so but then added 'of course, when I have all the men back from holiday they will soon make inroads into it'. I wonder. He hasn't stopped yet.

Our main problem is still that of increasing the CP output from the Bindery. I had a note from CHR yesterday saying that finance shouldn't hold me back if I needed more machinery. I don't, at the moment, and in spite of the new Bindery I should have difficulty in finding space for much more, at least on the ground floor.

A nice letter from Valerie Eliot, with warm praise for our work on *The Waste Land*. We are fortunate in having Beckley in the Filmsetting Room. His meticulous, rather fussy way, is just right for all the intricacies of this job, and he has certainly done it well. More praise for the Litho: another letter of congratulation from the British Museum for Vol. II of the *Beethoven*. So not too bad a Monday, even though Fulton has returned from his (successful) holiday in Spain.

☙

11 August, Tuesday

For me, an abnormally quiet day. I took the opportunity of visiting Eddles in his little Kate Greenaway house by the canal at Botley. He was in good spirits tho' still getting some pain in his knee. He is a great talker and I listened as best I could to the intimate recital of hospital and convalescent home doings. He is anxious to get back to work and I'm sure this will be good for him, tho' transport will be a problem.

I spent some time going through the batch of *Waste Land* material VE has now sent me. Later I had Ken Stewart (*Printing House chief designer*) in and we discussed the way in which we might lay it out. Some points need discussion with VE, as I have now written to tell her.

Sir Douglas Veale came in again just after lunch, bringing with him copy for the St Luke's Home appeal. He is a splendidly businesslike doer of good works, very pleasant to deal with. I hadn't realized, or I had forgotten, that the founder and head of the Home is Mary McMaster.

Philip Chester rang from Ely House, agitated by a request from Granville Eastwood, general secretary of the Printing and Kindred Trades Federation, for an interview to discuss the printing of our Hornby dictionary in Hong Kong. He asked me about GE and whether I would think of sending JH to sit in on the talk. I said no, it would be better to hear what GE has to say on his own. He has brought all this on himself and it will be good for him to have to cope by himself. It may even do this business some good.

A wonderful summer's day. Lunch and supper out of doors.

❦

12 August, Wednesday

Another fairly quiet day. Talked with Mrs Salmon (*deputy to John Hall, the Personnel Manager*) about the vast amount of paperwork brought upon us by the Industry Training Board. The work may be useful in those houses where little training has been done in the past, but for a place like this it simply adds another burden to the staff and prevents them from doing their real job. Mrs Salmon, as spick and span as ever, looks to my eye a shade plumper than she was when she came, so hard work can't be getting on her nerves. I can tell that she would like JH to delegate more to her but I doubt that he ever will. More work on staff salaries. Discussions on work and balance of work with Fortescue in the Bindery. He is a good, simple chap, who dearly likes to call a spade a spade.

Anne came in soon after 5, and Church drove us to the station for the London train. We saw Gielgud and Richardson in Storey's latest play *Home*, at the Apollo. Well worth the effort and the rattlebang journey back by British Rail.

❦

13 August, Thursday

Fulton came to see me about supervisors. The NGA has set up a section to deal with their interests, mainly of course to head off freebooters such as Clive Jenkins (*head of the rival union ASTMS*). Fulton was calling a meeting to which all NGA supervisors would be invited. I told him that all this was up to him and them, but I could not commit myself as to what my attitude would be until I had precise proposals in front of me. And so on.

More *Waste Land* proofs. Look very good so far.

❦

14 August, Friday

To London for the final judging in the National Newspaper Design Award competition. We met at Bedford Row. I distinguished myself by leaving my selection in a parcel on Oxford Station but managed to bluff my way through. First and 2nd went to the *Observer* (again) and the *Guardian*. Most time went on the weeklies; after a long argument I managed to get the *Southport Visitor* as no.1. Lunch with Dreyfus and Colley afterwards at the Royal Connaught in Holton, and back on the 4.15.

Kate and Tim arrived for the weekend. We look after Karin and Juliette for Sat and Sun while Jane and Rolf go over into Herefordshire for a break.

❦

17 August, Monday

Phone call from Brooke Crutchley to say that he had been pressing on his Syndics the need to spend money on developing computer-assisted typesetting, mainly on the grounds that the shortage of compositors would get worse as the demand continued to grow. They had asked him whether he would not do better to pool resources for the project with other printers. He replied that the only firm he would wish to go in with was Oxford, and what did I think? I rather poured cold water on the idea, mainly because I think so much money can be lost in that game; but I told him I should be quite ready to keep him posted about the little we are doing. He seemed quite content with that.

Continued quiet all round. Correspondence and the usual meetings. Heavy pressure on the letterpress side, and binding. Litho forward load still looking thin. It will probably remain so for the rest of the year.

Went over to the hospital to see Piper. In spite of having a tube up his nose he was sitting up in a chair and talked very cheerfully with me for 20 mins. He was 77 in January. In reminiscent mood. Said that in Johnson's time he had been told (by that gossip-scholar Fanny Williams) that the post of head reader on Gass's retirement lay between him and Harrison. H got it, much to his own surprise because only a week or two before he had been disciplined for bad reading on a Bible, and had been going about in fear of the sack. But JJ was said to have been sorry for him because he had two children! Sounds unlikely. He had been a close friend of Piper's.

❦

18 August, Tuesday

I thought of going up to London for Allen Lane's memorial service at St Martin-in-the-Fields, then decided against. Saw young Walker at 10 o'clock to talk over with him his latest paper on production control by computer. He has a great deal to learn about the trade but I don't want to discourage him. There is *some* good in his plans. What I fear from them is an elaborate, centralized system, producing masses of detailed information that then cannot be acted on. I told him we would go further when RR comes back from holiday.

Bratt on the phone about our extended specimen for the Bible Society's illustrated *NEB*. We had been told by London that he wanted the whole of Genesis set to show his committee. It now turns out that he wants the preliminary pages plus as many pages of Genesis as will make up a 32p section. I managed to alter course just in time. Dealing with such things through London can be very annoying.

Coldest day since Aug 1940. 48° (*The Times*) (9°C)

19 August, Wednesday

A large number of reprint orders down from the CP this morning. Badly needed, in the Litho at least. The first batch of *Waste Land* proofs back from Valerie Eliot. Very clean too, much to my surprise and relief. A storm blew up over a failed promise for the delivery of leaflets to Denman College. Promised for last Friday, now not going, says Bindery, until Wednesday of next week. Played hell all round and got the date back to this Friday. Placated the Warden over the phone & wrote a note to Taylor demanding a full investigation. Spearman, on the order desk, is too stolid and slow for this sort of thing. I may have to replace him.

Lunch with Fryman, who was making a routine call to see how the new Keyboard Room was coming along. Later he saw CHR to discuss my suggestion for extending CP offices over the Letterpress Machine Room. Fryman not very keen at the moment. Obviously he thinks it may jeopardize Phase II (*of the new extension – see Introduction*); and I sympathize.

A young man by the name of Brady came to see me at 2.30. He had asked me to give him advice on a personal matter. He is assistant to Siviter Smith, managing director of that firm. It is now part of a larger group and he fears he may be pushed out in a few years time because SS will be retiring and the new boys may not want him. I don't know why he thought I could give him helpful advice. He is only 35 but is worried because he is now married and feels the responsibility. I told him to try tactfully to get some indication now whether he is likely to be kept on, and if not begin to look around while he is still in the job. All very obvious to me, but he seemed grateful. A precise, rather fussy fellow, I thought. He seems to have had a fair number of jobs during his career so far.

Discussion with Ken Stewart on a new specimen for the *Progressive English Dictionary*. The London boys want us to use sans serif. I'm not keen but I suppose we must bow to the market occasionally. Also heard that Sir Douglas Veale's wife had died. I have never met her but

I imagine it will be a blow to him.

Robertses and Eltons to dinner.

❦

20 August, Thursday

I had Miss Morris over this morning because I had heard that she was uneasy about the future of the Exam Section. I took pains to go into great detail about the institutes and other bodies whose work I was turning away. She is such an excellent and loyal supervisor that I think my efforts were rewarded by the way she reacted. It was remiss of me not to have thought of her before. I might have remembered that Sugden, her section leader, would be bound to pass on my information in a wooden and probably stupid way. He is an odd fellow, tho' I must say he does keep our exam work relatively trouble-free.

I also had JH in to discuss our present litho machine-minder strength, & whether we should take on a young man who has just been given an NGA card. We already have 12 men for 8 machines, and as it is unlikely that we shall be able to run many of the machines in shift, at least for the rest of the year, I decided that we would recruit no more minders. Of course we may lose some of the men at short notice, but I prefer that risk to unrest and puzzlement in the chapel if we take on yet another man when we are quite clearly short of work. JH did not demur, tho' he had encouraged and assisted the young man to try the NGA, not believing they would accept him!

Taylor came in to report on his visit to Ely House. All fairly calm in that quarter just now, with no grievous problems to be moaned about. We went on to discuss the weaknesses in our new production control system, which is making me uneasy. I think the system is all right in itself, the real trouble lies in getting accurate information from some of the departments, particularly the Bindery. The progress chasers, being young and inexperienced, tend to be overawed by the managers, whereas an old hand will usually go beyond them to the shop floor to check for himself. I thought about this after Taylor had left me and later in the afternoon went over the ground with him again. What I think we want is another, older man in the Bindery office, and perhaps another as a progress chaser, tho' I am not so sure about the second. A real obstacle is the shortage of craftsmen in the Composing Rooms and Bindery, and this we can only overcome with patience.

Dick de la Mare wrote to say that Faber now propose to publish *The Waste Land* in May next year, and could I manage it? In fact, if dear VE had only produced her Introduction when she said she would, I am quite sure we could have had bound stock ready in October, just in time for Christmas. She is making few changes in the transcript proofs, and once we have cleared the composition all the rest is straightforward.

Brooke has sent me his revised draft on 'Scholar-printers' for the Canadian journal *Scholarly Publishing*. It deals with Oxford and Cambridge, and with Oxford generously.

A postcard from RR in Scotland. 'Weather will improve: it cannot worsen.' Two small children in a caravan in Scottish mist and rain. What bad luck.

The Seagull at the New Theatre. Good production, with Kedrova, Derek Godfrey, and an excellent performance from James Bolam.

❦

21 August, Friday

The Bateys looked in on their way to a funeral in North Leigh. Charles looking very pale: he says he is now under 10 stone and I can believe it. Otherwise correspondence and meetings until noon, when I left for home and N Wales.

Reached Bryn Coch[45] in good time at 7.30, after a short stop on the hillside overlooking Ludlow. Met the Melvilles[46] on Saturday morning and walked with them and Ben on the slopes above the house and huts. Back to the Melvilles' rented flat in Dolgellau for tea. On Sunday

---

45 Bryn Coch, Llanfachreth, near Dolgellau in Gwynedd, Wales – the home of Werner and Lotte Pelz, where Ben and Peter Pelz were staying.
46 Madeline and Alan Melville, old friends of AR and VR. Alan Melville (1911–1998) trained the BBC Singers for many years, having been chorus master of Sadler's Wells Opera.

morning we walked up on to the top of the hillside on the other side of the valley. If it had not been misty we would have had good views of the sea and Snowdon. Left for home at 2.45. Back at 7.45. Ben and Peter following reached us with the van two hours later.

☙

24 August, Monday

My post brought a letter of complaint from an author. In returning his proofs he said that the reader had overlooked a grave error. He was made to say 'I have had the disadvantage of Mr Storey's assistance throughout.' Mr Storey was his oldest friend and if this had gone through unnoticed 'I should have had to scrap the lot.' I passed this on in my letter to Colin, for his amusement.

Discussed the problem of producing Morison's Lyell Lectures to give bound stock in June next year. I feel we must do, tho' it is a large book with about 180 illustrations. If we filmset I think we can, but on the hot metal side we are already heavily loaded. At my managers' meeting after lunch I had to deal with several reports of broken promises, especially from the Bindery, which is in a bad way over holiday absences. But JH did produce four new girls for the department, and also two more for the Layout Section. This section is now the largest it has ever been, with eight designers. I am surprised that we have enough work for them, but it is so.

CHR came down late in the afternoon to tell me about his meeting with an NGA delegation last week. The union has now organized his drawing office and are pressing for an immediate rise all round and an increase in the minimum to £30. So far he has held firm and I don't think that at this early stage any hostile action will be taken against him. Of course the union is anxious to show what it can do for its new members, but they are not yet strong enough to bring the men out or anything like that.

Got home to find pear-picking in progress. Later in the evening a round of story-telling in Ben's room. Updike, Gogol, Perelman, Hans Andersen!

❦

25 August, Tuesday

I went to see Ian Philip at Bodley in the afternoon, to ask his advice on a successor to John Simmons. The person he suggests, as I hoped he would, is Paul Morgan (*of the Bodleian Library*). Morgan already knows something of our libraries here and might be able to spare the one morning or day a month that I need. Philip will sound him when he returns from holiday and let me know whether he is interested. If not there are one or two younger men in the cataloguing section who might serve.

In the morning I had Boswell in to report on the latest situation in the paper world. We can expect another price increase next January. He foresees plenty of trouble from the change to metrication, as I do. The Mill is very busy and have just sent us samples of their new black-coated process paper. Boswell hasn't seen it yet but he intends to have trials made as soon as he can lay his hands on the sample.

At home I found that Peter Pelz had finished (all in the day) the mural he had promised to paint for Colin over the fireplace in his room. Remarkable and firey – like Van Gogh operating with a blow lamp – and open to many interpretations. Colin will be excited when he sees it.

❦

26 August, Wednesday

Mostly spent in dealing with trivia of varying importance. Inspected the new mono Keyboard Room to see how the laying of the cork floor was going. All the tiles are down and the whole surface was being coated with some acid-smelling sealing compound. Heard that one comp., peering in at the magnificence, uttered 'I thought they were short of money'. You can't win these days.

Talked with Walker on a new computer-project, a Keats concordance. I wonder what real use these American-inspired concordances will be? John Hall came in to report a talk he had had with Fulton about the present attitude of some of our machine room apprentices. From what he said I gather he was able to enlighten F on several aspects of our training and attention to their progress that he apparently was unaware of. JH went off at midday for his short holiday in mid Wales.

Wrote and dispatched my notes on the Newspaper Design Awards to Allen Hutt, who had collared me on the telephone last night. I was the last judge to send his notes, so perhaps I deserved a touch of the whip.

Visited Jordan Hill after lunch. The firm putting in the sprinklers have now finished and almost departed. They have caused almost as much anxiety as the sparrows and starlings, who continue to do a lot of damage. They mess the place up, and build nests among the bundles of folded stock. Thompson also showed me how starlings had pecked off and taken away for nest building the strings holding the lagging around some of the heating pipes. As we have to work with the large doors open for most of the time the problem is practically insoluble. Even the Duke's sparrow hawks wouldn't trust themselves in such comparatively hemmed in places.

A party at home with Rolf, Jane, Peter and Ben. Cooking lumps of veal in fat kept boiling over a meths burner. Sauces, gherkins, butterballs & figs. Wine. Singing later. I fell asleep on my own in the sitting room...

27 August, Thursday

Every manager complaining about the effect of staggered holidays. They complain at this time every year. Keeping the work flowing is a problem but they all know what to expect by now – I suppose complaining acts as a safety valve.

I had Taylor in to report on his visit to Ely House. They are quiet up there and so there is not much about. Thompson complains that most of his other binders are letting him down over dates, which is some comfort.

Church took me to the station to meet Valerie Eliot and to take us on to the Saraceno, which is now very pricy indeed. But we had a useful talk over our expensive lunch. Afterwards I took her through the Works and up into the Monophoto room. Introduced Beckley to her:

she praised him for all the skilful work he had put into the book, which was just what I wanted. He is quite a sensitive man and was obviously very pleased. She has promised to work on the proofs, and on the elusive Introduction, over the bank holiday, but I doubt whether I shall see it for a week or two. She left a large bottle of champagne with me, which was civil of her.

Looked in on the most worthy Mrs Salmon, to see how she was getting on in John Hall's absence. She had no problems for me, tho' I could tell that many people were after her for one bit of advice or another. She says that the recruiting drive for young girls has gone better than she had expected. The problem now was whether to take on more than we need, to allow for wastage. I urged her to do this, knowing only too well that in a month or two Chalmers will be back to me with his old complaints of staff shortage.

A delightful, desultory evening on the terrace, eating out in the cool, clear air, and talking over family history with Ben and Peter, followed later by a look through old photographs.

༚

28 August, Friday

An unwelcome moan from John Lord about the delay in producing a prospectus for Dartington Hall. I did my best in a would-be tactful letter, tho' I felt the whole thing had not been well handled at Ely House. As usual, too many cooks and too much ambiguity in the instructions. Butler, whose care this was, is not good in correspondence and his memos tend to be craggy, which doesn't help. This is a pity because he is always most diligent on his customers' behalf, but it would be difficult to guess this from his letters.

Will Carter[47] came over to lunch from Cambridge. He brought with him the matrices of William Morris's Troy type, which he has borrowed

---

47 Will Carter (1912-2001), handcarver of lettering, also printed fine-press editions at his Rampant Lions Press in Cambridge. He carved the memorials for, amongst others, Henry James in Poets' Corner in Westminster Abbey, and Allen Lane.

from Brooke Crutchley. He had found a number of engravings by Burne Jones (by W Morris of BJ's drawings) at the Society of Antiquaries and intends to use them for an edition of Morris's 'Cupid and Psyche'. He wants me to cast type from the matrices.

Harry Carter was with us for lunch: he did not think there would be any difficulty in casting the type on the body required. After lunch we walked over to the Radcliffe to inspect an inscription plaque that WC had carved in slate at the instigation of Juel-Jensen.[48] He was telling me as he walked that he had taught himself to carve in wood and then heard, in the late forties, that David Kindersley[49] was taking a course of night classes in Cambridge on carving in stone. He had found K a great inspiration. As this plaque had been cut in Welsh slate I asked him whether he had ever worked with Cumberland slate. He had, but had found it very hard.

Later in the afternoon I had in the plausible Percy Best, to wish him well in his retirement. I had little talking to do, as he started immediately he came in at the door, telling me all about what he was going to do. He has now learnt off by heart a half-hour lecture on the history of Mr Punch, which he delivers at Rotary clubs and WI's; he intends to keep his Punch and Judy going, and his conjuring. He explained to me how the Chinese hoop trick was done, also the many-drinks-from-one-jug trick. The last has only 8 drinks in it, and they are controlled by a number of holes in the handle, which is played rather like a flute. His farewell remark, which I savoured, was 'Well, Mr Printer, it has given me great joy to say good-bye to you.' I then recalled that some years ago I had bawled him out in the Bindery basement. I found him sitting on a stack of printed sheets – a great crime – and told him at the top of my voice to 'get his great, semi-skilled arse off them'. So perhaps his farewell came from the heart.

---

48 Dr Bent Juel-Jensen (1922-2006), Danish-born physician and book collector, was a consultant at United Oxford Hospitals 1966-90, University Medical Officer 1976-90, and a great benefactor of the Bodleian Library.
49 David Kindersley (1915-1995) was a stone letter-carver and typeface designer, like Will Carter based in Cambridge. His son Peter co-founded the publisher Dorling Kindersley.

❦

29 Aug–1 Sept

Four days of holiday. Glorious weather for three of them. Looked at Philippa's prospective house next to Bladon Church – she managed to get it in competition with the Bursar of St Catherine's; then we all went on to Broughton Castle for a picnic lunch and a tour taken by a charming and rather shy sixth-former from Banbury School. More work on Colin's room, and other jobs about the house. On the Friday evening we had gone to see *Bob and Carol and Ted and Alice* at Kate & Tim's recommendation. Amusing, well-acted. Hollywood getting with it.

September 1970

❦

2 September, Wednesday

A cold, wet, and windy return from holiday. The keyboards are now being moved into the new room, which looks so splendid that I am sure to be asked to provide similar improvements elsewhere. 'Ben', Hinkins & Frewin's foreman, has been bustling about like a midwife. I am amused at the careful seating plan worked out by Harris and Brooker. Conscientious and hard-working operators at the back, talkers and walkers up front, close by the office. They gave the men no say at all, probably just as well.

All my letters announcing increases to the staff have now gone out. Miss Cox thanked me warmly for hers, rather to my relief because it did not seem particularly large to me. I have also had a letter of thanks from Gordon Taylor. Not all managers and supervisors do the same.

Wrote a tart letter to Davin about an appalling muddle that the CP has made over the printing of the plates by the Trianon Press for Keynes's *Blake Studies*. I was not consulted beforehand and the result is that they have been printed in such a way that the Bindery is faced with a difficult problem. Also wrote another tart letter to one of his staff who has been wasting the time of mine.

Richard back from holiday, claiming to have enjoyed the caravan life, even in wettest Scotland. He met Michael Milford (*cousin of Anne's*), who had bought the house at Methven where he had stayed many years before. Of course MM asked for a copy of *Hart's Rules*[50] which he has been after for some years. He *could* go to a bookseller but Richard has now rather committed me in the generosity of the moment. I could include a bill...

3 September, Thursday

Quiet morning dealing with correspondence. Have committed myself to producing Morison's Lyell Lectures by the end of June. That date will push Nicolas Barker,[51] the editor, pretty hard with his proof reading & indexing.

Various managers wrote or came in to thank me for their 'generous' salary increases. This word was used so often that I am beginning to fear I may have overdone it.

All the keyboards have now been placed in the new room. Looking at them spread out in their new positions I find it hard to believe we ever managed to pack them in to the old room, it seems so small.

In the afternoon I had a meeting, at his request, with Stiefel, the PA consultant, Williams of Neasden, and RR. S is obviously frightened of touching our intricate system of recording flat and folded stock and wants someone else to look at it for him. He offered a 'free' survey by a PA man. I had no objection, but I was non-committal on his general theme as I wanted to refer to my file to see just what PA had undertaken when they first took on the job. I don't much care for S. I don't quite know why, because he seems to be working well to his brief.

A & I went along to the Mayor's reception in the Town Hall to inaugurate the Salvation Army appeal in aid of the new building that

---

50 Horace Hart (1840-1916), Printer to the University, Oxford 1893-1915, introduced the use of wood-pulp paper as well as collotype and lithography at the Press. His *Rules for Compositors and Readers at the University Press Oxford* became a highly influential and popular bible of editorial style.

51 Nicolas Barker, bibliophile and historian of printing and books, later became Head of Conservation at the British Library 1976-92.

John Fryman has designed for them. He was there, and pointed out the hideous model that some SA worthy had made for the occasion. If the building turns out like that it will indeed be awful. There were lots of speeches, and 'musical items' sung by Capt Joy Webb and the Joystrings. She has a good voice and I bore it with composure. Basil Blackwell was there, also Bryce & Church in their SA uniforms.

Afterwards Fryman asked me to go along to see the new building he is putting up in the back garden of Univ, off Magpie Lane. I don't think I had ever been along Kybald Street before – the site is at the end on the north side. Fryman has had to preserve two large elm trees and a high curved stone wall. His building goes over the wall and around the trees in a very ingenious way. It is difficult to judge the full effect because it is only half built, but I liked the plum-coloured Leicester brick he has used.

Packing for the holiday in the evening with only one break for relaxation and a late supper. I shall have the luggage rack put on the car just in case Colin's luggage is bulkier than we expect.

❦

4 September, Friday

Left for home soon after 12, and for the Lakes at 2.

❦

21 September, Monday

Back at my desk again after the wettest holiday in the Lakes I can remember. Not too much correspondence to deal with. Roberts and Davin also back from their holidays so that our usual meeting was more scrappy than usual, each of us wanting to get back to our own affairs. Richard anxious about Stiefel's performance on the Warehouse assignment, the comps' FOC (*Father of the Chapel*) anxious about work for the keyboards. I saw him later in the day and assured him that any fall-off in work would soon be put right – he wants, or hinted at wanting, a stop put on work going outside for keyboarding. I played this one gently as I know it could be a sore point if operators here are not getting overtime.

Frost in difficulties in the Counting House and at home with a sick wife. John Hall has taken in more people, male and female, for the Bindery; and at my managers' meeting the work situation did not sound too bad. The Litho has picked up again and there is now quite a good load for Oct and Nov. The outer office and lobby have been painted in my absence, which pleases Pat Cox.

To Stratford for *A Midsummer Night's Dream*. A 3-hour bout between Peter Brook and one Bill Shakespeare. The latter survived after a lot of punishment and brilliant ring-craft by his over-clever opponent, but only just.

❦

22 September, Tuesday

Main meeting of the day was with the Registrar and his officers (inc. Campbell) in the Clarendon Building. It was at my request, to discuss ways of dealing with the growing amount of University work. I'm afraid not much of real benefit came out of it, but at least I had made clear that we were now very close to the limit and unless they could do more to help themselves there was a real risk of breakdown. Both Campbell and Rosemary Noyce were helpful. I was amused at the irritated tone in which they replied to Sandford, whose reputation for getting on with people – or at least his staff – is not high.

A quiet evening. Colin active in arranging his room. I am nearly at the end of *War & Peace*, vol II. The battle of Borodino is about to start.

❦

23 September, Wednesday

Talked over plans for the Safety Services dinner at the end of October with JH. This is to replace the annual coach outings which had been so poorly supported during the past few years. A dinner at the Freemasons Hall will be a bit of a bore for me, but the men are enthusiastic and so I hope it will turn out to be a sensible change.

To London in the afternoon for the *Companion to Art* launching party at Burlington House. Held in the recently re-gilded & decorated Reynolds Room, a beautiful setting and just the right size for the number invited, tho' windows had to be opened as natural heat was generated. Osborne, the editor, gave me gracious words of thanks. I was equally gracious in return. He has now started on another Companion, this time of the useful arts, and he hopes to have it completed in about 2 ½ years. Bruno told me that advance sales of the present one are now over 12,000, which is not bad for a £6 book. I had sent Butler and Mitty from the Litho Office; they had done excellent work in piloting the material through the department and seemed to be enjoying themselves, particularly Butler, whose rich colour was obviously the result of the champagne.

RR and I travelled back with the Davins. Dan is in the middle of yet another novel. I felt guilty that I had not read anything of his since *Roads from Home*, and then turned back to my Tolstoy.

❦

24 September, Thursday

A brief visit from Turner, the PA supervisor of our warehousing changes, and a colleague, Apps. Their underlying intention is to sell me more consultancy, but this was a social call and we exchanged only pleasantries on the state of the economy. I am to expect a report from them in a few days, and then we shall meet again.

Close on their heels came Paul Morgan of the Bodleian. I had asked him to lunch with Simmons and me so that we could examine the possibility of him taking over from S as our library consultant. He cannot spend the 3 hours a week S has been giving us, but even the one hour he suggests would I think be quite enough. He is willing to do this and I shall now write offering him an honorarium of £100 a year. I am a little embarrassed by this because he grew up with Simmons and they are close friends *and*, I now find that we have really been underpaying S for all the time he has been putting in – only £125 a year. And so I have decided to make him an ex gratia payment soon after he leaves us next week which will be free of tax. He has never asked for an increase, and being part-time, he somehow escaped our annual review.

With Anne to see Alan Badel performing brilliantly at the Playhouse in Hauser's version of Sartre's version of Dumas' *Kean*. A good production and a packed house that on a lovely summer evening, and a Thursday, is encouraging at the beginning of the new season.

❧

25 September, Friday

Peter Barnard gave me lunch at the Randolph. He is advising the government of British Guiana on a new printing plant and wanted the architects (Oxford Architects Partnership) to see our new building. A curious man, who every now and then comes out with some embarrassing piece of flattery about my doings. He seems to be doing well as a consultant. I have come to expect these periodic visits, when he usually wants my opinion on this or that. Recently he has been talking with *The Times* people, and told me that he had passed on my criticism of it (I had forgotten I had ever said anything to him) to Denis Hamilton.[52] They must have had many criticisms to judge by the new dress it now appears in.

After lunch I got Church to run me up to Fred Allen's bungalow. His wife, who suffers badly from arthritis (and can't read or write, says JH), received me civilly in their spick and span sitting-room, though she was obviously almost overcome with the worry of trying to cope with a sick man. She released some of the tension by blaming the doctor. I listened patiently, hoping that I might be able to see Fred and noting the innumerable trinkets and ornaments covering the shelves and pelmet boards while she talked. A touching change came over her when we went into his room. He hardly knew me, or her, but she spoke gently to him and tried to ease the pillows under his shoulders. He cannot

---

52 Sir Denis Hamilton (1918-1988), Editor in Chief and Chairman of Times Newspapers Ltd, having previously been Editor of the *Sunday Times* from 1959.

last more than a few days, I'm quite sure, mercifully, because there is no prospect of recovery. She has friends and relatives, and I believe owns the smart bungalow they live in.

※

28 September, Monday

JH came in first thing to tell me that Fred Allen had died the previous night.

CHR back from Frankfurt. He had seen Richard, who is due back tomorrow. Gloomy about present sales and our cash position. Fears that the Longman-Penguin publishing programme will have a damaging effect on our sales of educational books.

My afternoon managers' meeting disclosed the familiar problems of lack of balance and shortage of skilled men in some sections. Although we are short of new composition it is difficult to clamour for more when we still have difficulty in pushing through fast enough what is already in the pipeline. No quick solution, I fear, just a steady plod to get the balance right, or better.

※

29 September, Tuesday

Boyce in to see me in the morning. Hacker, the (good) reader we have put in the Litho Department, is not happy with his surroundings: too noisy and depressing. I have already moved him once and it really is a problem to find him space in the new department that is free from noise. I said I would see what else might be done but I may have to move him back to the main Reading Department, which would be a pity because a reader is needed on the spot now that litho is such a large part of our work.

Finance Committee after lunch. Bruno looked in before the meeting. He too is rather worried by stagnant sales and steeply rising overheads. This was reported at FC, also the present severe strain on the cash position. We shall now have to seek extended overdraft powers from the bank. CP annual accounts were scrutinized. The same story, profit down, costs up. I felt slightly embarrassed that my figures for August were not worse: profit still well above budget, also profit as a % of sales.

The new manager of the S African branch was seen, a barrister. Seemed full of new ideas for selling Oxford books in SA. He made a very good impression on everyone.

Wrote to Mrs Allen. The funeral is tomorrow, as I guessed it might be, when I shall be in London. Signed invitations, 42 in all, for the Services dinner at the end of October.

Richard safely back from the Frankfurt fair. Felt he had got some value from his visit, tho' not much. Awful lot of pornography in the bookshops, he says.

❦

30 September, Wednesday

To BFMP for General Services and Legislation committees. No startling news or events. Met Gordon Taylor at Oxford station on return. He is gloomy after his visit to Ely House because another of their Bible binders has discovered some blemished sheets of *NEB*. It looks as though our stock of sheets will have to be sorted, an expensive and slow job.

October 1970

❦

1 October, Thursday

Halsey produced a polemical anti-Jewish book review destined to go in the next issue of *The Islamic Quarterly*. I read it, compared its virulence with other reviews in previous issues, drafted a letter, then decided to let it lie. I am not eager to comment on the text of journals I print as the book under review was published by OUP. I felt it more prudent to do nothing.

A long, long talk with RR about computer applications for the printing business, in preparation for next Tuesday's meeting of the full steering committee. The young men at Neasden want to get the situation 'clarified'. I want to keep things fluid, taking a short step at a time, and not embarking on any 'long-range plan' with a commitment to spending thousands of pounds in the vague hope of a return.

Today is the beginning of my 13th year as Printer. Probably long enough, really, as I don't feel quite the same zest for the job that I used to. I think it is partly because of delegating so much, to RR and JH in particular – one often has the feeling of watching over things from the sidelines. Another thing is that as the OUP as a whole has expanded rapidly, this business, in spite of the new buildings, has remained static in size. The result is that, rightly or wrongly, I feel it has somehow diminished in prestige and importance. I also have the uneasy feeling that if I were a more political animal I should have done more to stem the tide.

JH came in later in the morning to say that Fulton and Gibbons now want to see me about their argument over 'working through' the double shift on the folding machines. Their case is a weak one and I hope I can settle the matter without generating too much heat.

At the end of the day I had RR over to discuss the problem of Hacker, and what to do with him. We went over to the Litho Dept and I suggested we might build an office in an existing bay of the make-up room which now houses a spare make-up table. Ventilation will be a problem but we agreed on giving it a trial.

Paul Morgan has accepted my terms for his duties as part-time Librarian. He starts next week.

Vernèdes[53] in for coffee in the evening. Colin busy packing for his move to Cambridge tomorrow.

2 October, Friday

Fulton and Gibbons had asked to see me. I saw them with JH at 9. Long

---

53 Raymond Vernède (1905-2003), Bursar of St Peter's College, and his wife Nancy. Their son Nicky was Colin's oldest friend, and spent five months with him in 1970 on archaeological excavations in Turkey.

and rambling discussion from F on 'working through' a double-shift break in the folding section. The ironic fact beyond all the talk and argument is that JH had to fight to get 'working through' accepted by the men. We had to pay an extra 10/- for the 'inconvenience' and now they find it so convenient that they don't want to give it up, or the 10/-, whereas the arrangement is no longer of any value to the business now that treble-shift working has stopped. I listened patiently, made one or two points that JH had already made at earlier meetings, and then said I would consider the matter and let them know. What I have in mind is to let the present arrangement run until Christmas, and then start fresh in the new year. I expect there will be some huffing & puffing but their case is a weak one and Fulton knows it.

Dick de la Mare breathing down my neck for *The Waste Land* estimate. Dear Valerie has still not produced her Introduction but I suppose we must give him an approx. figure.

Pat Cox goes on a week's holiday this evening.

❦

5 October, Monday

Meetings! – all day. Office. Secretary's. Production. Works Advisory. Managers. Letterpress Machine Room. And almost continuous until 5 o'clock. It looks as though the Machine Room chapel, led of course by Fulton, will try to resist the introduction of more minders and an apprentice. I may have to make it a head-on clash, to clear the air, tho' I should prefer not to. The danger comes if I allow myself to be put in a position where the chapel can decide just what the strength of the department should be. I feel I am already close to it, and so a bust-up, or explosion, or fight, however tiresome & unpleasant, may be useful in the long-run.

The Readers' chapel have reported 'an obnoxious smell' outside their windows. O'Dogherty remarked, caustically, 'probably fresh air'.

Rang de la Mare at Much Hadham, but he had gone out to tea.

❦

6 October, Tuesday

Dick again eluded me, but I got the Eliot figures through to his secretary. Yesterday I had another letter from Valerie, sending me a list of corrections – but still no introduction. She is now waiting on someone in France to confirm a detail of TSE's movements in Paris, or so she says. I'm beginning to wonder whether she will ever put pen to paper. All the rest is now in our hands.

A long meeting on next year's budget at Help the Aged office. From 11-12.45. I do my gallant best but find it difficult to hold the details in my head from one meeting to another. What is clear is the very rapid expansion of schemes under Stallabrass's powerhouse direction. Had snack lunch afterwards at the King's Arms, where I was surprised and pleased to meet Henry Ward,[54] who is now in the middle of directing *The Jesse Tree* at Dorchester – the music, that is. We talked about the way it is going: too many hands in the direction, he thinks; and Betty Maconchy has been attending more rehearsals than are good for her nerves. In my easy way I told him it would be all right on the night. And of course it will be.

A rather perfunctory but long meeting of the Electronic Data Processing committee in the Delegates Conference Room, with Bruno rather distantly in the chair. He gave me the impression of wanting to get away, which in the end he did, leaving us to have quite a fruitful if informal talk over the many problems and options facing us in the application of the Neasden monster to our affairs. I was impressed by young Reeve, the highly paid expert in charge of the section at Neasden, but I am determined to go cautiously as far as the Printing Business is concerned. Poor Jimmy Huws-Davies had a strike of SOGAT members on his hands in the warehouse. I gave appropriate murmurs of sympathy.

Anne reported, after the dress rehearsal at Dorchester, that things *had* gone much better. One of the problems is the cold, because the

---

54 A conductor, and contemporary and friend of Ben Ridler's when they were at Clifton College, Bristol together.

electricians need to keep a door open to pass through a cable for lighting the east window from outside. Unfortunate because it is turning much colder this week. John Piper[55] and his wife were there. They and many others were complimentary about the work. But it is hard going, and Alan Kitching,[56] who is producing, says very little and never speaks a word of encouragement, and rarely of criticism, to his actors.

❦

7 October, Wednesday

Around the Works this morning. Bindery badly congested with stacks of books awaiting inspection and despatch. A cheerful sight, all the same: when the men see work all around them they are more inclined to keep their output up. The trouble is that books tend to get damaged when they are stacked in gangways.

Mansfield told me at tea this morning that his chapel committee had raised no objection to the introduction of a letterpress machine-minder. He had met them earlier in the canteen and had gone over all the reasons why we felt it necessary to increase the staff. I think they would have preferred to resist, but they have no decent case for doing so, and they know it. We may have more difficulty over the next recruit.

Later in the afternoon I met the junior supervisors and gave them what information I could about the state of OUP as a whole – sales and prospects – and about the state of our own departments. My report was more cheerful than I anticipated some months back. Sales are not good but I have no need to be too pessimistic, altho' I did stress that no one could tell just yet what the effect of recent price increases would be. The meeting livened up towards the end, as often happens, but I closed it at 5.30 as I felt it had gone on long enough.

---

55 John Piper (1903-1992) was a painter who focused on the British landscape and designed stained-glass windows as well as opera and theatre sets – including the Tree in *The Jesse Tree* at Dorchester Abbey in 1970.
56 Alan Kitching (1906-1997), opera producer, and his wife Frances were pioneers in the revival of Handel's operas, staging them at the Unicorn Theatre in Abingdon.

To Dorchester in the evening, for the first night of *The Jesse Tree*. I was quite overcome by the power and clarity of words and music. Betty Maconchy's music was more dramatic than I had expected. The effect at times was that of quite a large orchestra. Clarissa Melville was playing the flute and piccolo – she is staying with Jane and Rolf. Ben came with us, and goes back to Bristol tomorrow.

Several critics from London were said to be in the audience, also dear old Frank Dibb (*Oxford Times*). I *hope* they all give the production a warm welcome. The only blemish for me is John Piper's spindly Tree. As Ursula Vaughan Williams[57] said afterwards, it is too frivolous, particularly against the splendid background of the east window, which is lit from outside. All the soloists were good, and Anne Pashley, who sings marvellously, also acted a difficult part with great intensity. Both Betty and Anne seemed pleased, and relieved after the stresses of rehearsal.

🙶

8 October, Thursday

JH brought rather disturbing news that Mrs Salmon, who is again away, may be more seriously ill than we had thought. Her husband is coming in to see John this afternoon. If this is true, and she has to give up her work, it will be a blow to us and particularly to John, because she is so good with the young girls and indeed with all the staff. John assures me than Miss Robbinette, who trains the Bindery girls, can take over a fair amount of Mrs S's work, and so relieve him – which relieves me, because he has so much on his hands. Anyway, I should know more by the morning.

Chatting in to coffee at 9.45. He reported progress in the Work Study Section now that we have a new man – ex de la Rue – to make a start with method study in the Bindery. He himself is concentrating mainly upon studies for the Filmsetting Section, which has been without them for ten years and more. Chatting is a good man, trusted by the shop

---

57 Ursula Vaughan Williams (1911-2007) was a poet, novelist, and biographer of her second husband, the composer Ralph Vaughan Williams (1872-1958), for whom she also wrote libretti.

floor, and I hope now that we can really make the changes needed, at least in some departments.

A meeting with RR to discuss Apps's (of PA) report on production control in the Bindery in relation to the Warehouse changes at Jordan Hill. He proposes an 8-10 week assignment for one consultant (at £380 a week!) and I suspect that after talking it over with Apps tomorrow morning, we will accept, because a great deal certainly needs to be done and my own people cannot get the job done in the time required.

A Works Advisory Committee at 3.30. To hurry things along I said I would have to leave for another meeting soon after 4.30. We got through most of the agenda briskly and without acrimony. Walker, dear dim Walker, clumsily attacked me for the shortage of work in the keyboards. I waited to reply until I made my usual report on the state of the business as a whole. My report was rather long, and I sensed that my putting Walker in his place (he had called the lack of work 'disgraceful') was felt to be just by the other members on their side. I got RR to describe our plans for the Warehouse and then vacated the chair for him. JH had suggested an adjournment but I felt it far better that the business should all be dealt with there and then. I left for St E Hall and a Stated Meeting, the first in our new common room. A pleasant dinner afterwards talking to Hackney mostly, and to our new domestic bursar, Rear Admiral Leslie, whom I take to very much.

At lunch we had the Lefanu's,[58] Henry Ward, Clarissa Melville, and Ben. Much rejoicing and toasting at the good notice by Alan Blythe of *The Times*, which I read out. Success with a project like *The Jesse Tree* is a lovely feeling. Such a relief to get a notice that, if hasty, is not silly, as they so often are.

Later in the afternoon, Werner Pelz came to pick up Ben and carry him off to Bristol. A gallantly burnt rubbish in the garden because of the dustmen's strike.

---

58 Billy and Betty Lefanu (ie Elizabeth Maconchy). Their daughter, Nicola Lefanu, is also a well-known composer.

❦

9 October, Friday

Apps of PA came in with RR at 11 to present his report on production and control in the Bindery. The nub is that they want 8-10 weeks and £380 a week to do the job. Apart from that there was not much we found to quarrel with in his proposals. Our own production control in that department is not what it should be, and with the reorganization at Jordan Hill we would have to revise our methods in any case.

Eaglestone in to coffee. I asked him what he had thought of the Works Advisory Committee meeting on Thursday. He said that Fulton had given him a lift home afterwards. On the way he remarked, 'Well, Phil Walker asked for it, and he got it', adding that 'his choice of words was unfortunate'. It was!

In the evening to Dorchester with A, for a party at the Borns, primarily to meet Eric White.[59] I found him a little thinner but just as talkative as ever. We did not stay on for the performance in the Abbey because Kate and Tim were due to arrive later in the evening.

❦

10 October, Saturday

The final performance of *The Jesse Tree*. As moving as before and just as beautifully done. The audience made up of many friends and relations: Kirstie, Marion, David Milford, Wilkinsons, Melvilles, Vernèdes, Katharine Ross – almost like a funeral. We stayed on afterwards for a performance party in the guest house but it was too crowded to hear much of the farewell speeches. I congratulated Alan Kitching (*the producer*) as he came away. He replied, characteristically, with a grunt, and made for the cheese board. Colin had come over (by bus) from Cambridge. I should have been terribly disappointed if he had missed it. Good review in *S Times* by Desmond Shaw-Taylor.

---

59 Eric Walter White (1905-1985) was an arts administrator and writer on numerous subjects, particularly music. VR had published two books by him, *Wander Birds* (1934) and *The Little Chimney Sweep* (1936), at the Perpetua Press before the war.

❦

12 October, Monday

At CP meeting this morning rather disturbed to hear that my compo-sition charge for the *Concise Dictionary of English Literature*, which was filmset, is very much higher than a check quote from BAS – £5.19.0 a page against £3.17.6. This kind of confrontation is always difficult to cope with because printers' estimates seem to vary so wildly from job to job. There is little I can do about it, unfortunately. Profit on composition is not high, so that there isn't much scope for cutting.

In the afternoon an Edwin Smith, area representative of the Industrial Society, came to give me details of the lunch meeting planned for February at which I have agreed to take the chair. He brought with him the representative from the Midlands area, newly appointed. I found that this man had been personnel manager at Collins for twelve years and had come south for personal reasons. He told me that Collins diary business now accounted for 25% of their profits.

A call from the City Engineer. He wanted to know whether, if the present council workers' strike goes on we could withhold the discharge of our 'trade effluent' which includes a tiny amount of cyanide, from the drains. I said I should have to investigate. I suppose the cyanide comes from the electro foundry but I can't remember exactly. I only hope the strike is settled this week.

Began reading Tolstoy's *Childhood, Boyhood, and Youth*.

❦

13 October, Tuesday

Brooke Crutchley here in time for lunch with JH and me. Good talk during afternoon. Amazed us by saying that they had decided to go over almost completely to computer-typesetting within 5 years. Main reason seems to be that he thinks their image, in the eyes of the young craftsmen, is too 'fuddy-duddy', and unless he does something like this he won't be able to keep his men. Total cost he puts at £300,000. Well, well.

Fiasco in the evening. After an early and good dinner at the Saraceno,

A & I took Brooke to see Hauser's *Othello*, with Alan Badel. So bad we came out after the first act and went home. It really was *dull*.

⚘

14 October, Wednesday

Brooke went off at 9. I went to London later to lunch with John Shepherd of the BFMP and a COID (*Council of Industrial Design*) man to talk over the design exhibition next year. I am chairman of the selection committee and we make the selections in January. The exhibition is planned to coincide with IPEX. I hope we shall get enough entries, but the successful ones – we only want 20 – have to pay £100 fee for the display in the COID hall. For 6 weeks it is cheap publicity but the idea may deter many people.

In the evening to Monotype House and the exhibition of Curwen Press work timed to coincide with the retirement of Herbert Simon, who is being elevated to the new post of 'president'. Basil Harley collared me as I was going in and asked me to propose Herbert's health. I hate doing such things at short notice, but I did it, not very well, I fear.

HS was given a set of lithographs by David Gentleman. I asked the Curwen organizer, Rosemary Simmons, about them and she said she would get me details. Later Diana Crutchley was puzzled and as much amused as I was when Rosemary came up to us and said to me 'I believe you said you were interested in the Gentlemans.' I said that it was an unfortunate weakness in our sex to be so. The Curwen exhibition is impressive. Couldn't see it properly, of course; far too many friends and acquaintances packed into too small a space.

Later in the evening Basil H put on a splendid dinner for us at the Charing Cross Hotel, where I was staying. I sat between Mrs Schmoller and Timothy Simon's widow, Susan, an attractive American woman interested in American literature. Francis Meynell,[60] now 78 or 79, was also there with his wife. The only weakness in the arrangements was

---

60 Francis Meynell (1891-1975) founded the Nonesuch Press in 1922, which went on to produce over 140 elegantly designed books until the 1960s. Meynell was revered by fellow typographers.

that we were placed around a table at least 40 feet long and 5 feet wide, which curbed the feeling of 'togetherness'. Short speeches from Basil and Herbert. The latter tactfully referred to Cambridge's *Printing and the Mind of Man* and Oxford's *Fell* (*see Introduction*), as well as to one Curwen book whose title I now forget! We broke up at 10.30.

※

15 October, Thursday

To see KST at Ely House in the morning. In his usual emotional state. I assumed from what he said that Bruno has told him he will be retired at the end of the year. The relationship between Ely House and ourselves is still not good and I shall have to work hard to improve it.

Management Research Group lunch afterwards, again at the Charing Cross Hotel. The speaker was personnel director of the Br Airport Authority at Heathrow and gave us an excellent run-down of the Carr paper on industrial relations. Well attended, good discussion afterwards.

Back on the 5.15 with Peter Spicer.[61] Not much conversation as I was reading *Childhood*!

※

16 October, Friday

The new editor of Crockford (*Clerical Directory*) came in to see me. A young man, Sussex University, read philosophy. Banking in S America and then in London, but 'very fond of books' and a poet, so tried for this job and got it. Hard to judge how he will handle what is really a humdrum routine of collecting material, updating and feeding us at the right time. He does *not* write the controversial editorials, which are always anonymous.

JH having a quarrel with Willetts of the NGA over payment of our graduate readers. W accuses him of breaking the agreement I and Bonfield signed personally last November by not giving them the

---

61 Peter Spicer (1921-1993) worked at OUP 1947-81, and was head of the Schools and Further Education Department for part of that time.

national increases agreed for this November. We pay on the Burnham scale, more or less, and have always made annual increments, irrespective of NGA agreements. I told JH that they can't have it both ways. We shouldn't argue but pay the increases demanded now and then do nothing next year until the next payment under national agreement is due. The whole thing is silly but the NGA doesn't really like the idea of graduate readers and has the power to cut off recruitment. There is no sense in making a prolonged tussle out of it which I can't possibly win; and in the long run it makes no difference to the business whatsoever. Yet it is still galling to be bullied!

❦

19 October, Monday

A wet morning after two beautiful days of mellow sunshine, fine enough for June. We had lunch out in the garden on Saturday. Lunch on Sunday at All Souls with Charles Monteith (*Faber Editorial Director*). He introduced us to the Fennells. Mrs F is a relative of Tolstoy's – great excitement and talk. Helen Gardner[62] also there and in good form. Professor Zaehner there too: he began complaining to his neighbour (Rosemary Goad of Faber) of the slowness of the Oxford Press. After I had told him who I was it turned out that he was talking of poor Geoffrey Hunt. GH does indeed take months to deal with anything but is very thorough when he at last gets around to it. Fortunately the book I am doing of his for the CP, *Concord-Discord*, has gone through quite smoothly and should be out next month. All very polite and amiable. Charles Monteith told me they (Faber) are thinking of appointing Nicolas Barker as David's successor. I have my doubts but CM says that he has done very well at Macmillan.

No particular crises during the day, just one or two exasperated memos about broken promises, due I'm afraid mainly to the state of congestion in the Letterpress Machine Room. I thought it wise to fly off the handle

---

62 Helen Gardner (1908-1986), literary critic and longstanding Delegate of the Press, was Merton Professor of English Literature 1966-75, and the editor of *The New Oxford Book Of English Verse* (1972).

a bit, particularly in those cases when information of changes had not been passed on in good time – a point I have to keep pounding away at.

At the Secretary's meeting I pointed out that in the Book Design exhibit catalogue both CP and London had named designers, contrary to our long established rule. It was also unfair to Stewart and others on my staff, who had never had public acknowledgement of their work. Both CHR and DMD entirely agreed and will put a stop to it.

Drafted a letter to send out on behalf of the Industrial Society. Received a draft from John Shepherd for the Carol Service 'Introduction' at St Bride's. Not bad but I must get Anne to look at it. He is very persistent.

❦

20 October, Tuesday

To Bristol for a S W Alliance exec meeting. JH went with me. We went via Bladon to drop Anne at Philippa's new house, where she is helping with the moving-in; then Witney to pick up Raymond Cripps and take him with us to the meeting. Uneventful – best part of the day was the travelling to and fro in the autumnal sunshine. Dawson gave me a vivid account of the troubles he had had with his Rover 3500 in Austria. The automatic gearbox broke down; parts had to come from Vienna and London; he had to extend his stay, then leave for home with all the family by train; then his son had to go back for the car. When it was back in England exactly the same thing happened again. Fortunately for D he had gone out under the RAC Cordon Bleu scheme and is putting in a bill of over £400. The car is out of guarantee.

❦

21 October, Wednesday

Had a pleasant letter from Mrs Mills, widow of P S Mills, our accountant for many years. He died suddenly, leaving his affairs in surprising disorder. She was writing about *The Jesse Tree*, which she had not been able to see but had bought the libretto. She sounded lonely tho' content. Her children are grown up and far away.

Late in the day the new University Information Officer (a post proposed by the Franks Commission) came in to see me. He is an ex-headmaster from Leeds, Sabben-Clare by name, and I should think a good choice for the job. We talked a little of those publications that will now be his concern: the Prospectus, Calendar, and Handbook. I told him of some of our troubles in trying to cope with an increasing amount of rush work. He has only just taken over and so said very little about his own ideas for doing the job.

Wrote one or two 'difficult' letters, and sent off the draft letter to Edwin Smith of the Industrial Society.

❧

22 October, Thursday

Redrafted one of the 'difficult' letters. Gardner (*possibly Ron Gardner, a Press employee*) then pointed out an error of fact in it, so that I had to do it again, for the third time.

Took the chair at the FC sub-committee at Help the Aged to go through the budget for 1971. Managed to get away by 11. Otherwise a fairly quiet day, touring part of the Works and discussing with RR possible moves in the next stage of our computer development at Neasden. The nub of the problem is: 'who is to have ultimate control'. Publisher, Printer, or neither? I should like to have full control of the product, but it might be impractical, as the computer is at Neasden and so closely tied into the Publisher's departments.

Mrs Clothier in to see me and to complain about her helper Mrs Cobb, who on the evidence put in front of me is illiterate. Spoke to JH who promised to move her. Also saw Mrs Salmon, back from her sick bed and showing the marks of it, I'm afraid. She is coming in on Thursday and Friday for the time being. She also wants to attend the Services dinner next week: I want her there but as she gets very tired it may be overdoing it.

Chalmers in to see me. I had sent him a Work Study report, critical of the department. He was annoyed, reasonably, as it seems, that the report had not been seen by him before it was given to me. I did my best to get things back on the rails, tho' I thought Eaglestone or Chatting had been inept in going over his head. Surprising too, because E is wily and C is straightforward. Forgetfulness, I expect, tho' that doesn't excuse it.

Glad to see during my tour of the plant that Monophoto are now well on with Morison's Lyell Lectures. In fact the section is getting short of work. Beckley told me that we have over 6000 pages of various jobs out on proof. Bratt had rung me earlier in the week to say that I could expect the *NEB* Stirling Bible copy and drawings early in January. He was not asking Cambridge to requote in the bigger size discussed. He had made his own calculation and would tell the committee that going larger would price it right out of the market they were aiming at. I hope he isn't being too sanguine, and I shan't be happy until I see the copy arrive. Still no sign of Valerie Eliot's Introduction.

Passed the advance copy of the Hart *Century of Typography* reprint, with a fine introduction and notes by Harry Carter. The title page was not perfectly placed, and this annoyed me; but the error is not great enough to do anything about. The machining of the new text (the fac-simile is done by litho) is not perfect either, but then Mansfield is not a *printer*, good administrator tho' he may be. The output of his department is curate's egg stuff. He blames his minders. I blame him. Annoying because he can get good work if he tries.

※

23 October, Friday

Both JH and RR off to the Alliance w-end conference at Sidmouth. Met Beesley and Webb with JH earlier, to discuss procedure at our forthcoming Safety Services dinner. I only hope Beesley doesn't hold forth too long on the doings and virtues of the Fire Brigade. Otherwise a fairly quiet day, at my desk and round the Works. The flow of copy to the keyboards is still meagre, tho' slightly better than it was last week.

Gerard Frost came in to say goodbye before he went off to Surrey on a week's holiday.

1 The Printer in his pomp: managing a business with some 900 employees was a constant struggle – with recalcitrant unions, demanding publishers, makers of new machinery, bankers – all the while maintaining staff morale and production standards. Once, when dissatisfied by poor workmanship on a prestigious job for the Roxburghe Club, VR went on to the shop floor and hurled the offending book to the ground, knowing news of such action would spread like wildfire round the Works. Yet that same evening he might visit a sick member of staff in hospital.

2 Best Man at his best friend's wedding: VR with David Bland and his bride Mary, 1947. Bland – who died in January 1970 – had been shot down as a bomber navigator during the war and incarcerated in Stalag Luft III. He and Ridler had run the small Perpetua Press together in the early 1930s, before Bland joined Faber's and Ridler the Press under John Johnson.

LEFT
3 New man in charge: VR in 1958 on his appointment as Printer. In reality he had been running the Printing House as Assistant Printer for several years after Charles Batey, the then Printer, became ill. Batey had persuaded a reluctant Ridler to rejoin the Press in 1948, when the memory of being fired by Johnson in 1937 for marrying the London Publisher's niece was still raw.

4 The Printer in his office: VR holds
the Coronation Bible – on which the
new Queen swore her solemn oath
in 1953 – which he had designed,
with a special binding by the artist
Lynton Lamb, regular illustrator
of book jackets in OUP's World's
Classics series. A 1959 painting of the
Letterpress Machine Room by Alfred
Daniels, commissioned by VR, can be
seen on the wall behind.

RIGHT
5 The BFMP President and his
lady: Vivian and Anne at the British
Federation of Master Printers annual
conference at Torquay, held during
his year in office in 1968-69. As the
Diary reveals, VR continued to serve
and advise the Federation in 1970-71,
during a time of major upheaval in the
industry. See also plate 31.

6 At the helm between the wars: Humphrey Milford (London Publisher, 1913-45), RW Chapman (Secretary to the Delegates, 1919-42), and John Johnson (Printer to the University, 1925-46) after receiving honorary degrees in 1928. Milford and his Clarendon Press publishing counterpart and overall head of the business, Chapman, got on well; Johnson, who produced books for both of them, often felt he was treated as an inferior, excluded from management decisions. He guarded his printing domain fiercely.

OPPOSITE
8 Postwar supremos: Colin Roberts (Secretary to the Delegates, 1954-74), his immediate predecessor ALP ('Thomas') Norrington (Secretary, 1948-54), and Char Batey (Printer to the University, 1946-58), admire a book in Batey's grand office (rather too grandiose his successor Vivian Ridler felt) in about 1954.

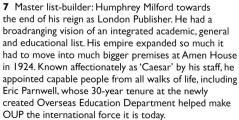

7 Master list-builder: Humphrey Milford towards the end of his reign as London Publisher. He had a broadranging vision of an integrated academic, general and educational list. His empire expanded so much it had to move into much bigger premises at Amen House in 1924. Known affectionately as 'Caesar' by his staff, he appointed capable people from all walks of life, including Eric Parnwell, whose 30-year tenure at the newly created Overseas Education Department helped make OUP the international force it is today.

ABOVE
Printing House team:
9 The Press Archivist and historian Harry Carter, much admired by VR;
10 Assistant Printer, and later Commercial Director, Richard Russell wearing Press Fire Brigade helmet; and **11** Personnel Manager, later Director, John Hall, whose sudden death in 1974 robbed the Printer of a close and supportive colleague (see Appendix 2).

12 The Executive Committee of the Press in 1975: left to right GD Webster; President of OUP New York Jimmy Huws-Davies (formerly Neasden Warehouse Manager); East Asian Branch Manager Raymond Brammah (soon to be head of a new Education Division); Vice-President of OUP New York Byron Hollinshead (soon to be President); Finance Director David Mitchell; Publisher to the University Sir John Brown; Printer to the University Vivian Ridler; Secretary to the Delegates George Richardson; Deputy Secretary and Academic Publisher Dan Davin; and UK Publishing Services Director Eric Buckley (who would succeed VR as Printer in 1978).

13 Beyond OUP: many of VR's friends from the wider
world of books are seen here at a launch party in
1972 for Steingruber's *Architectural Alphabet* published
by Sue and Monty Shaw at their Merrion Press, edited
by Berthold Wolpe and printed at OUP. From left
to right: Wolpe; Shirley Tucker; Bodley Head Art
Director John Ryder (see Appendix 1); Susan Eaton;
Sue Shaw; Faber director Rosemary Goad; Faber
Editorial Director Charles Monteith; Monty Shaw; and
printing historian James Moran. VR and Anne Ridler
had got to know Wolpe – renowned for his type
designs and Faber jackets – in the years after he came
to Britain as a refugee from Nazi Germany in 1935.

Cambridge men: *LEFT* **14** Will Carter, skilled letter
carver and limited-editions printer at his Rampant Lions
Press, who visited VR as the Diary records on
28 August 1970. *RIGHT* **15** Brooke Crutchley, Printer to
the University at Cambridge and close friend of VR (see
Appendix 3).

Nasty letter from H M Inspector on my dilatoriness in having all our Miehle two-revolution machines properly fenced. I have deliberately taken this slowly because I am still not sure how many we intend to keep and at several hundred pounds a time the guarding of machines you intend to scrap is an expensive luxury.

🐝

24–25 October

A & I had lunch at the Wolvercote Motel on our way to Edward & Bertha[63] at Cheltenham. Spent some time at the Roman remains at Chedworth. Good mosaics. Lovely autumn colours in the surrounding woods. Walked along the disused railway track above the ruins for a short distance. On return found I had locked the keys in the car. Panic. A motorist lent us a screwdriver and we managed to prise one of the front vent windows open without breaking it. Lucky. Delightful and funny evening at the Everyman: Joe Orton's *What The Butler Saw*. Very good house too. Early service at St Paul's College Chapel the next morning, then back to Oxford. Found Col's new carpet left in garage. Struggled it up the stairs and laid it in its own scent of india rubber. A then found starter of car wouldn't work. Rolf brought children up for lunch and for them to stay for two nights while J helps K & T at Fentiman Road (*at a house in London they had bought*).

🐝

26 October, Monday

Church fetched me and later had the car starter put right – a nut needed tightening. Letter from Valerie E saying that the Introduction should have been with me this morning. It wasn't. RR and JH had enjoyed the conference weekend in Sidmouth. The Victoria Hotel had done them proud and the business sessions had been good. Mrs Salmon unwell

---

63 Anne's brother Edward Bradby (1907-1996) was Principal of St Paul's teacher training college in Cheltenham, where he and his wife Bertha lived. He retired in 1972.

again, and JH hard-pressed. It is own fault, as I told him – he simply doesn't or won't delegate enough.

To London on 12.30 train for BFMP Finance Cttee. Dull. Saw Lubitsch's *The Love Parade* (1930) at the Nat. Film Theatre. Stood up very well, tho' Chevalier ghastly. *Lupino Lane* excellent. I first saw it in 1931 at the giant Regal in Bristol.

❦

27 October, Tuesday

BFMP Council at 10. Walked up thro' Covent Garden – streets filthy with uncollected refuse caused by council workers' strike. Surprising number of questions on my Legislation report, none of them difficult to deal with. Sat next to Tony Norris at lunch and discovered he had been in Nigeria during the war (*as had VR*).

To Fentiman Road in late afternoon. K & T not there. Waited 2 hours reading *Master & Man*, then left a note and returned to Charing Cross and another visit to the N F Theatre, where I saw *42nd Street*, made in 1933. I remember seeing it in Bristol at the time and apart from the outstanding absence of talent in Ruby Keeler, the principal, it was enjoyable.

❦

28 October, Wednesday

An all-day conference on 'Print for the partially-sighted' at the Royal Commonwealth Hall. Organized by the Libraries Association. Alison Shaw, who at one time was Bickmore's assistant in the Cartographic Department of the Press, had done some research in the subject and gave one of the papers. I took the chair for the final session and wound up proceedings at 4.30. Not too well attended, I thought, though those who did take part were lively enough.

Got back to find a note from A to say that she had gone to Fentiman Road for the night to help with the decoration, after hearing from Jane what they were grappling with.

❦

29 October, Thursday

In some gloom this morning, brought on by a long, civilly-worded letter from Davin on our shortcomings as seen from the CP side. Several of the points he makes are difficult to answer, but to my mind the root cause of these continuing problems – in the main, Composing and Reading Room problems – lies in the large number of titles we are handling for *one* customer. As I don't really want to reduce that number because our raison d'être is primarily to serve the CP, I have this dilemma, and finding a solution, or partial solution, is not easy. I have shown the letter to RR and JH. Today I shall let GB Taylor see it, and then next week I shall arrange a special meeting to discuss not only my reply but what lines of action we should follow to meet the criticisms.

Handed indentures to two good lads later in the morning. A long Playhouse directors' meeting at 5, long because we had to discuss forth-coming rent negotiations. When that was over I went almost directly on to the Freemasons' Hall for the first Safety Services Dinner I have arranged to replace the outings. It seemed to go well in that rather barn-like place. About 35 of us sat down to a quite reasonable meal, with beer or cider to drink. I then spoke of the purpose of the dinner, the importance and value of the Fire Brigade, St John Ambulance Division, the Safety Committee, and the medical room under Sister Westley. I got Beesley, Webb, Sister W and JH (as ch of the Committee) to say a few words, and ended the formal part of the evening by handing out some medals to members of the Fire Brigade. We sat around chatting until about 10.

A had just returned from an exhausting time at Fentiman Road. Our spirits weren't exactly raised by the Bergman play on TV, which A was watching when I came in. Called *The Lie*, it seemed to be about the savage break-up of a marriage or marriages. Hypnotic but depressing. Well acted by Frank Finlay and others.

❦

30 October, Friday

Decided to cancel my attendance at the S Reg Ptg Adv Cttee mtg at Reading. Spent the day seeing many different people. Decided to remove Spearman from his post at the Jobbing desk – he seems to lack the qualities needed for pushing small jobs through at the right pace.

November 1970

❦

2 November, Monday

Looked in on Piper on Friday evening. He is dying and I was saddened to see the change that had come over him since I had last visited him. It was the day of his official retirement. Philip Walker was there and I was irritated that he did not leave when he saw I wanted to speak with P alone. Still, he is so thick-headed I wasn't surprised. P has begun writing his reminiscences. I fear he has left it too late.

Saw a new recruit, Bunker by name, who will eventually take charge of production control in the Bindery. One of Hazell's redundancies. Not a 'high-flyer' but I guess he will do the job we want done.

At the CP meeting this morning I took up the question of misleading specifications when I was asked to give estimates for purposes of comparison with those of outside printers. In a recent case my binding price was said to be twice that of others. I found that we had quoted on quite a different specification. This criticism was well received and accepted.

Colin is very worried about our bad cash position. Sales are down and stocks are up. The consequences for me are not good: they mean a cutback on reprints, and possibly on new books, at least for a time. Difficult to plan for. At present we are building up staff, in the Bindery, where we have about 1,300,000 books in hand for the CP alone, and in the Composing Rooms. Here the men are resistant, naturally seeing the short-term prospect only, and complain that no more comps should be taken on while they themselves are not doing overtime.

Met JH, RR and GBT to discuss Davin's letter and memorandum. No conclusions at this stage. Colin told me earlier that London had also prepared a broadside and this should be with me in a day or so. I want to deal with them together.

The audited accounts for the last financial year are ready and go to F Cttee tomorrow. They are good, and in going through them with Frost I found little that needed detailed explanation. The period accounts & summary for last month are also good, and provisional profits well above budget. My anxiety now is being faced with a sharp fall-off of reprint work in the new year.

❦

3 November, Tuesday

A brief visit at midday from John Brett-Smith (*President of OUP's New York branch; VR first met him there in 1960*). His usual sardonic self; and his usual moans about Britain and British inflation. This irritated me, as it always does, and I asked him what they were doing about American inflation which by all accounts – and I showed him one – is still raging. No adequate answer, of course. He confirmed that sales of our academic books had fallen away badly, partly as the result of unrest in the universities, and partly because of financial restrictions. He spoke to this effect at FC in the afternoon. The V-C attended, with Bowra, Hicks, Chadwick, and the Senior Proctor. A long agenda, and a long discussion on the cash position, which is indeed quite alarming. Bruno gave an account (cheerful) of his recent visit to Nigeria, where sales and production are now going well. I presented my audited accounts, 'the one straightforward item on the agenda' as the chairman remarked, and gave my usual brief account of our present state, which really isn't at all bad for the half-year to date. In fact the net profit is well above my budget, and higher than I had forecast. As the annual accounts showed, and as I emphasized, high volume is the key to profits.

In the evening the Ogstons[64] took us to Stratford in their new and

---

64 Sandy Ogston (1911-1996) was a biochemist, and President of Trinity College 1970-78.

comfortable Fiat. They practically introduced us to the Stratford Theatre, in 1953, when we saw *Richard III*. We saw the same play this time, and in almost the same seats. Norman Rodway played the part – very well – with Richardson as Buckingham. A really brilliant production by Terry Hands, whose *Winter's Tale* had irritated us so much. He even made the moaning queens tolerable and believable, and his treatment of the ghosts episode was simple and most effective. There was nothing over-clever about his approach, tho' perhaps more gore than was necessary. Back by midnight.

❦

4 November, Wednesday

Talked first thing with JH about the shortcomings of Carlton in the Bindery office. I think we have tolerated him far too long. J says that he is almost at retiring age and isn't keen on moving him elsewhere. The trouble partly lies with Chalmers. He isn't strong enough or ruthless enough to put the fear into a man like Carlton, and has to be pressed to do anything about it. His supervisors, Fortescue and Coggins, are both better in that respect. One really needs a mixing of their qualities.

I also complained bitterly to Harris about some dirty proofs I saw in his outer office, and told him that if he had work of that standard coming out of the Keyboard Room he should shake the operators up by getting rid of a man or two, and that I would back him if he did. There is really no excuse for such sloppy work and they all know it.

Allan, of the British Academy, wrote to advise me that an enormous project, Paul of Venice's *Logica Magica*, would be coming along in six months. It is in two parts, each of ten fascicules, each fascicule containing 300 pages of Latin and 300 pages of English. The sort of thing that should see Richard out of office, let alone me.

To Neasden with R, mid-morning. Long talk with Huws-Davies and Tony Reeve about computer-typesetting and what the next step should be. Concluded that Reeve should send a system analyst to Oxford and that we should send Walker to Neasden for 3 days a week, beginning next February. By doing so we should make better progress than we have over the past year. We had a brief tour of the w'house which I'm afraid looks in a bit of a mess. It is going to be reorganized to link up with the new scheme for Jordan Hill, and not before time.

Management Club in the evening. Campbell spoke well about the future of the car industry. Henderson very rude in persistent question and comment, to the chairman's (J Allen) embarrassment. A late meeting and I didn't get home until 11.30. Earlier I had been along to the Dragon School to see how David Evers's printing group was getting on. Not too well really. I managed to dissuade him from trying to set up and print 2000 copies of their forthcoming *Mikado* programme.

5 November, Thursday

A little more new work flowing in, tho' still not very much from the CP. At any rate, the keyboards have been kept going, and elsewhere we are quite busy. I looked up a trial sheet of the *Rossetti* plates which Coles has just produced before printing the job in earnest. I think they are good, and a great improvement on our earlier effort. My main anxiety is in making sure that we don't now lose the man we have carefully trained to print this kind of high-quality illustration. He is very keen, and at the moment satisfied, but I know that he casts an envious eye at the shift workers on the large machines.

To London later for a lunch with John Ryder[65] of Bodley Head at the Garrick. I ploughed my way through the smelly rubbish of Covent Garden to get to their offices in Bow Street, almost next door to the Royal Opera House. Max Reinhardt[66] was about and we had a drink in his elegant room and the usual animated conversation that always

---

65 John Ryder (1917-2001) was Bodley Head art director and the author of *Printing for Pleasure*, for whose second edition of 1976 VR wrote the foreword (see Appendix 1).
66 Max Reinhardt (1915-2002) had bought the Bodley Head in 1957, and published such well-known authors as Graham Greene, Alistair Cooke, Eric Ambler, William Trevor and Maurice Sendak.

starts when we meet. He had been at Paul Hamlyn's[67] wedding party in Hampstead the night before. 500 guests, ox roasting on a spit, oysters and champagne, the whole, gloriously vulgar, lot. The comic thing was that practically all those who had been sacked from IPC,[68] or done the sacking, were there, presumably invited. Max said that Jarvis, managing director of the IPC books division since Hamlyn pulled out, came up to say that he had been sacked that morning. Hamlyn is now with Murdoch at the *News of the World*, a more suitable home for him, I imagine. Max also told me that Francis Meynell has nearly finished his autobiography, which they hope to publish next spring, after some cutting and chopping.

Over lunch John told me of his visit to Pinewood when Chaplin was filming *Countess in Hong Kong* with Brando and Loren. He had never seen anything like it. It was as though they were all suddenly living in the '20s – a tatty story and tatty sets. All the technicians were dumbfounded at the old-fashioned way Chaplin went about things. He acted each part in detail, to show his actors just how he wanted it done. Sophia Loren was very nice about it but Brando was furious and remained surly all the time Ryder was there. The purpose of his going was to take a young writer who was planning a book covering all Chaplin's films, and the history of them, right from the beginning. But it has all fallen through.

We talked of Mardersteig,[69] Moran and Mosley, until 3.15, when I left to call on Henry Jacob, the publications officer of the British Museum at his office in Bedford Square. He said wryly, 'splendid house, no staff', and indeed he has to run the office on a shoestring. Besides

---

67 Paul Hamlyn (1926-2001) was one of the commercial geniuses of British publishing after the war, creating successive companies (Hamlyn, and from 1971 Octopus) that pioneered the printing of popular colour-illustrated books in volume at low prices. His sojourn as joint managing director at News International lasted only a year (1970-71).

68 Hamlyn had sold his eponymous company to Cecil King of International Publishing Corporation (IPC) for £2 million in 1964 and become Chairman of its book publishing wing. King's successor Don Ryder took over IPC in 1969 and made many staff redundant.

69 Giovanni Mardersteig (1892-1977) was revered by typographers and printers for the fine books he produced on a hand press at the Officina Bodoni, which he had founded in 1922. He also designed the typefaces Fontana, Dante, Griffo and Zeno.

the Quarterly I am now doing several books and booklets for him, and litho reprints. In fact he says that my account is by far the largest. He speaks highly of our quality, and of the help & attention he gets from Halsey, and so I came away in good spirits.

With A in the evening to a subscription concert in the Sheldonian. Janáček (delightful), Tchaikovsky's cello variations (trite), Shostakovitch's 1937 Symphony (impressive). Good playing.

Still no Introduction from Valerie Eliot!

❦

6 November, Friday

A nasty blow. JH came in early to report that Pill, our best keyboard operator, had handed in his notice and was going to Aldens. The reason being the falling off in overtime here and hence a fall in his take-home pay. I think he is being foolish because the slackness here is only temporary, and JH has told him so. But he has made his decision and we must make the best of it. Unfortunately we already have too great a proportion of the less skilled men, and this new loss will make the fight to maintain quality that much more difficult.

Entertained Baylis, the new Controller of HMSO, and one of his lieutenants, Macaulay, to lunch. B is a great talker, hails from the Board of Trade, and already seems to have a fair grasp, if not grip, of the industry. Over lunch he emphasized that the office had now definitely come away from accepting the lowest tender received, and took more fully into account such things as quality and service. Useful meeting.

I toured the Works. Much impressed by the *Rossetti* plates now coming off machine. They really are better than I had hoped for.

To Holywell Music Room in the evening for the Allegri lecture. Mainly on Beethoven Op.59 no.2, and Verdi's sole quartet. Hugh Maguire (*leader of the Allegri string quartet*) had not prepared what he was going to say, so that illumination came in flashes, but these things are always fun.

❦

7–8 November

Bodley lunch at Brasenose on the Saturday. Sat between Nicholas Kurti (*Oxford Professor of Physics*) and the Warden of Merton. Trevor Aston (*Oxford historian*) opposite. Looked over Blackwell's new music shop in Holywell afterwards. Ingenious use of space – tiny-looking outside, capacious in.

To the Allegri concert in evening. Mozart K468 and the Beethoven and Verdi. Encore was a delicious Haydn minuet and trio from Op.76 no.2.

To Dragon School on Sunday afternoon to help David Evers with his little printing crew, who are trying to set up a programme for *The Mikado* which DE is producing. One of the class is Matthew Porteous, John Christie's[70] grandson. Bright lad and very quick. Finished soundtrack for Spanish film.[71]

❦

9 November, Monday

CHR let me know that because of the continuing cash shortage the CP would be slowing down the flow of reprints and spacing out new books. He therefore suggested that I should go slow on turning away my exam customers! A perfect example of the dangers of interfering with our mix of work. Exam work is regular and predictable; and although disruptive of book work it does give us an assured flow year by year. For the same reason I want to maintain the number of journals we handle. In the last few months the Keyboard Room has been kept going with journal copy.

An ex-Oxford keyboard operator, now at the Nuffield Press, wrote in this morning to ask whether he can come back. He can indeed, and he won't be too bad a replacement for the man I'm losing.

Handed over his indentures to a rather depressing machine minder

---

70 John Christie (1899-1980), Principal of Jesus College, Oxford 1949-67, was Ben Ridler's godfather. He had been a House Tutor at Rugby School when AR was a child living there, and became a lifelong friend.
71 VR made high-quality 8mm home movies, not just holiday diaries like the *Spain* film but short 'feature films', involving a shooting script that he drew out meticulously.

apprentice, Slay by name. He doesn't appear to have the energy to slay a fly and we may have to send him off if he doesn't bestir himself.

JH still struggling with the graduate reader problem. The NGA has now agreed with us, but Walker, the comps FOC, doesn't, so that the introduction into the Reading Room of the young woman we have had to put out to grass with Burchfield is still delayed.

At my managers' meeting I gave them an outline of the present financial situation and warned them of possible difficulties to come. I have to be careful not to dishearten them. At the same time, one must prepare them to some extent for changes which can cause a good deal of unrest in the departments.

A better intake of work last week. I hope we may now be over the slump, particularly as the exam papers have started to flow in, tho' we are still a few months away from the peak load.

In the evening, ran through the *Spain* film with the soundtrack. Neither of us liked the music track. Must start again.

JH had earlier put into my hand a scruffy notice from SOGAT headquarters calling on all members to strike on Tuesday 8 Dec against the Industrial Relations Bill. A stupid bunch. I must talk to the FOC.

❦

10 November, Tuesday

Talk with Eaglestone, my most reliable grapevine, and the Bindery supervisors about SOGAT's strike-call. Bindery chaps apparently very much upset, tho' there are conflicting views. Beal, the Branch Secretary, has told the chapel that the order is a firm one and must be obeyed. If they try to come in, pickets will be sent from London. All this sounds like nonsense to me. I have decided not to approach the FOC or the chapel committee. Instead I want first to find out whether such a strike is constitutional, written in the union rules. If it isn't, then my hand will be strengthened if I find it necessary to intervene at all. I also want to raise the issue at Thursday's meeting of the Association, to suggest that a letter of protest be sent to the Branch Secretary.

I wrote to the Secretary to point out that I should be given first priority if there is to be a cutback of composition, otherwise I shall have trouble in 'maintaining my credibility' with the men just after getting rid of some exam work which is assured and regular. He came down later to give me strong assurances on this point. We will see.

John Bell looked in at midday. He wanted advice about a nephew who, he said, was 'stupid'. That is, he can't pass exams. I asked him whether that was why his immediate thought was of the printing industry. The young man's father is planning to set him up in business as a fine binder and wants to know how to set about it. I recommended Ivor Robinson at the Polytechnic, also a management course at the same place.

Death of De Gaulle. Long, interesting film about his life was shown on TV. Denis Healey most impressive in a '24 Hours' discussion afterwards.

❦

11 November, Wednesday

Complaint from Pugh of Victoria County Histories (*RB Pugh, general editor of the VCH 1949-77*). I groaned, because he is such an old woman, tho' not a bad fellow to meet. He reported fingermarks on the six advance copies of the 'General Introduction' volume. I have now written to suggest we might change the cloth, because the present one is susceptible to marking, even if the packers are careful. But I doubt whether he will agree.

Wrote to an American in San Francisco who had inquired whether I could tell him anything about the setting of music. It so happens that we are about to melt down most of our founts because they are no longer used. I have therefore offered to let him have a fount of Ruby, laid in three cases. To judge from his letter this will send him into ecstasies.

Dined in. Who should be there but Pugh, a member of the Hall. We kept off the subject of VCH and fingers, tho' he winced when he saw me.

❦

12 November, Thursday

Made a précis of the main complaints made of our service by the publishing departments and sent a copy to Taylor & Halsey with a request for comment. Went over to the Machine Room to see Castle, who is back after a 3 months' illness. He is a splendid, cheerful fellow, and now looks well, tho' he told me that he still has to go into hospital again for a gall-stone operation.

Had Fissenden, our chemist, over for coffee at 9.45. He is still busy with paper testing and is trying to keep up with the constant changes being made at the Mill. I suspect we don't work him hard enough but what he does do is useful.

Jimmy Huws-Davies looked in at 4, with Richard. He seems quite pleased with the way things are going at Neasden and Jordan Hill. Whether we go ahead with the full scheme of reorganization at JH now seems doubtful, in view of the cash shortage. I have suggested to Colin that we might consider a lease-back arrangement with a financial company. The snag is the high interest rates we would have to pay.

To the Wolvercote Motel in the evening, for the AGM and dinner of the Association. Again a splendid attendance. John Alden presided: he does the job well and keeps everyone in good humour. Parchment gave me a vivid account of his expansion plans. He was shaved this time and looked quite presentable.

Home in time to see Michael Parkinson interview Gene Kelly on ITV, with some high spots from his best musicals, including the title dance from *Singin' in the Rain*. Marvellous, but not enough of it.

※

13 November, Friday

Several meetings, uneventful. Lunched with Stallabrass and his hench-men at the Golden Cross to discuss next week's finance meeting of Help the Aged in Baker Street. I get hints of stresses and strains between the London and Oxford personalities, particularly now that the Oxford end grows.

❦

14-15 November

Heavy rain all day on Sat. Critical leader on OUP in the *Oxford Magazine*, nicely (?) timed for next Tuesday's debate. Queries our efficiency, etc.

To Dragon School on Sunday to help the young printers with their *Mikado* production. Ben home when I got back, and thrilled to have been given a lead part in Bristol University Opera group's prod. of Moniusko's little-known opera *The Haunted Manor* next Feb.

Reading Tolstoy's 'Strider. The Story of a Horse'.

❦

16 November, Monday

Came to the office with a stiff neck, and wearing a red scarf. As usual, discovered that many members of the Press had suffered in the same way, and so I received plenty of advice. Saw Sister Westley who advised warmth and gave me some pain-killing pills, two of which I took later in the day without noticing any effect.

Colin suggested after our main meeting that we might get a consultant to look at the production problems of the three departments together. As this had already been in my mind I agreed, tho' I did not agree that a man from the Anne Shaw organization would be preferable to one from PA. Why I am particularly in favour of an outside opinion is that on balance it will produce a better understanding on the publishing side of my problems, whatever shortcomings may be disclosed. CHR is going to propose this plan at the next FC, before the new FC comes into being. The debate on the Press will be led from our side by Herbert Hart,[72] a good choice, being moderate and rather 'left', which may appease any wolves that turn up.

---

72 Herbert Hart (1907-1992) was Professor of Jurisprudence at Oxford 1952-69 and became Principal of Brasenose College in 1973. His most famous book was *The Concept of Law* (1961). During the war he served in MI5 at Bletchley Park alongside Alan Turing, and in MI5 at Blenheim Palace, sharing an office with the spy Anthony Blunt. His wife, the civil servant and historian Jenifer Hart, was a one-time member of the Communist Party.

Later in the day Anthony Hobson[73] and Tilly de la Mare[74] came in to discuss their project on Italian Handwriting. As usual the plans had changed since my estimate of last year and we shall have to start again. Most of the money to prime the pump is coming from a rich American. I urged them not to sell the book too cheaply and I think they will take that advice.

To Teddy Hall in the evening, for the Feast. Black tie, guests from our sister college, Fitzwilliam, quite amusing speech by the Principal, and reasonable tho' not prima food and drink. The new hall, splendid in its way, is not ideal for high-table intimacies – no pools of light, just the shadowless, boring fluorescence over everything and everyone. Still, we had candles in the SCR, which was some compensation.

☙

17 November, Tuesday

Mrs Blanche Henrey called in. She is working in Bodley on some of the illustrations for her botanical volumes. She needed advice on the right way of collecting and arranging the plates for the printer, and this I was able to give. As Bruno says, *he* is going to lose a packet of money on this vast project, to which he is committed by a contract made in Cumberlege's[75] time, while I shall probably do well out of it and at least get my money back. I hope so, but it is the sort of thing that usually generates a good deal of unchargeable work.

An early lunch so that I could get to the debate on the proposed new Statutes for the Press, arising out of the Waldock Report, at 2pm in the Congregation House. John Hall and I were the first there. A few minutes later Burchfield and Cordy (*Clarendon Press Classics editor*) appeared, then another CP contingent of editors, then Colin and Bruno, then

---

73 Anthony Hobson (1921-2014) was the world's leading expert on Renaissance bindings and a bibliophile of great distinction.
74 Tilly de la Mare (1932-2001) was a librarian and palaeographer who specialized in Italian Renaissance manuscripts.
75 Geoffrey Cumberlege (1891-1979) was Publisher of OUP's London Business 1945-56, having succeeded Humphrey Milford. He had successfully reinvigorated and expanded OUP's branch in India in the 1920s and rescued OUP's New York branch in the early 1930s.

Helen Gardner, Blackman, Jack Thompson,[76] and Herbert Hart. The V-C arrived fairly punctually, hemmed in by his beadles and proctors, to open the debate with a brief statement of what we were to consider. Bamborough, the only member of the Waldock Committee in sight, made a brief formal statement. He was followed by Lucy Sutherland who read well from her carefully prepared script putting the Council's support for the Statutes. Opposition came from Rosenbery of Linacre, who spoke loud and clear but produced no strong reason as to why the Press should make regular subventions to the University, his main point. Then another critic, Cooper of Trinity, and a one-time fellow of All Souls, made a drawling ineffective speech, again poorly argued. Why had the Delegates spent a million on the Mill (why indeed?) and how much better if they had given that sum to Bodley. And if the Bible was no longer profitable because [he seemed to assume] of 'technological change', what was the sense in spending £2.3 million on the Printing Works? He ended on rather a sneering note by reminding the house that the Delegates of the Press were the only members of the University to receive 'fringe benefits', by which he meant the much-coveted free books.

Herbert Hart then spoke for the Delegates. He went over a number of significant points on which he had been carefully briefed by Colin, the main one being that we had to be self-financing. He also mentioned the high return on capital made by the Printing Business, and defended the decision to put up the new Mill with some force. But I was rather disappointed in his performance. He gave the feeling that he was not all that sure of his brief and he does not speak particularly well. However, apart from one comment mumbled by John Wright, also of Trinity – its gist was lost on me – no other comments were proffered by the few non-Press members present and the Statutes were duly accepted. Rather flat really, after those months and years of rigmarole, and I can't see much positive good coming from it all.

---

76 Jack Thompson (1909-1975) was chairman of OUP's Finance Committee, a mathematician whose sound financial judgement Colin Roberts came to rely on.

18 November, Wednesday

To London on lunch train. Presented budget to V & CS on behalf of Help the Aged Housing Association. Then to Charing Cross Hotel to change for Printers Pension Corporation dinner at Connaught Rooms. Mansfield, now president of Printing Managers Association, came with me. Best collection of after-dinner speeches I have ever heard. Redcliffe-Maud,[77] with his remarkable mimicry, was very funny. The Prime Minister (*Ted Heath*), who got a great reception, threw away his prepared speech and was also very funny as well as apposite. Then Lord Goodman finished the thing off with one of his rapid, skilful, sometimes acid, speeches.

The managing director of the *Daily Telegraph* was sitting on my left. Goodman is chairman of the Newspaper Proprietors Association. 'Accepted by all and trusted by none' he said. Edward Pickering, director of magazines at IPC, was my other neighbour. He says they are doing quite well, tho' the great days of the 'general interest' periodical are over. The PM stayed on afterwards, chatting to all and sundry in the bar. Very adroit, and should help him retain a few votes when the crunch comes.

19 November, Thursday

Breakfast with Mansfield, then on to Ely House to see Philip Chester. Interested to hear that they now regard printing in Hong Kong with some caution. They don't think it will last, and I suspect they can't get what they want when they want it. Friendly meeting, with exchange of views on Eric White, who is now Philip's neighbour. EW has been very kind to the Chesters and his sister-in-law, Joan White, works at Ely House.

Management Research Group lunch meeting. Talk by an ICI accountant obscure and not helpful – to me at least. Champagne at lunch in celebration of Group 9's 100th meeting.

---

77 Lord Redcliffe-Maud (1906-1982) was a civil servant who chaired the Royal Commission on Local Government in England 1966-69.

Colin (*Ridler*) came over for a lecture by Lévi-Strauss. I met him and Anne at the Town Hall to hear the Philharmonia Quintet playing Bruckner, Weller, and Mozart's K515. Superb team with most beautiful tone. Pity they didn't play all Mozart.

Back home C gave us a disturbing account of some of his King's companions. Thieving and pot smoking. A big change since Ben's day, alas. Letter from PM's office asking whether I am willing to accept CBE.

Brief talk with JH earlier. Graduate reader dispute with NGA settled at last, thank goodness. No further news of SOGAT strike action on 8 Dec. BFMP has written to Flynn, the secretary, but it may not have much effect.

☙

20 November, Friday

Hasty 10 o'clock meeting as I had to catch a train for the Newspaper Design Award lunch at the Savoy. Butler had been at Ely House and his notes, issued the next morning, were rather too indiscreet for my liking. I explained that they were given quite a wide circulation and not everything that came into his head should be put down on paper. He seems to have been given a good if 'warm' reception in London. Halsey is keen that he should make regular visits and I think he is right. I left the matter open until I got back.

Advance copy of Lord Leicester's Roxburghe volume, *The Holkham Library*, appeared on my desk. The plates, printed by offset in black and in colour, are good on the whole, tho' I can't help regretting the passing of collotype, not that we always got good results from it. I hear that Leicester is v pleased.

The Award lunch went its usual way. Dreyfus spoke for us judges, quite well. The other speeches were more or less routine, the sort of showbiz congratulations and thanks to all and sundry. I sat next to the new managing director of Linotype and Machinery, one Brace by name, from Marconi six months ago. Intelligent man with plenty of drive, I imagine: they certainly need it. John Maud was there, to my surprise.

He is one of next year's judges and wanted to know what was involved. When I told him that we had voted the *Observer* as Top Paper, thus giving it a hat trick, he said he thought it looked awful. So the new lot of judges should have an interesting time.

I stayed in London to see Sternberg's *The Last Command* at the NFT. I saw it in 1928 when it was first issued. Emil Jannings and Evelyn Brent weathered the years. Sternberg's handling of his crowd extras did not. One quickly got used to the sub-titles and the piano accompanist made the whole thing seem like old times again.

21–22 November

To doctor in the morning, about my neck. Not much help really. Looked in on Piper. His flesh hardly clothes his frame now, poor man, and yet he talked of feeling better and of what he would be doing when he was up and well again.

With A to Bladon, to photograph Philippa's house for her Xmas card. The sun (of course) came out more strongly soon after I had finished.

Back to Oxford and Antonioni's *Zabriskie Point* at the ABC. The celebrated, or notorious 'love-in' was tiresome and ineffective, but the rest was fairly compelling and well shot.

23 November, Monday

The new PA consultant for the Bindery production control, Slight, was brought in by Wilkinson, their supervisor. He seems a bright fellow (ex-Cambridge) and during the next 10 weeks we shall see what to make of him. Colin told me at our meeting that Turner, PA's supervisor on the warehouse job, is keen to look at the printer-publisher relationship himself, which is very good news. We all trust and respect him.

At my managers' meeting I referred to the serious shortage of cash in the organization, and told them that they must keep stock to the bare minimum, and close as many orders as they can as quickly as they can.

To the Staff Club AGM at 5.30. Uneventful, quite well attended.

Earlier, de la Mare rang up to ask me whether I know anything of a man at BAS typesetters who they are thinking of taking on as David's successor. I had never heard of him and so couldn't help. Apparently they are not now going to engage Nicolas Barker. Also heard that Valerie Eliot has broken her arm *but* – Dick says – her Introduction is finished and Fabers are helping to get it typed. Dashed off a note to her.

Bratt also rang to say that the *NEB* Stirling meeting is definitely fixed for 8 December. I told him I would come myself, which seemed to please him!

☙

24 November, Tuesday

Butler brought over the proof of a trial colour plate for the illustrated Ruby Bible. Many years ago, on my advice, London had the illustrations printed by photogravure. Now they are anxious to cut costs, in order to compete with Collins' rival edition, and I have given them my estimate which shows a considerable saving. This proof is to give them a comparison, and although offset can't produce the depth and intensity of gravure our result looks attractive. I am sure London will go for it.

Took an extremely well-designed book, *The Napoleonists*, printed by Clay and designed by Roger Davies at Ely House, into my layout section. I am rather afraid we are too unadventurous these days, and without some prodding from me everyone, even the bright young things, tend under the otherwise admirable Stewart, to follow the old and set routines. The results are sound enough, but I don't like to see CP and London outside-printed books as the only selections in the annual book production exhibition.

Drove out to Sutton Courtenay in the afternoon to see Mrs Mills, the widow of the accountant in office when I came in 1948. He died early, and suddenly. She is now 75, suffers from lack of thyroid and loneliness, and told me she was 'ready to go' any time now. She is fond of reading but not TV. I was surprised that she has no set but she said she didn't want one. She was born in St Aldates, where the Memorial Garden now stands. Her father was Alderman Brown, one-time Mayor of Oxford. The school she taught at in St Ebbes has now vanished with the demolitions. Her room, very tidy and pleasant, was full of elephants in various shapes and sizes.

When I got back JH reported that the SOGAT chapel don't really know what to do about the threatened strike on 8 Dec. They are holding a chapel meeting in the canteen at 4.30 tomorrow.

*

25 November, Wednesday

To London for BFMP Legislation cttee meeting. As Chairman I distinguished myself by leaving my agenda and notes behind, but Eric Dixon came to my rescue and we got through the business very smoothly. Afterwards the President invited Alastair Stewart and me to have a drink with him. I thought we were going to a pub but we approached a plain façade off Holborn and walked into a brothel-like passageway which led into something called the Epicure Luncheon Club. In the end we all stayed for a snack lunch. Harry seemed to like the place, but I can understand why Kenyon and others are less enthusiastic not that it was anything but seemly.

I picked up a new suit at Hornes and caught the 3.15 back. Thompson from Ely House had been on one of his regular visits. I had just missed him. Skelly and Taylor reported on their talks: fortunately no great crises or troubles, tho' some of our schedules have been upset because of delay with paper deliveries.

*

26 November, Thursday

A thin post this morning, which allowed me to spend rather more time in the Works. I had quite a long talk with our SOGAT FOC about the impending strike called by their executive. He told me that the shop floor are very upset about it, particularly as many of his members voted the present govt into power. They think the whole thing is commu-nist-inspired – interesting, coming from his side of the fence – and he has told Beal, the Branch Secretary, that he isn't going to call the men out himself, and if necessary he will resign. I hope he doesn't because, although he is not a strong FOC he is at least level-headed and honest. There is to be a branch meeting tonight, so there may yet be a change of plan.

John Alden (now president of the local Master Printers Association) rang me to ask whether I thought a letter should now be sent from the Association to Beale in protest. I said yes indeed, and he rang me again later to read out his draft, which I thought a good one. It may have no practical effect but at least we shall have gone on record. I invited him to the next Management Club dinner at Worcester College.

A letter from Charles Batey. Poor chap, he has just had his last teeth out, but sounds in good form. But I still wonder whether he was wise to move to such a remote place. He writes 'There is little social life here and the village church provides no spiritual refreshment or comfort. The first is not important at our age; the second is.'

Had Sinclair, assistant manager of the Litho Dept, down for coffee this morning. We recently put him through a course in the Work Study Section and while he was there he unearthed quite a number of anoma-lies and defects in the Litho incentive scheme. I wanted to congratulate him and also to test how he is settling in, because being a Scot there is always the risk that he may want to head north again. But he seems settled, and talks of buying a house at Thame. Rather too convenient for Hazells for my comfort, but I think he likes it here: he is certainly a good manager and will get even better with more experience.

Drafted a brief for Turner of PA against the time when he starts his investigation of our production methods. I have turned it over to RR for his comments.

Lunched next door with HGC and Edmund Poole of Chatto & Windus. Glad to hear that Poole thinks highly of Oxford's machining – which is more than I often do. He suffers a lot at the hands of his few printers or so he says. He is interested in the printing of music and was down here to study at Bodley.

Looked at some trial desks of a new design, for our Reading Dept extension. They are too big, and RR is going to have them cut down in size to something less elephantine. Even then they will look pretty hefty.

Mrs Salmon has had a good report and sympathetic treatment from Bart's. She looks better, which is a great relief because the pressure on the Personnel Section grows and grows, what with the flood of paper from our ITB, and recruitment problems.

☙

27 November, Friday

Storms and tears this morning! Halsey came in with a long face to say that Butler was going to leave. He had been insulted over the phone by Taylor and this was the end! Halsey had told him to sleep on it but he had come in this morning determined to depart. O dear. I told him to send Butler along to me at 9.45. He came in with set jaw and gleaming eye. He loved his work, he had served under three printers and tried to do a good job, but to have Taylor bellowing and ordering him about when Halsey was his immediate boss was too much. With tears in his eyes he painted a sad and vivid picture of Butler stumbling out on to the hard, cold streets of Oxford, realizing that any job he might find would be more lowly paid but still...! I hastily dissolved the lump in my throat, assumed my best plain, no-nonsense dutch-uncle manner and told him not to be such an ass. I also said that I wouldn't in any case accept his resignation on such an issue and that he must try to stem his self-pity, however justifiable his grievance against Taylor might be. I think the week-end will bring him back to earth. The trouble is that Taylor *is* a blunderer when it comes to dealing with some situations, and Butler can be quite uppish himself in such encounters. But he is a very good man and I should be sorry to lose him. He said something else that interested me. 'Some years ago, Printer, at your Monday morning meeting, you asked me a question about a book I was dealing with that

I couldn't answer. I felt that was because I had been drinking too much over the week-end, and from that time onwards I practically gave up drinking so that I should be able to answer your questions.' Dear Butler had got a bit of a reputation as a boozer in the Victoria Snug, so it was just as well that he found a good reason for mending his ways.

Sent off a draft brief for Turner of PA to CHR. I shall be interested to get his reaction on Monday. Also wrote a longish letter to Batey and began drafting another to Gibbons on the projected SOGAT strike.

Later in the day RR reported that a 10,000 reprint of the *Companion to Art* was on its way, which is good news for the Litho. New book-work is still not plentiful but everyone has a job.

Harvey, one of our old and reliable caster operators is not at all well. I think he has had a mild stroke, at any rate he looks vacantly about him and has made one or two bad mistakes. He is now 66 and we had been hoping to keep him going for several years more, but dealing with molten metal can be dangerous and we may have to retire him after Christmas.

❦

28-30 November

The Pennants[78] arrived last night. Alice came with us to the OU Opera Club's performance of *Armide*, with Marion Milford[79] in the title role. On Saturday, to *The Tempest* at Stratford. Much underrated by the critics. Fascinating set, Ariel, Caliban, and of course Ian Richardson as Prospero. Dined at the Arden beforehand. Very wet Sunday, with rain almost all day. I stayed at home on the Monday, trying at A's behest more intensive treatment on my neck, including external application of an electric heat pad and internal ditto of cabbage water (Philippa's remedy!). Finished soundtrack for *Spain*, after much trial and error.

---

78 Alice Pennant (née Stainer) (1912-2001) was a friend and contemporary of AR's at Downe House School. She married David Pennant (1912-2001), who became a circuit judge.
79 Marion Milford was AR's cousin, a professional soprano singer and niece of the composer Robin Milford (1903-1959).

December 1970

☙

1 December, Tuesday

Butler is still here – and silent! For the time being at least. Later in the morning CHR came down to say that the London publicity committee wanted to put the spring and autumn lists with another printer, Watmough, and what did I think? Talk about *consultation*! This was the first I had heard about it. I told him plainly that we could deal with these lists just as speedily as anyone else if we were allowed to. The trouble always is the heavy amount of correction made at the last minute. As a matter of fact I really wouldn't mind losing the composition, which is a nuisance, but to lose the printing of 30,000 copies is another matter. C is now going to send me a note for my 'considered' reply.

Finance Cttee in the afternoon. The V-C forthright and lively. Whatever may be said about Bullock[80] it is good to hear someone on this cttee speak his mind loud and clear. Much indeterminate argument about our woeful cash position, which is really quite serious. Not yet clear what is to be done about it.

The investigation of the Printing Business's relationship to the publishing departments was also tabled and passed. The Chairman asked the V-C whether Council might be asked formally whether it still wished the Printer to print for the University. Bullock neatly turned this round by suggesting that it was for the Delegates and the Printer to say whether they wished to do it. He added, pointedly, that he thought any proposal to do *less* for the University would look rather odd, coming immediately after the Waldock Report. Poor Jack Thompson hastily pointed out that he had only raised the matter in this way because the report had suggested the possibility of a small offset unit being set up by the Registry. I know of course from Campbell that this is the very last thing they want.

---

80 Alan Bullock (1914-2004), author of the first comprehensive biography of Adolf Hitler (1952), was founding Master of St Catherine's College, Oxford, and the first full-time Vice-Chancellor of the University.

I left soon after 4 to go with Anne to Bristol for Ben's University concert. He sang the Evangelist in Schütz's *Christmas Story* and sang it most beautifully. His first real public performance as a singer, and an auspicious one. We stayed with him at his pleasant flat on the Downs, 1 Brecon Road, which he shares with Meg Davies and Werner Pelz, very happily. Sent a letter to the SOGAT FOC on next week's strike, appealing for sense!

☙

2 December, Wednesday

Overslept, and so did not say farewell to Ben until just after 9.30. Went straight home for an early lunch, then back to the Press in time to look at my post and pick up my papers for a Help the Aged meeting at 2.15. Took pills and cabbage water for my stiff neck which obstinately refuses to unstiffen.

Help the Aged meeting went on until 5.15. It was prolonged by a discourse from Faulkner, director of the main charity, who feared that our wish to have an established salary structure would be moving away from the charity spirit to that of a local govt office. We all demurred at this. Obviously the main charity feels that Tom Stallabrass's exceptional drive is taking us too far too fast. I don't think it is, and the underlying friction is probably because Faulkner senses that power is moving from the centre.

We gave a dinner party in the evening for Philip Larkin.[81] The Nowell-Smiths[82] and Philippa were our other guests. PL is slightly deaf which makes him seem more taciturn than he probably is. But the evening went quite well. A had worked out an exotic meal (with some help from Philippa) of pheasant and raspberry flan. Afterwards we showed them

---

81 Philip Larkin (1922-1985), poet, novelist and librarian, who edited *The Oxford Book of Twentieth Century English Verse* (1973).
82 Simon Nowell-Smith (1909-1996) was a bibliographer and former Librarian of the London Library who wrote two books about publishers (Cassell and Macmillan) and amassed a great collection of rare books. He lived with his wife Marion in Headington.

The 13th Candle, The Flycatcher, and *1851*.[83] Of the last PL declared that he thought it 'a work of art', which was gratifying. Molly Austin came in to help behind the scenes, which meant that we weren't faced with a load of washing-up after everybody had gone (at 11.30 – quite late for us!). RR had given me some liniment the vets use which I rubbed carefully into my neck, hoping for the best.

❧

3 December, Thursday

Overslept, and have been feeling drowsy all day. I put it down to the pills I'm taking – 8 a day – at the doctor's request. I haven't felt any benefit so far, unless the urge to nod off can be called a benefit.

Not much new work about. The departments are busy, and should be until Christmas, but I feel anxious about what may happen in the new year. During the day I talked with Fulton, and even he ventured to say how lucky we were compared to many firms in the area. So the lesson is sinking in at last. He is busy producing 'Toy Town' as the footballers' Christmas pantomime. He tells me that under the reorganization scheme of its branches planned by the NGA he will lose the presidency, which is to go to a man in Banbury. He didn't seem enthusiastic about it. He also told me that SOGAT were recalling their delegate conference to a meeting on Friday. This is hopeful because it may mean that they will now vote against the decision to strike next Tuesday. Not surprising either, now that the Newspaper Proprietors Association has slapped an injunction on several members of the executive which could make each of them liable to heavy damages.

Turner of PA came to lunch. We had a long and thorough talk about his proposed assignment. I emphasized the two separate aspects of the problem, the friction caused unavoidably by the circumstances of the relationship, and the friction caused by inefficient machinery or

---

83 All 8mm films by VR. *1851* was his most ambitious production, involving filming selected scenes from lithographs – mounted by VR on a special wooden rig – that had been made at the time of the Great Exhibition. The soundtrack used extracts from Queen Victoria's diary of her visits to the exhibition, chosen and read by AR.

communications in our methods of production control. Later he was good enough to thank me for the clarity with which I had put the issues. He will now make a quick survey of the ground to decide just what his brief should be.

🦗

4 December, Friday

Had Taylor in at 9.45 to report on his meeting with the publishers' production managers. The CP now wants us to prepare a specimen for *COD* in the 'Galaxy' paperback size.[84] The first batch of copy for the new edition should be ready in two years' time. This means that I must now decide fairly quickly exactly what type of new rotary press to handle the larger paper size we should put in. The design and manufacture could take all of 2 years. The other matters on their agenda were less important.

The usual meeting at 10. Not much new work about – and still no sign of Valerie Eliot's celebrated Introduction. According to Dick de la Mare, Faber were typing it for her some weeks ago.

After the meeting I went along to Bodley to discuss with Michael Turner and Miss Briggs the design and production of a catalogue for an exhibition on the John Johnson Collection[85] to be opened next May. The catalogue is to have an account of its origin and of course as many illustrations as they can afford. I suggested that the cover should be associated particularly with Johnson, whether by photograph or drawing, and Turner is going to see what material he has available. He is also thinking of following the catalogue with a series of picture books, which could be exciting.

Toured the Works after lunch, not too successfully because I was treated to dismal news wherever I went. In the Jobbing Ship (*short for 'Companionship'*) I was told that the new lino operator who only started

---

84 The 'egg-head', slightly larger paperback size used for the OUP American branch's Galaxy paperbacks, first introduced in 1956 (see Introduction).
85 Johnson had during his time as Printer systematically collected historic printed ephemera from a wide variety of sources. VR transferred this entire unique collection to the Bodleian Library in the 1960s.

on Monday had given a fortnight's notice because he found the work too difficult; Mrs Fulton complained that half her sewing machines had been standing idle for most of the week; and when I inquired of one of the engineers what was wrong with a nipping machine he was repairing he said 'I reckon this is *serious*. They are getting through a pair of shearing pins on this machine about once a fortnight, and they cost £15 a pair. At that rate we shall be paying for the thing twice over.' I know we have a reputation for exerting great pressure on our nippers, but I hadn't realized it was that bad. I hastily slunk away with a mental note in place.

Alice Hadfield came to lunch at home. I had not seen her for many years. She told us that Charles had retired from David & Charles over three years ago, but was still working on his history of the inland waterways.

5–6 December

A to Magdalen College School production of *A Man For All Seaso* which she is reviewing for their magazine. I worked on *The Ma* *Man's Revenge* as we want to get it finished in time for Christmas. (the Sunday evening I again helped to judge the entries for the Cow Centre Cine Club. Not a very good batch but the two prize winner both short comedies – had been done by a man and his wife. Bob Ell from my design section had done quite an ambitious piece on 5 N but made it far too long. Got back home only a few minutes after one of the Eisenstein documentary had begun on TV.

7 December, Monday

Discussed the production of the seasonal catalogues with CHR Chester at our 11 o'clock meeting. If the Joint Management (really believes that the copy will in future be virtually correct wh t is ready, then there is no reason why we shouldn't do each list i 7 weeks. But I very much doubt whether the copy will be left alone. I shall now suggest that we produce the Autumn List here (the Spring one is already printed) and see how we get on. It is easy for a rival printer to say that he can do the job in a certain time when he has never done it.

Much to-ing and fro-ing about tomorrow's strike. Some of my chaps want to come in but are afraid of what might happen later. They really need an unofficial shopfloor spokesman to rally them, and no-one is in sight.

Six more new books coming down from CP. Two in from the Univ of Wales, so the load should improve a little to help us over the slacker time after Christmas.

Catechized Ashby about the wasteful use of shear-pins on the nipping machine, and stirred him to do something about it.

Looked at the monthly accounts with Frost. Good on the whole, with the provisional net profit continuing well above budget. He warned me to expect a long letter from our new auditors suggesting various changes in our stock and work-in-progress accounting.

Examined with RR the report from Neasden's computer expert, Reeve, on ways in which our experimental work can best be continued. Quite sound, though I must be rather cautious in what I disclose of our management accounts. This is the trouble with having what is in effect a management consultant based in the offices of one of your main customers.

JH left with me O'Reilly's project thesis on keyboard operator training. Elegantly bound (at my expense). I hope the contents do it justice.

❦

8 December, Tuesday

A group of cold-looking pickets were drooping against the railings when I got in at 8. Later I heard that all the SOGAT people had stayed out, most of them reluctantly and under the threat of a £20 fine. All very stupid, but there was nothing more I could do about it.

Slight, our resident PA consultant (at £380 a week) came in with RR to report on progress with production control in the Bindery & Warehouse. I think he is on the right lines, and now that the Publisher is to become responsible for Jordan Hill he may be more disposed to accept some of the ideas that Slight has resurrected and which I had put to him years ago. I had to cut the meeting short because I decided that if I was to be sure of getting to the Bible Society meeting by 1 o'clock I had better catch an early train. I had also arranged for the Publisher's chauffeur, the inimitable and cockney Dykes, to meet me at Paddington and take me across London. This he did, and on our way we encountered such a traffic hold-up in the Strand, where busloads of police were decanting to deal with the strikers' procession, that we turned round and got down to the Embankment. The road was clear, and as we purred along Dykes said 'What d'you think of those Post Office fellers striking because Lord 'All got the sack? He got 50,000 quid and they lost a day's pay. Blimey! I asked the Publisher what he thought would happen if 'e got the sack and 'e asked me whether I'd come out on strike for 'im. Not likely, I said, I wouldn't lose a day's pay for you. 'E laughed but I don't think 'e liked it much.' That last remark was surprisingly acute because I don't suppose poor Bruno *did* like it all that much.

We were quite a large gathering at the Society's HQ. (I had looked in on Mosley at the St Bride's Library to kill a little time as I was then so early.) Bratt took us down to the new canteen of our Stage II extension. All the lights went out while we were having coffee.

We then went upstairs to a daylight office. Besides Bratt and four of his assistants there were Bowers of CUP, Hunt, Street, and me. Most of the discussion was of editorial matters, but we got on to production later and it looks as though we shall have a good part of the copy before Christmas and the completion by the end of May. Everyone seemed most enthusiastic about our filmset specimen. This rather surprised me because I think the type is too small. However, I decided to keep silent on this point. But we shall have to produce a revised specimen because some important if minor changes in style have been made. I left the meeting quite pleased with the result, although I always tend to pale before the mass of clerics inhabiting Bible House.

Went to Whitehall Court, read *Anna Karenina* for an hour and made my way to the Bath Club in Brook Street for an Office Bearers' dinner with the Federation President. The main, indeed only, business of the meeting is to decide upon a nomination for the next Junior V Pres and there was unanimous approval for Henry Davey of the North-Eastern Alliance. He is chairman of the Public Relations Committee and a solid if rather serious fellow, very much concerned with design. He should make a good president.

Elliott Viney gave Lord Ebbisham and me a lift back to our hotels. I didn't sleep well because although I turned off the radiator my room seemed to remain stuffy and airless.

❦

9 December, Wednesday

To the Fed offices for a meeting for the General Purposes Committee. Val Curtis – an excellent chairman – presided. I presented the report of the Legislation Cttee: not many questions tho' some discussion. Because of the unpredictable power cuts I decided to cut the Organization Cttee meeting in the afternoon and caught the 1.15 back to Oxford.

Herbert Newman told me earlier that CUP were desperately short of composition. This seems to be confirmed by their approach to us to see whether we could send them some proofs for reading.

In the evening I took John Alden to the Management Club dinner at Worcester. A Christ Church don, Oppenheimer, spoke fluently and well (in spite of a heavy cold) about the Common Market. He saw very little advantage to us in joining and argued his case with some conviction.

When I got home I found the house completely blacked out except for a night-light burning by the hall mirror. A had retreated to bed and was reading by candlelight – there had been a blackout since 10.30. Odd feeling, just like wartime.

☙

10 December, Thursday

Carol rang me to say that Richard Russell was staying at home with a cold and sore throat. During the morning I had a talk with Aubrey Beesley about Fire Brigade affairs in anticipation of the AGM in the evening. However stupid in some ways, he really is a most loyal and conscientious fellow. Also had a talk with Mrs Fulton who was having a struggle to keep the sewing machines going. I was surprised at this, but in talking with Chalmers I discovered that he has no large dictionary orders going through at the moment, and a lot of 'perfect'[86] binding on paper-covered books which bypass the sewers. Fortunately we shall be starting on the new impression of *COD* in a day or two, so that I don't think the situation is desperate.

Drafted my reply to CHR on the proposal of the Joint Management Committee to transfer the production of the seasonal lists to another printer. I showed it to GBT, who seemed well satisfied, and sent it off. I want to hold on to the work if I possibly can.

After lunch Turner of PA brought in another PA expert, Marsh, to discuss the forthcoming project on the relationship of the businesses. Marsh questioned me closely and in fact I had to close our talk when we came to 3.30 because I then had to meet the other trustees of the John Johnson apprentice award scheme to decide on the best senior and junior apprentice of the last year.

The trustees are Howard Buckley, now retired from the Polytechnic, and Fulton. One unusual and rather amusing point this time was that the comps chapel had recommended Ron Harris's son for the junior award. As manager of the department he had recommended another boy, so it was a tribute to him that the shopfloor had chosen in the way they did. We had to give the award to Harris's nomination because there was no doubt that on paper he was the better candidate. Fulton told me beforehand that he and his wife had been to Stratford for the first

---

86 'Perfect' binding is a contradictory-sounding term used in the book trade to mean books that have glued rather than sewn binding – generally creating a less durable, and therefore rather 'imperfect' binding.

time, to see *Richard III!* Heavens. He gave me the impression that they had been rather bewildered but had enjoyed themselves.

Then to a Playhouse directors' meeting where Frank H had wonderful schemes for taking over or going into the New Theatre if we cannot reach a satisfactory rent agreement with the Curators of the Univ Theatre. I have never met anyone who can so convince himself, and sometimes others, of so many contradictory arguments at one sitting. We listened and talked and in the end decided to await a pending move from the Curators' side.

Then a brief call in at Richard Gray's sherry party, and so home. No blackouts, and at 9.15 a ray of sunshine in the form of Ben. We were soon discussing Eisenstein, whose *Ivan the Terrible* was to appear on TV at 10.30. We looked at the opening part, pictorial but v slow moving, more pageant than movie, gave up and went to bed.

🌱

11 December, Friday

The electrical power workers' go slow continues, but so far there has still been no cut at the Press. At my 10am meeting Butler reported on his visit to Ely House. We still need new composition and I was glad to hear that another two Oxford English Novels were on the way. Added to two CP manuscripts in the box this morning they make good news for the Composing Rooms. We also discussed my estimate for the reset edition of *Oxford Illustrated Dictionary*. Butler was delighted when I said that we must certainly print it by offset lithography.

JH and I had a long talk afterwards: wage rates for filmsetting, merit rating for keyboard operators, and the health of Mrs Salmon. Her husband reported another setback yesterday and I very much fear that her illness may be more deep-seated than any of us thought. If she doesn't come back we shall feel the loss in many ways. At least JH now has O'Reilly working for him, which is some relief. Later he brought in Neale, winner of the senior JJ award. He is a quiet, reticent lad, son of one of our machine feeders and destined, we all hope, to become a

good keyboard operator. He had not I think realized that the prize was
£10 and seemed delighted.

Halsey was entertaining two members from the production staff of
Jonathan Cape, one of them being John Saunders, recently of my layout
section. They seem anxious to print with us, tho' as most of their work is
straightforward I can't quite see why. We may, says GJH, get one book
after Christmas, and possibly be asked to quote for litho reprints. I
have told him not to appear over-anxious to get their work; and in any
case I must be cautious because I don't want to affect our learned work
unnecessarily if I can help it. On the other hand, fringe customers come
and go, so that the occasional new publishing account can be useful.

Richard still away: he should be back on Monday.

❦

12-13 December

Dined at All Souls with John Simmons. Now that he is Librarian the
College has given him an elegant and comfortable sitting room and a
well-equipped office leading out of it. John Dreyfus was there as Seznec's
guest. After dinner I had a long talk with Michael Holroyd,[87] who had
been brought by Rowse.[88] He has now started on his life of Augustus
John, which he is planning in 2 volumes, one the biography and the other
a selection of drawings and paintings with a commentary. He is younger
than I had imagined. Philip Larkin came up and said nice things about
the *1851* film and apologized again, poor man, for not having realized
that his fellow guest had been Simon Nowell-Smith. At dessert I sat
next to Charles Monteith. He said they had taken a man from George
Rainbird as their successor to David, one Phillips, a plain production
man, not a designer. He also assured me that Valerie Eliot had now completed her Introduction. He felt she had had great difficulty in writing

---

87 Sir Michael Holroyd first established his reputation as an outstanding biographer with *Lytton
Strachey* in 1967-68, and consolidated it with biographies of Augustus John and Bernard Shaw.
He is married to the author Margaret Drabble.
88 AL Rowse (1903-1997), a fellow of All Souls College, Oxford, and later a lecturer at Merton
College, was a prolific author, publishing over 100 books. He is best known for his work on
Elizabethan England.

about Vivienne Eliot,[89] which isn't surprising. Agreeable evening with no power cuts and no fog. Colin had arrived back from Cambridge at lunchtime and so the house is filling up.

On Sunday we recorded the voices for *Magic Man*, including Karin's and Jane's, and in the evening I began laying the track, interrupted by Garbo as *Anna Karenina* (rather good, and magnificent sets), and the second part of the documentary on Eisenstein. Earlier we had sung (even I tried) Ben's skilful 'Winter Canon', which he has also printed as his Christmas card. Our own, 'Mary's Song' from *The Jesse Tree*, followed his on the press – a good weekend's work altogether.

❧

14 December, Monday

RR back this morning, earlier than the post, which was late. Lord Rennell wrote asking me whether I would be willing to print the Transactions and Proceedings of a club in Herefordshire; I discovered I'd completely forgotten about the annual party for the managers and had to rush invitations out for tomorrow week; at the Sec's mtg I pointed out that Morison's Lyell Lecture proofs had been completed a full fortnight before the due date. And in the afternoon I had a long discussion with the managers on discipline, particularly the slackness in leaving departments early and crowding around the front entrance. Inconclusive but helpful.

At 4.30 had four apprentices in with their fathers for indenture signing. Two of them had fathers already in the business. Quite bright lads and doing well so far. I noticed that the first to sign, a compositor apprentice, wrote his signature slowly and with difficulty, but I am assured that he is just as good as the others. I trust so.

---

89 Vivienne Eliot (1888-1947) was TS Eliot's first wife, whom he married in 1915. She had multiple health problems, and Eliot separated from her in 1933. Later she was committed to an asylum, where she eventually died. Valerie Eliot (his second wife, whom he married in 1957) was granted copyright on Vivienne's diaries after TSE's death in 1965.

☙

15 December, Tuesday

Confusion! Disaster! Rushings to and fro! That fiend in sub-human form, Colin Thomas Ridler, had taken the plug from my alarm clock. The result was that I looked at my watch, thinking I was very early, and found that it was 7.45, and I had to catch the 8.15 for Paddington to meet Dudley Moss for a visit to the Whitefriars Press at 10 by Charing Cross Station bookstall. With A's gallant help in telephoning, I made it, and Taylor and I had an interesting day at Tonbridge. Our main purpose was to study their production control system, which Dudley told me had been installed by PA some years ago. It looked fairly effective but their problem is simpler than ours. They have only about 60 books going through at any one time compared to our 300, and they use a larger staff than we do to control it. I am not impressed by Albert Lord, Dudley's works director, and never have been; but they are turning out good-quality work and appear to be prosperous. Dudley himself is a charming man and insisted on buying return tickets from Charing Cross. We caught the 5.15 from Paddington so that I was back in time to finish the soundtrack of the *Magic Man*. General verdict – quite a success.

☙

16 December, Wednesday

JH in to see me early about announcements for tightening up workroom discipline. I redrafted one of them, addressed to the managers, and sent it on for distribution. Received at last the first batch of material for the Stirling *NEB*, copy and illustrations. We can do with it because pressure of new work is still slack and keyboard operators have been complaining of lack of overtime. Halsey brought back an inquiry from Cape's for a litho reprint which was also welcome. Later in the morning I 'inspected' the Composing Rooms. They had been tidied up quite nicely but the truth is that they never are all that untidy. In the afternoon I did the same with the Litho and Bindery. They too were looking quite smart.

Gave sherry to Miss Rosson of Legal & General; she came to discuss various pension scheme proposals and JH led her away to lunch next door.

The Royal Society of Edinburgh wrote to ask whether I would be willing to estimate for their journal and transactions. The answer I fear must be 'no'. They are now printed in an undistinguished style by Neill and Sons. I'm surprised that the RS should want to come south.

Saw Bell, the junior JJ award winner, and said pleasant things to him in spite of his long hair. He runs a discotheque as a hobby, poor chap.

RR brought Slight in to present his first report on binding procedures. Nothing startling but his recommendations will require some important policy decisions from the publishing departments. Also discussed with RR the outstanding policy questions on co-operation with Neasden on computer-assisted typesetting.

Wrote warmly to Dudley Moss, thanking him for his hospitality and suggesting a return visit in January.

❦

17 December, Thursday

A & C to London, where Ben is singing in *The Messiah* tomorrow night, so lunched at the Club. The post was late again, and meagre when it did turn up. Inspected the Letterpress Machine Rooms, which were about as smart as they could be when the machine removal men were busy dismantling three old presses. Had Frost in to go through the consolidated accounts in preparation for the special FC meeting with the auditors. This meeting, held in the conference room at 2.30, was well attended by Delegates. Chorley and a colleague represented the new auditors, the redoubtable (in City terms) Cooper Bros. They did not knock their predecessors too hard though Chorley said that the arrangement of our present accounts was difficult to understand. He passed around a set of papers showing a new plan: this is certainly simpler and clearer than the old, and was adopted without dissent. Coopers being what they are, Chorley was anxious to bring our presentation of accounts more into line with The Companies Act. He seems a sound man, far less smooth than his predecessor, which is something, although his exposition is rather hesitant and not always lucid. Several of us, including the chairman, had to confess ignorance at various times because of this. The V-C was helpful in relating the discussions to the needs of Congregation. He is very much a political animal.

To a special Playhouse meeting at 5.15.

A special dinner at St John's, organized by CHR to say farewell to the three Delegates who now go off the Delegacy under the new Waldock scheme. The V-C presided, and those present included Helen Gardner and Prof Paton, who sat next to me, with Hart on the other side. Bowra[90] gave a brilliant and very funny farewell speech, saying how skilfully and tactfully the 'execution' had been carried out. None of this pleased the V-C at all. He looked very cross and made no comment later. The second to speak, Blackman, was brief; he said a few sensible and unmemorable things. Kenneth Wheare (*see footnote 130*) was the third, and gave his usual teasing performance. Bowra seemed to be speaking from the heart when for one serious moment he referred to the uniqueness of the Press and the excellence of its printing. He also used the word 'correctness', which, alas, I felt was not now entirely true.

I had an interesting talk with Hart. He had been a contemporary of Isaiah Berlin who, he said, had been 'born old' and was exactly the same in learning and eloquence as he is now. He hated writing and H feared that he would now never write the book he was uniquely fitted to do: a history of the antecedents of the Bolshevik Revolution.[91] At his Sheldonian lecture on Turgenev on 29 Nov he had an audience of over 2000, and spoke for most of the time without notes. Hart said that his talk, in a much extended and revised form, would be coming to us for publication. Later in the evening Helen Gardner told me that Valerie Eliot had been to consult her. She felt it was a pity she hadn't done so earlier because Helen would have made her eliminate many

90 Sir Maurice Bowra (1898-1971), Classical scholar, literary critic and wit, was Warden of Wadham College, Oxford 1938-70, and Vice-Chancellor of the University 1951-54.
91 Sir Isaiah Berlin (1909-1997), Chichele Professor of Social and Political Theory at Oxford 1957-67, founding President of Wolfson College, Oxford, and President o the British Academy 1974-78, was one of the 20th century's greatest historians of ideas. As a child he had witnessed the Bolshevik Revolution in Russia.

of the minute trivia she had been fussing over. She also said that she herself was going to edit the *Four Quartets* 'in conjunction' with Valerie – though she would have only her own name on the title page! She has two anthologies with Faber and said how much she noticed the difference between their printers and me. Brandy is potent stuff.

At the very end of the evening I managed to get some talk with Davin. He really is thinking of persuading Colin and FC to let him retire at 62. (He is a month older than me.) He wants to write more and feels that the Delegates won't really want to have him bridging the gap for a short period when Colin retires. He may be right, but I was rather surprised at his vehemence in saying that he wasn't really a 'Press man', with the Press as his life. I rather feel he has thought himself into this state of mind as more and more younger men, such as John Nicoll, have come in. He feels constantly guilty, he says, at his inadequacies. Well, perhaps, but I am sure, crafty and even lazy tho' he may be, he is still a remarkably shrewd judge of many situations.

I got home in time to see a few minutes of *The Boyars Plot*. Visually splendid but just as ponderous and pageant-like as *Ivan*. I don't think I could have stayed the whole course. Afterwards I went down to the station to meet Anne and Jane off the late train. They had been in Stepney to hear Ben singing in *Messiah*. He had done well, and 'came on looking very business-like', A said.

❦

18 December, Friday

Went to the surgery at 9 as my neck shows no sign of getting better. A long wait for Kirkham as other patients disappeared from the waiting room at high speed on their way to his partners. He was suffering from the same complaint, and had been for the past 6 weeks. He gave me a form for an appointment at the Orthopaedic for an X-ray, but didn't hold out much hope of a quick cure.

A contingent from PA came in at noon to discuss Slight's work. Not much substance to discuss, in fact. Earlier JH reported redundancies at Harrisons' High Wycombe plant and asked me whether he should try for letterpress machine minders. I suggested that we would have to check very carefully with Gordon Taylor as to his estimate of the future load in the department in view of the reduction we had to expect in publishers' orders.

To the Randolph after lunch to settle the menu and other details for next Tuesday's managers' dinner. Then drafted a letter to Sec and Publisher on the new web-offset press I want to order. Everything depends on the *NEB* size being acceptable for the new editions of *OD* and Hornby's *Advanced Learner's Dictionary*.

The usual bottles of Xmas cheer arrived from Rod Henderson. Post still running very late.

❦

19-20 December

Colin back from London for a late lunch. Me to see *The War Lord* at the Moulin Rouge, not the best use of a fine afternoon. A on tower duty at St Mary's, and preparing for the party of Ben and his friends expected from London at tea-time. At the Ex-Service Association dinner in the evening, this year in the Officers' Training Corps HQ for the first time. Very cosy and intimate, with a brisk performance by the little group from the Operatic Society. The CO of the Corps, Col Richards, was our guest.

I have forgotten to record the fine mess I (I think) made of our plan to attend the Xmas Dinner in Teddy Hall on Friday evening. We had carefully dolled ourselves up in full kit for the occasion, arrived in good time, crossed the quad, entered the ground floor of the common toom, looked at the seating plan posted at the foot of the stairs – and couldn't find our names! Consternation! Panic! Chagrin! What to do? Risk embarrassment by going up, or slink off? We slunk off, and after a brief and somewhat tart discussion about having an egg at home, discretion and chivalry found us eating cannelloni at the Saraceno. We felt fine in our togs, eying less well-dressed customers with disdain.

Fortunately we hadn't seen another don or reveller at the Hall, either going in or coming out.

Carols on Sat evening with Peter, Danny, Elaine, Judith (*all Ben's friends*), the Tites (he is a don at Magdalen and they are friends of Elaine's) – I managed to join them after my Association Dinner. Mulled claret afterwards – great fun.

Everyone busy with his or her ploys on Sunday. The Länge parents and chicks came up for tea. We showed *Spain* and *The Magic Man's Revenge* before the party broke up.

❦

21 December, Monday

Post again very late. Not much of substance when it did come. Ashby came in as usual at 9.40. We went through the list of jobs his dept hopes to deal with during the shut week after Christmas. After the 10 o'clock meeting JH showed me the draft of a notice that Fulton wanted put up in the departments. This was to make a special appeal for help to two of our people who have been away for some time, and for the widow of Mick Foster. I was very doubtful about the last, not through lack of sympathy but because once you begin to include dependants it can mean such an additional strain on the resources of any charitable fund. JH decided to take the draft away for second thoughts.

At the CP 11.30 meeting we talked mainly of binding methods for the *OED* microform edition. The problem is the reading glass to go with the set. No one in the CP office has got down to serious thought about it, and until this is settled we cannot know whether the two volumes should be boxed or put into a slip-case. It must be decided fairly quickly because the binding work is very heavy and completed sets are wanted in June. After this meeting GBT stayed behind and I went through his progress records of CP new books. There are about 150 of these and they seem to be going pretty well according to plan. When we had finished I opened the door and there was Col on the threshold, clutching a large straw mat which he wanted me to take home in the car. He got home by bike just as soon as I did. After lunch I took Ben's Judith to the train and then held my usual managers' meeting. No great crisis to report, but as the CP and London are closing on Thursday we shall have a rush to get everything we should away on Wednesday night.

At 5 I went upstairs for a talk with CHR, mainly on Slight's first report. He is in favour but the cash implications are a worry. All the same, I hope he and Bruno will go ahead with the scheme because it will simplify our warehousing problems very much.

As Ashby cannot attend the managers' dinner tomorrow night I invited Boswell to take his place. He should have been asked before but I have always been anxious about making the affair too big.

Dudley Moss had sent me the three enormous 'Spotlight' volumes (*listing actors and actresses*). Awful to throw them away but I don't want to keep them indefinitely. Perhaps Colin will have them in the cellar for pressing his enlargements. The family out singing in the evening. I packed up various presents and read until they returned.

❦

22 December, Tuesday

Not much in the post this morning, but two more manuscripts down from the CP. We now have quite a build-up, but the Keyboard Room is still very much hand-to-mouth and Brooker has a struggle in trying to keep them going. I wrote to Lord Rennell, telling him that I was prepared to take in the Transactions of his Herefordshire club, but not expressing myself as too willing so that he realizes it is a favour.

After this I went round the departments, looked at the final sheet of the *Rossetti* plates now coming off the machine, and the 64pp sections of *COD* coming off the old Timson rotary; talked with Aubrey Beesley on Fire Brigade matters, exchanged pleasantries with Miss Morris in the Exam Despatch Room, and with Mrs Fulton, who kindly inquired about my neck and told me that she has to go into hospital again in January with a recurrence of her back trouble; and then got back to my desk for more paperwork.

After lunch at the Club next door – where we were treated to champagne: a present from the architects – RR and I had a talk with Slight of PA about E J Walker, our graduate computer-expert. He feels frustrated and now tends to be 'disloyal', or disgruntled, in consequence. We don't keep him under sufficient pressure, but I am hopeful that his new chore at Neasden may bring some improvement in his outlook. We went on to talk about our production control problems. Slight thinks, as we do, that liaison between the managers is not good enough, and pressure on them to keep dates not strict enough. One of the difficulties here lies with Gordon Taylor, who doesn't know how to get what he wants by tact and has no authority over the managers. Slight thinks we can only overcome the problem by making RR more closely involved with production control. If this is so, then he must bring in a younger man under RR to spread his considerable load. Slight is a good man, and should be at the price, and I think his advice is soundly based.

On my way to the managers' dinner at the Randolph I looked in on Cyril Piper. He was looking much better, lying snugly in bed with his devoted wife knitting some enormous piece alongside him; but of course he is still very thin and drawn.

The dinner, held in the Osbert Lancaster room, was a great success. The only thing to disturb the harmony was that O'Dogherty, who had unusually taken a cigar, was violently sick all over himself and had to be led out in confusion. The meal was voted excellent, which it was, and our shop-talk afterwards, mainly about paper and paper-buying, was quite useful. Chalmers drove me home as A had the car to take the boys over to Philippa at Bladon.

❦

23 December, Wednesday

A talk this morning with JH on three men past retiring age who want to stay on. Pat Cox's father is one of them, and he is still doing well. The most difficult is old Harvey, in the Caster Room. He is suffering from hardening of the arteries, and we are all worried that in his present state he will burn himself on the molten metal. But his doctor says that if he leaves, that will be the end of him, and he may well be right. We decided that J should have another talk with Harvey and his supervisor, and report back.

A letter from Kenyon to say that Bernard Nicholls has had a nasty accident while hunting, and was in hospital with several broken bones. I have written to him.

A meeting of Help the Aged gen purposes cttee at 2.15 to discuss, mainly, the relationship of the Association to the main charity. The intriguing figure in all this is Faulkner, obviously an autocrat with high motives, one of the more difficult types to cope with.

On my way back I bought a record case for Ben and a record token for Caroline (*Bland, VR's goddaughter*). Took Ben to the station in the evening: he is spending Xmas Day with Donald Reeves and Peter, but coming home again on Saturday.

☙

24 December, Christmas Eve

I managed to begin my tour of the Press quite early, and had greeted a good number of supervisors and FOC's by 9.45. At 10.15 I slipped off to take a cake up to poor Simmons. Visiting him isn't easy, because he cannot speak but simply has to sit about looking at TV or being attended to by his splendid wife. All one can do is to smile and nod and say a few heartening things, and there are limits to what one can do in that way. But I chatted with his wife for a few minutes and came away in the hope that I may have cheered him up a little. Then I completed my tour, quite pleased that most people – even in the Bindery – were getting on with their work. Fortescue held me with a long but interesting discourse on his neck and shoulder troubles, so similar to mine; and Fulton gave me the latest details of the pantomime he now has in rehearsal for the children's party on 9 Jan.

Towards the end of the afternoon I saw four people who were retiring. The first, R T Humphrey, a compositor, had been away since

January with thrombosis. He is a cheerful, garrulous, man, and I had the greatest difficulty in bringing our, or rather his, conversation to an end so that I could receive the next in the queue. This was Mrs Mason who has been heading the girl section of the Work Study Department. She was rather overcome with emotion at leaving, and I had to steer the conversation firmly into unsentimental channels. She is an excellent person and I am sorry to lose her. She is sorry to be going but now feels she must go to help her ageing brother in W'hampton.

Then came Greenman, another comp, and very much a cut above the average, a fine craftsman and extremely conscientious. He told me that he had been 'mad about printing' ever since he had been given a John Bull printing outfit when he was seven. He had been apprenticed in Caerphilly, then went to the Electric Press in Cardiff, which closed down. Times were bad in S Wales and he managed to get a job with Clowes at Beccles. He spoke more warmly of Beccles than anyone else I have heard talking of it: the kindness of the locals seems to have made a lasting impression on him.

Lastly came dear Remington, now 85. A very sad case, because he is a lovely man. He had retired once, in 1956, and then asked to return on a part-time basis in 1957. The trouble was that his work had deteriorated rapidly in the past eighteen months, and this was proving a worry to Boyce, who had to read over most of his work again. I don't know what he can or will do with himself. He should go into an old person's flat where someone could keep an eye on him and provide some company, but he is not keen on anything like that just now.

Handed over my present to Pat Cox (liqueur chocs) and Sid Church (Milk Tray); then found Frost suffering from incipient flu and pushed him off home.

❦

25 December, Christmas Day

It started to snow last night, while we (including Kate but not Tim, who was held in London) were enjoying a delightful party at the Länges, with food and decorations beautifully prepared by Jane and Rolf. The snow – a sprinkling – was still there when A and I set off for the 8 o'clock service. Afterwards the Länges arrived and present-opening began in earnest. Juliette much taken with her carpet sweeper, and swept all and everything before it; and Karin with a wondrous drawing toy called a 'Spirograph'. Tim arrived in time for lunch, with a welcome bottle of champagne. After lunch the children did cutting-out while I filmed them. Then I took A & Col to Helen Wright's for a walk with Peter and Julia Reynell and family, and went on myself to visit one of my readers, Jakeman, who is in the Warneford suffering from depression.

After tea, carols, supper, Morecambe and Wise, reading and bed.

26 December, Boxing Day

Kate & Tim went off to Bath after lunch. In the evening watched with Colin part of *Bad Day at Black Rock*,[92] still very gripping in spite of its age.

27 December, Sunday

Jan, Diana, Ken,[93] and their two children came over from Tidworth for a buffet lunch with ourselves and the Länges. The roads were not good because of the snow and ice but they arrived on time. In the afternoon we showed the children *The Magic Man's Revenge*, and they left soon after 4 to get some of the travelling done in daylight.

28 December, Monday

A party at Margaret Powell's in the evening, with agreeable recorder & harpsichord music. The weather had thawed, unexpectedly.

---

92 An 8mm film made by VR in 1959 called *Big Day at Bad Rock*, featuring Ben's French exchange Aymar as a villain, was a play on the 1955 Hollywood movie title *Bad Day at Black Rock*.
93 Jan Bradby was AR's sister-in-law, widow of her elder brother Matt Bradby (1899-1963). Their daughter Diana married the British Army officer Ken Marchant.

❦

29 December, Tuesday

Editing the Greek film in the morning. Ben went off to Manchester. Finance meeting in the afternoon, with long discussion on production budgets for the publishing departments. Bruno announced that the Publishers Association had just made a warehouse agreement with SOGAT which would give the men another 14%. The reason, he said, was that publishers were not prepared to stand up to a strike. I couldn't refrain from pointing out that for years, publishers had been complaining of printers for not doing just that.

Looked at Houdini film in the evening. Read *Anna Karenina* and did a little more work on the Greek film. Colder again, and sleeting.

❦

30 December, Wednesday

Still cold. Spent day indoors, still working on Greek film.

❦

31 December, Thursday

A fetched the children and we took them to Disney's *Cinderella* at the Moulin Rouge. A success, in spite of some boring vulgarities. Showed them some home-made films later in the evening. Karin took a long time to get off to sleep and was busily trotting up and down stairs for part of the time.

January 1971

❦

1 January, Friday

Took the children home soon after 12 and went on to collect Arnold Prosser for lunch. He insisted on presenting us with one of his 'treasures', a Balinese brass bell originally given to him by a professor of ethnology at Leyden. Quite a handsome piece in its way. He resurrected his stock account of the way he had been cheated out of his rightful job at the Press – by that creeper Wheeler egging on that super-creeper Frederick Hall – while he was away in the army. Still, he enjoys life and talking, and a cigar, and I took him home in a happy frame of mind.

Earlier in the morning Madeline Melville had rung to congratulate me on my CBE in the Honours List which she had just seen in *The Times*. Phone calls and nice letters – a particularly nice one from JH – continued to come in during the day.

2 January, Saturday

Col & I took Anne to the station for her London appointments, first with Enrica[94] at her club, and then with the BBC at London Wall, where she was to be filmed being interviewed by Tom Fleming about *The Jesse Tree* and the ideas that lie behind it. I then went to the Press, did the post, looked around to see what the engineers and maintenance staff had been up to, received congratulations from Sawyer in the Lodge, and returned to the town to meet Col again. Our purpose was to look at tape recorders for him. We did, at Curry's and Bakers, but came away to ponder on what we had seen.

I had lunch alone and got through most of my thank you letters afterwards. C came back for tea and we occupied ourselves pleasantly until I had to go to the station to pick up the returning A. All had gone well except the car that should have brought her back. A broken hose and a half-hearted drive (it was a cold and foggy night) persuaded her to take the train. *It* broke down too, but she was less than half an hour late in reaching Oxford.

3 January, Sunday

Freezing fog and icy roads all day. Did not venture out. At 11am

---

94 Enrica Garnier, an old friend of AR's through a connection originally with Norman Nicholson, the Lake District poet published by Faber. She was Kate Wilson's godmother.

watched A's programme on TV. She looked charming, and C & I felt even more proud of her, if that were possible. The sweet noise-makers arrived in force for lunch. In the evening and the silence we watched the Omnibus programme on TS Eliot; it was made by the inclusion of many unpublished early and late photographs, supplied by Valerie, who made a too-brief contribution, we thought.

And so ended, for me, a most blissful Christmas holiday. Enrica and Ben are due to arrive tomorrow.

❦

4 January, Monday

Back to work in more cold and fog – the coldest day for 8 years says the *Oxford Mail*, and it felt like it. Spent quite a time answering letters of congratulations. Touched to get one from Francis Meynell. Quiet meeting with CP, tho' their cutting back on the next printing of *COD* is disturbing: it will leave a nasty gap in the Letterpress Machine Room and in the Bindery. But four new books are coming down this week which is some consolation. Nice letter from Clauson on the completion of his Turkic Dictionary proofs: 'incomparable work' etc etc.

Managers' meeting as usual in the afternoon. Rather quiet all round, which is not unusual for this time of the year, and few absentees.

Enrica came and went, and Ben arrived at 9.40pm, full of his time in Manchester.

❦

5 January, Tuesday

A good part of the morning taken up discussing with JH & RR our main projects and likely capital expenditure for the year. The publishers have now confirmed that the medium-size dictionaries such as *COD* will go up to the larger page size already suggested by the production managers. This means that we must now order the new web offset press, which is likely to cost even £100,000 by the time we take delivery in about two years.

Continued answering CBE letters – I've now had exactly one hundred, including two telegrams. John Garne, Henderson, and Richard Gray also rang up during the day.

Glad to see Mrs Salmon back again. She has a heavy cold but otherwise looks very much better. Frost is still away but there are fortunately no urgent problems in his department just now.

To Wolvercote Church in the evening to take part, with A, Jane & Col in one of dear Peter Shingleton's fiendish 'presentations'. He will pack so much into his programme: Eliz Jennings[95] was brought in as a special guest and would have gone on reading in a thin monotonous voice for ever if PS had not, at last, muttered something to her about 'the last poem'. We did an extract from *The Jesse Tree* under A's guidance. It sounded effective and Jane did the part of Mary exceptionally well. But the church was cold and draughty. John Wain[96] read well also, and kept down to a reasonable length. Back to Jane's for a warm-up afterwards.

6 January, Wednesday

To see Mr Grieve, in Welbeck Street, about my neck. Ben travelled up with me and we spent a pleasant hour looking at possible tape recorders for Colin and having lunch together afterwards. I was only on G's couch for 20 mins but he imparted his quiet confidence to me, and I shall follow his instructions to take the special pills he is having made up. My neck muscles were definitely less painful after he had squeezed, pulled and pushed them and other parts of my neck and shoulders. I caught the 4.15 back to Oxford. Now very much warmer, with rain.

7 January, Thursday

More and more CBE letters, which I am answering as they come in – I

---

95 Elizabeth Jennings (1926-2001), a prolific and popular Catholic lyric poet, suffered from bouts of mental illness throughout her life.
96 John Wain (1925-1994), a novelist as well as prolific poet and critic, was Professor of Poetry at Oxford 1973-78.

must have written about 120 letters by now. Found on glancing through *Printing World* that Miss Cox had allowed me to drop an awful clanger. There at the head of their honours list for the industry was C H Baylis, CB. He had written to congratulate me earlier in the week, and I had replied without mentioning his own award, which neither I nor Pat Cox had seen in the lists. I managed to write a suitably apologetic letter, after abandoning the idea of phoning him.

Talks with RR and Gardner on binding prices for the Hornby dictionary. Went round the Works, which looked and felt busy, and for the moment is. But work in the Keyboard Room is still low, although the exam papers are beginning to come in thick and fast.

Also discussed with RR Slight's work on production control, and the possibility of changing the agenda of my Monday afternoon meeting with the managers. I'm not against a change but I want to be sure that I don't cut myself off from the day-to-day happenings too much. R's brother Nicholas, now at Longman's, called in while we were together. We had an interesting talk: he is getting quite a lot of straightforward work done in Tenerife by German technicians supervising Spaniards, and he says the work is well done. Longman's organize their publishing into subject divisions, each with its own director, editors, designer, and production manager, and the groups are given almost complete freedom to select and produce books in their own way. In England they put a lot of the simplest home market books with Camelot, who will produce to a schedule of 10 weeks for an average book of 176 pages. Clowes also give them good service. I thought N had matured very much since I had last seen him some years ago.

Nicky Vernède at home in the evening – excellent supper of turkey, sweet, and wine. Showed the *Dragon's Life* film,[97] and later the first Greek one. Col & N go back to Cambridge on Saturday.

---

97 VR's film of Colin's life at the Dragon School in 1959.

❦

8 January, Friday

Banging on the table about the lateness of some *Periodical* proofs. Too casual an attitude developing towards broken promises which I must put right.

An interesting and unexpected telephone enquiry, in from the Almalgamated Society of Woodworkers. Their general secretary wants me to quote for the annual printing of their rule book – 300,000 copies, 176 pages. Our job now is to persuade him to keep to its present page size, which just fits our web-offset press. Seduced by all the talk of 'international paper sizes' he wants to make it larger and to an international size. Nonsense really and quite unnecessary. I'm hoping that money will talk because I should be able to quote him an attractive price if we print on the web. We can do with such work for that machine, particularly as there is already a slow-down in publisher's work. Halsey is pursuing him and it urgently.

Quiet evening listening to Ben's present to us, the Fritz Busch *Figaro*.

❦

9–10 January

A took Colin back to Cambridge in the morning, and was back in time to attend the children's party in the Institute.[98] This year the pantomime put on by Fulton and his merry men was 'Toy Town'. It seemed interminable, and indeed went on for nearly 2 hours. Slightly redeemed, as usual, by the ingenuity of the Reeves brothers, who produced some good sets and devices, such as Stephenson's 'Rocket', which rolled across the stage very convincingly, and a moon rocket with the letters TT 1971 VR CBE on its black flank. Far too much talk, which couldn't be heard anyway because the children were making such a racket. A gave the presents to the boys and I to the girls. This cut down the time a

---

98 The Clarendon Institute in Walton Street was built by the OUP Printer Horace Hart as a place of recreation for his employees. Today it houses the Oxford Centre for Hebrew and Jewish Studies.

little, but the party didn't end until nearly 8.45 – and it had started at 4 o'clock. A was presented with the most lavish bouquet, absurd really, but they obviously like doing it.

Sunday was a wonderfully mild day, balmy air and soft sunshine. As the Länge's didn't come up we went walking in the Botanic Gardens, and sat afterwards, like Darby and Joan, on a seat under Merton's walls, looking out over the Meadow and the slow promenaders along the Broad Walk.

❦

11 January, Monday

At CP meeting spent most of the time examining various samples of reading glasses and discussing the most economical way of including one in the slipcase of the two-volume *OED* microform edition. Came to some sort of preliminary decision and CP now going to get a quotation for the glass. CHR muttered something afterwards about pressure from the Far Eastern offices to print over there some of the books, such as Legouis's *History of English Literature*, that had previously been done here. I don't like it, but I can't stop it, so that's that.

Managers' meeting after lunch. Very busy all round. I told Harris that after seeing the amount of new copy coming in, I thought his Keyboard Room would soon be as congested as ever. He agreed. The Letterpress Room is also under pressure, but Mansfield, characteristically, was still moaning of how little work lay ahead, etc etc. Incurable!

To Jordan Hill later in the afternoon, to see the start of the air-balloon warehouse erection. But the men – from Scotland – were only bolting up the metal entrance doors, and nothing of the plastic balloon, which is to be kept up solely by the pumping in of warm air, was to be seen. The foundation area, at the back of the playing field alongside the golf course, looks vast.

Nice day again, but cold.

🍷

12 January, Tuesday

To Bristol for Alliance meeting with JH. Fog and drizzle made a rather dismal journey in both directions. Had lunch with Field and Land, who insisted on marking my CBE with a bottle of wine.

St John Ambulance Division AGM at the Institute in the evening. A good meeting, well attended. Five new members, three of them ladies, the first we have had.

🍷

13 January, Wednesday

Discussion with Slight and RR on Bindery progress control. A good deal now turns on the acceptance by the publishers of the 'sewing-out below 2000' scheme. CHR won't commit himself because of the extra working capital required and we have to try to convince him, not an easy job. Agreed that O'Dogherty should be moved to Jordan Hill, but I want a meeting with the Neasden management before I tell him. He should be pleased because he lives on the estate.

Cornell University sent over a specimen batch of xerox ms concerning Marcello Malpighi. It will eventually make 5 vols of about 2800 pages in all, similar in scale to the earlier project we did for them 5 years ago. The copy won't be ready until early 1972 but what they want now is an approximate idea of our composition charges. Very welcome.

At Kettners in the evening for a dinner to meet the Design Exhibit judges, Betty Dougherty of the Council of Industrial Design, Jock Kinneir,[99] Walter Partridge, Tony Williams, and me as chairman. LEK, Eric Dixon, John Shepherd and two other COID members also present, as well as William Maxwell, Director of the Machine Manufacturers' Association, the sponsors. Straightforward discussion, no great problems, finished by 9.15. Early night at Whitehall Court reading *Anna K.*

---

99 Jock Kinneir (1917-1994) was a typographer and graphic designer who, with his colleague Margaret Calvert, designed many of the road signs in post-war Britain, especially for the motorway network.

❦

14 January, Thursday

To the BFMP at 10 o'clock to begin selection of design exhibits. Continued until 4.15 with break for a working lunch in the Alliance Council room. A wearying job and Jock Kinneir wanted to reject practically everything. He got a few sparks off poor Walter Partridge, otherwise temperaments were kept reasonably under control. I had to push occasionally for a decision but not often. We ended with 24 items out of 250 entered, covering a fair section of printed products.

To Management Club meeting at Teddy Hall in the evening. Interesting and lucid talk by Charles Villiers, chairman of the doomed Industrial Redevelopment Corporation. Joe Edwards there, full of his meetings with Onassis (*Greek shipping magnate*) and Jackie Kennedy. He thinks O is certain to get Harland & Wolff.

❦

15 January, Friday

Geoffrey Keynes[100] looked in at noon, to talk over a few minor points concerning the Godine book. He told me that he sees the Meynells regularly – they meet for lunch once a month – and that he was dismayed to see how rapidly FM was ageing. As GK is nearly 85 and FM is nearer 75, he said this with a certain sprightly cheerfulness, and he *is* remarkably spry for his age. He spoke highly of the Roxburghe Lord Leicester volume that he had just received. We have had several very complimentary letters about it.

Help the Aged meeting at 3.15. Didn't get away until 6. Help the ageing, I felt as I staggered out... went to bed at 10.15 and had a marvellous sleep.

❦

16-17 January

A wet and dank week-end, just the sort of weather to usher in the postal

---

100 Sir Geoffrey Keynes (1887-1982), pioneering surgeon, was a famed bibliographer and authority on the artist William Blake. He was the younger brother of the economist John Maynard Keynes.

strike which is due to start on Wednesday. Stayed indoors on Saturday; to Cathedral to hear Henry Chadwick[101] preach (well) on Sunday morning. Rolf & the children to lunch & tea (Jane in London, helping K & T to wallpaper). Hard at it reading *Anna K*, that wonderful book.

Wrote to Colin, who, having had his hair cut unusually short, is now a marked man at King's, to bolster his morale.

18 January, Monday

Further talk with CP on sewing-out, and rate of overs. I think we are now getting somewhere, and it looks as though Slight's proposals will go through, much to our relief.

Marsh of PA came to see me during the afternoon. He brought with him his survey report on the relationship of the businesses. Nothing out of the way in it, the business-end being that they want 5 or 6 months to do the job at a cost of about £11,000. It *may* be worth it, but I'm rather doubtful, not entirely.

19 January, Tuesday

To Federation Council and lunch. Presented legislation report – no questions and only one brief comment. The lunch afterwards is the one to which we traditionally invite trade guests. I was photographed with Baylis of the Stationery Office (CB) and Charles Pickering (OBE), and I was able to make my apologies once again to Baylis for having been unaware of his honour when I had written to thank him for mine.

An old acquaintance from Robinson days at my table was A R Taylor. I couldn't have put a name to him when we met, altho' I remembered his face well. He told me that they had closed down my old workplace, their Bedminster factory, some two years ago, and were doing practically no direct retail trade.

---

101 Sir Henry Chadwick (1920-2008), Dean of Christ Church, Oxford 1969-79, and subsequently Master of Peterhouse, Cambridge 1987-93, held chairs of divinity in both universities during his academic career. He was an authority on the early history of the Christian Church.

Our chief guest was Sir Max Brown of the Dept of Trade & Industry. None of us seem to have heard of him but he spoke well and was even polite enough to mention my CBE in somewhat generous terms. As we have never met I thought his air of sincerity and feeling skilfully done.

On getting back I heard that Bratt has now phoned confirmation of the revised Stirling *NEB* page. We can now go ahead and this big job will keep the filmsetters going for some months.

Wrote to Val Curtis, who is convalescing from trouble with his water-works, poor chap. A & I went to see Godard's version of Moravia's *Ghost at Noon* called *Contempt* over here. It held us, but seems a bit pretentious.

❦

20 January, Wednesday

Postal strike now on. A few bits and pieces of post arrived, and we have our own arrangement with Ely House so that their orders arrived as usual. Exam bodies are also making special arrangements, and RR has laid on Securicor for vital stuff. As long as the telephone remains we should be able to manage. If telephones are shut down life will become very difficult indeed.

Most of my day taken up with the return visit of Dudley Moss and Albert Lord. They came mainly to look at our oldest litho perfector which they may like to buy for Whitefriars Press. I'm not all that anxious to sell because it is proving useful as a reserve machine, but I told Dudley that *if* I let it go I should want £5500. This may deter him, but a new, slightly larger and higher speed press would cost him £30,000 today. They seem quite keen – and left saying how impressed they were with our housekeeping, and the place is certainly kept in quite good order by Tibble and his men.

Dined at Teddy Hall. Rather dull, tho' I sat next to Hackney at dinner and I always enjoy arguing with him. The bursar gave me my key to the new guest room: it is well equipped and looks comfortable. I only hope I can make some use of it when I have visitors. He kindly drove me home in his large Citroen afterwards as A had the car to go to Worcester College, where she was speaking and reciting to the Univ. Poetry Society, not a very rewarding bunch to speak to.

❦

21 January, Thursday

Wilkinson of PA, David Slight's supervisor, came in with him and RR at 10 o'clock to discuss their report on production control in the Bindery, and to put forward another report on our general production control procedures. Their plans for the Bindery are sound and I had no particular comment to make on them. The only problems – minor ones – concern people: O'Dogherty and one or two others will leave Walton Street altogether and be based at Jordan Hill. The remains of the warehouse function here will revert to the Bindery manager, and we shall bring a strong man from Jordan Hill to assist him. Their scheme for the main production control would mean the amalgamation of our present production control with the forwarding office. We could probably save several bodies by doing this, but there are snags over the Taylor/ Halsey relationship, and we shall have to think about it more carefully than Slight or Wilkie have had time to do.

Before they came in I had asked Cowley, Taylor's comparatively new (6 months) progress chaser, in to coffee. I questioned him closely about his work. He struck me as shrewd as well as intelligent. He obviously has a difficult job in getting dates and information out of some of the managers, especially Mansfield, who is more disgruntled than ever now he has been told that our next web press will be a litho one. Anyway, I murmured encouragement and said we would talk again in a few months' time.

Turner of PA came in for a brief talk on Marsh's Printer/ Publisher Relationship report. It contains some naiveties but they are hardly worth altering at this stage. The report now goes to FC next Tuesday.

JH rang in mid-afternoon to say that Axford, who earlier in the day had been complaining of chest pains, had been rushed into the Intensive Care Unit at the Radcliffe, presumably after a heart attack when he got home at lunchtime. No further news. I wrote to Mrs A.

I should have recorded earlier that RR has now taken the plunge and bought a house at Wolvercote. I am pleased and rather relieved by this news, not only for his sake but for the business. He has what in the winter months is a tiring 3/4 hr journey each way, and he cannot easily attend evening meetings, altho' he is always very willing to drive back late at night if he really must. Now he will be near to Jordan Hill, and to the schools. They are keeping on Lamb's Cottage, so that they will not be cutting themselves off from a county base altogether.

A out judging a debate at Weston College in the evening. I lay doggo and finished *Anna K*, reluctantly.

❦

22 January, Friday

JH told me first thing that dear old John Barker, compositor, JP, and faithful St John Ambulance officer, had died in his sleep. He was 63 and apart from trouble with his legs last year he was in good health. He was a careful and conscientious comp, and we shall miss him in the Exam Ship, where he had worked for many years.

Blanche Henrey's vast manuscript, 35 folders, appeared on our table this morning. A fine piece of composition for the keyboards. Illustrations, masses of them, still to come.

I went over London's requirements for the new settings of the Revised Church Hymnaries. These originate in Scotland, and because of the nationalist fervour London had quite a fight against Collins and others to hold at least some of the work south of the border. As usual, time has been very much wasted on the editorial and planning side but the authorities still want to publish in May 1972. I'm not at all sure that we can cope with all the settings in that short time, hence my meeting this morning with Taylor and Skelly to assess the amount of work facing us. Most of the long-run printing is to be done in Scotland which doesn't make the job all that attractive at the moment, altho' we will benefit from reprint and other editions later.

Brian Campbell, assistant registrar, came to lunch with RR & me at the Club, to discuss schedules, which are now painfully tight. As usual, BC is a model of realism and we understand each other well.

Help the Aged meeting in my room at 3.15 to discuss our proposed salary structure. To my surprise we finished by 4.40!

❦

23–24 January

Fine day on Sunday. Walked in flooded Port Meadow in the morning in clear sunshine. Not too cold but everything *very* wet. Visited Scala 2 on Sat pm. Bergman's *A Passion*: marvellous and gloomy.

❦

25 January, Monday

Mild, showery morning. Strike still on, no post other than London and CP. Therefore no money in, few invoices out, which could put us in an awkward position if the strike continues much longer.

Large batch of ms in from CP, including Wordsworth's collected prose. This will make three volumes and should keep a few keyboards occupied for some months. But the reprint lists are dwindling, with little sign of anything substantial to come.

Complained at the CP morning meeting that the book jacket for the Surtees *Rossetti* book should have gone to Cotswold for machining by collotype when we were short of litho work. This put me in a thoroughly bad temper for Monday morning, particularly as the excuse was that Cotswold had been to see them, saying that they could do short-run jackets just as cheaply by collotype.

Long managers' meeting in the afternoon because we were going through the departmental committee reports on their talks with the chapels. Not a great deal of substance, though we seem to be having another bout of pilfering, including four wooden chairs from the girls' section of the Bindery. Scratches on halftone blocks, another old problem I thought we had licked, has also come up again.

157

O'Dogherty reports great confusion at Jordan Hill, where the Dexion people have just arrived with the first 16 tons of Dexion to start putting up the new racking for the pallets of bound stock. The floor of the balloon warehouse is giving trouble and has to be planed down, but he has already transferred about 100 pallets of *OED* into it. Talk with Frost on overhauling our charging methods, which are antiquated and expensive.

❦

26 January, Tuesday

In even worse temper this morning when an innocent memo from Geoffrey Hunt, raising a query on a word in *Hart's Rules*, disclosed that London have apparently agreed, without any discussion with me whatsoever, to let the Japanese (of all people) translate it. I also had to send a note of protest to Bruno about the sarcastic memos we are getting from one of his young men. Spent the rest of the morning, apart from fuming, and having Webber, Halsey's assistant, in for coffee, in going through my papers for Finance Cttee.

At FC the chairman wanted to get finished by 4, which pushed things along fairly briskly. The publishers reported on their proposed cuts in production, in order to bring the very serious cash position under control, and I can see that my Machine Rooms at least, and possibly the Bindery, may be even more badly affected than I had thought. When we came to the PA survey on dept relations I was pretty forthright in pointing out that any suggestions for a radical change in our relationship must be treated with caution because PA would only be proposing, leaving us to carry out any new policy. A committee is being set up, not in my view a very strong one, of Jack Thompson, Hart, and Hicks, not one of whom has ever run a factory. The man I *would* like, Bullock, being the V-C is not available. He is much more down to earth and said that he thought a lot of the survey was 'a load of guff'. As a matter of fact the bulk of it isn't, and I shall be very interested in the result of their 5-month-and-£11,000 investigation, but he has the right approach!

Brief talk with Bruno later, mainly about the new Church Hymnaries.

He thinks that production by next May ('72) is ridiculous, which is some comfort.

With Elsa Booth to the Playhouse *Merry Wives*. So, so.

❧

27 January, Wednesday

Full dress meeting with Jimmy Huws-Davies, John Williams, of Neasden; Stiefel, Slight, and Wilkinson of PA; JH, RR and me, to discuss future plans and policies for the warehouse reorganization and changeover. We agreed that responsibility for Jordan Hill should pass to the publishing side on 1 April. This talk went on for the rest of the morning and through lunch at the Club next door.

After lunch I cycled on to a Help the Aged meeting at 2.15. Miraculously this ended by 4 o'clock and I was able to get back to my desk in time to deal with correspondence and estimates.

Dawson and Fryman to dinner for a film evening. Jumbo Dawson had been particularly anxious to see our Greek film and was duly appreciative. Fixed another appointment to see Grieve about my neck for tomorrow at 12.

❧

28 January, Thursday

Memo down from CP saying that Nicolas Barker would be at least another fortnight late with the Morison Lyell Lectures. Publishing! So that programme has gone by the board, as I suspected it would.

To Barclays head office in Lombard Street for a talk with the one-time chairman, A W Tula, about the production of their history. Stanley Gillman, who was secretary for many years, and manager of the Old Bank in Oxford until the early '50s, has written most of it, and he was present. It will not be a long book – some 50,000 words – and not all that many illustrations, tho' some will be in colour. I was glad to hear that they would like to show examples of their cartoon films, and suggested that they should try to get us some of the original drawings so that we can reproduce from them and not from frames of the films. After our meeting Gillman showed me more of the upper floor, including the board room. Never have I seen such areas and masses of thick carpeting, polished tiles, pillars, pictures, old walnut & mahogany, liveried porters, etc. etc. No wonder the banks want to put their charges up. The enormous carpet in the board room was woven in one piece, weighing according to Gillman several tons. The secretary's desk, looking faintly like a broken-down Wurlitzer, had a series of buttons & coloured lights on one side. I thought these must be for transmitting instant and vital decisions to the far corners of the earth, but I was told that they were for operating the window blinds by remote control. As the sun moved on its majestic course and shone into the eye of a certain director its beam would be interrupted by a blind, slowly descending and rising again when its work was done.

Double Crown Club in the evening. Sat next to Lynton Lamb and the managing director of Guinness. Good dinner, rather dull talk on books illustrated with skeletons. Illustrations too monotonous. Left before the discussion to catch my train.

A overnight at Fentiman Road, to help with decorating. I saw Grieve at midday. He thumped and pummelled, and seemed confident that he had done, and was doing me, some good. I wish I could believe him.

No sign of an end to the postal strike.

29 January, Friday

Discussion with JH and RR on the Litho workload over the next few months, and how we might deploy any surplus men. The work prospect in the department is certainly not good, tho' one or two large jobs may come along without previous warning.

Lunched at Teddy Hall, in the new senior common room. Pleasant, and possible to read without interruptions afterwards.

Saw Halsey and Walker to talk over the problems arising out of HMSO's request that we tender for the updating of all the statutes,

6 Clocking-off time, late 1960s: the Press moved into this neoclassical building on Walton Street, designed by Daniel Robertson, in 1830, having outgrown its former premises in the Clarendon Building in Broad Street. The Printer's office lay behind the Corinthian pillars on the right, and his press car, a Rover, is parked on the forecourt.

17 Inner quadrangle: view towards the entrance. Designed to be more like a college than a factory, 'it was curiously unlike either,' according to the Press historian Peter Sutcliffe, having 'more in common with the great railway termini.' The 'outward front of dignified piety advertised its evangelizing mission.'

18 Blowing the House down: Secretary George Richardson, Delegate Lord Blake and OUP New York President Byron Hollinshead try to extinguish the 501 candles on the mock Walton Street building birthday cake at an event held in New York in March 1978 to celebrate the Press Quincentenary. See also plate 26.

19 Checking proofs of the Coronation Bible: an important and valued part of the service the Printing House provided for authors and publishers was the careful correcting of proofs. Yet by the 1970s – when so much printing moved abroad and publishers increasingly undertook proofreading themselves (or neglected it entirely) – such a service was outmoded and uneconomic.

OPPOSITE, ABOVE AND BELOW
20 Ken Scroggs checks a stereo plate: as manager of the Stereotype and Electrotype Department (1951-71) Scroggs oversaw the 'dirty and smelly' foundry where such plates were cast from pages that had been set up in actual type. These plates were far more durable for long letterpress printruns than real hot-metal type. **21** A Monotype keyboard in operation: a brilliant but noisy American invention slowly introduced in Britain from the early 1900s, this mechanical way of keyboarding individual letters – which were punched into the paper roll at left that then drove a typecasting machine – immensely speeded up typesetting. Stanley Morison introduced many new typefaces for the Monotype Corporation from the 1920s onwards.

22 Working the Stones in the 1950s: the stone was a slab of flat metal where pages of type already made up by a compositor were laid out or 'imposed' in a set order to make up 8-, 16-, 32-, and 64-page signatures that could be sent to the machine room ready for printing.

23 Checking a printed sheet in the Letterpress Machine Room: flatbed printing was largely supplanted by rotary letterpress (introduced in 1961) and lithographic web-offset (from 1963) printing, especially for long printruns of dictionaries and bibles.

24 The sewing section of the Bindery in the 1960s: the machines, operated by female members of staff, were driven by overhead shafts and belts. Compositors were not allowed in the Bindery, for fear they might loiter there with the 40 or 50 women in the department.

25 Wrapping *The Oxford Book of Carols*: general view of the Inspection and Dispatch Department with its 60 women packers, who were supervised by the foreman Aubrey Beesley. He was also a leading light in the Press Fire Brigade.

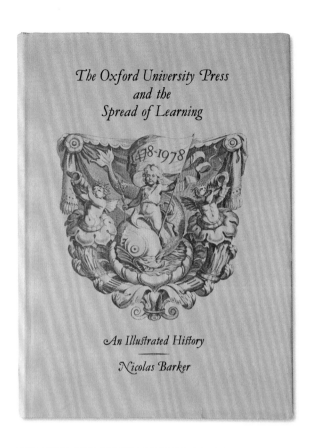

The Oxford University Press
and the
Spread of Learning

1478-1978

An Illustrated History

Nicolas Barker

26 Quincentenary celebration: the jacket of the substantial and learned catalogue produced at the Printing House for the special exhibition held at the Pierpont Morgan Library, New York, in 1978 to mark 500 years of Oxford printing.

BELOW LEFT **27** Typographic mastery: VR's title page for a book he printed at the Bunhill Press in 1938 for the bibliophile Theodore Besterman's Guyon House Press. It shows one of the earliest uses of the typeface Albertus, commissioned by Stanley Morison for the Monotype Corporation and designed by Berthold Wolpe (a pupil of Rudolf Koch). Wolpe drew ornamental devices for the book as well. See also plate 13.

BELOW RIGHT **28** Printer honours poet: VR's title page for the limited edition, printed at OUP, of Anne Ridler's libretto for Elizabeth Maconchy's opera *The Jesse Tree*, first performed at Dorchester Abbey in 1970 (see Diary, 6-10 October). The publisher was Tambimuttu at his Lyrebird Press; he had first published Anne's poetry in 1941.

MAGNA CARTA

AND OTHER CHARTERS OF ENGLISH LIBERTIES

THE GUYON HOUSE PRESS

ANNE RIDLER

The Jesse Tree

WITH DRAWINGS BY
JOHN PIPER

THE LYREBIRD PRESS

29, 30 Pinnacle of the printer's art: *RIGHT* jacket of the great *John Fell* folio, published in 1967, and *BELOW* an example of a two-page opening from inside the book. Entirely set by hand in the so-called Fell types bequeathed to the Press in 1686 by the Dean of Christ Church, Bishop John Fell, it was, wrote Charles Batey in a letter to VR, 'a monumental work…the most handsome and satisfying book to come from the Press within my knowledge, both physically and aesthetically.' And as VR's predecessor as Printer, he knew whereof he spoke. Priced at £25, it was limited to an edition of 1,000 copies.

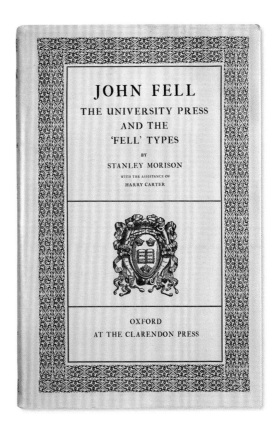

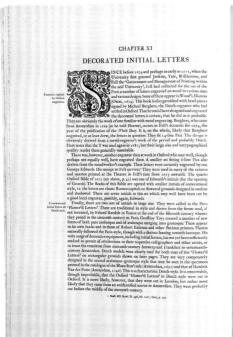

31 Vivian Ridler, engine driver: as part of the festivities at the British Federation of Master Printer's annual conference, held at Torquay during VR's year as President in 1968-69, a steam locomotive was hired and named The Master Printer in handsome gold lettering on a board that hung at the head of the engine. That board later adorned Ridler's small printing house at Stanley Road in Oxford, where he printed limited editions at the revived Perpetua Press during his retirement, using a Cropper platen press.

using computer setting and printing by litho. I am quite keen to do the job – it would last for at least 10 years – but I should have to come to a most carefully worked out provisional agreement on pricing, because we have virtually no past practical experience on which to base a reliable estimate.

Also saw Coles, back from a visit to Kalle, near Wiesbaden, to see their new litho plates and to see them in use at nearby printing plants. Quite valuable, according to him. Ran into trouble on the return journey at Heathrow because of the BEA strike – he hadn't heard it was on and nobody told him when he got back.

🦌

30-31 January

Wet, wet weather. Bought two gasfires, heavily marked down by Southern Gas Board because of the coming conversion to natural gas. Saw *Patton* at the Super. Remarkably good; splendid performance by George C Scott, and some interesting shots of La Granja, north of Madrid, where several interiors were made. Also redecorated part of the hall. Watched Apollo 14 launch on TV. Finished Turgenev's *Fathers and Sons*. Began Cairns's *Berlioz*.

February 1971

🦌

1 February, Monday

A little colder. Postal strike still on and Ford being shut down. General gloom at the mess we don't seem to be able to get out of.

CHR had flu or something like it and only Davin and Chester attended the morning meeting. When D and I were alone I protested at John Ashton's latest folly in interviewing one of my staff when JH had told him that he did not want him to approach her. D confessed that he had begged CHR several times to get rid of JA and engage a stronger and more experienced man. The sad thing is that JA means so well and personally is likeable; but he exasperates everyone by his sheer ineptness.

Lunch with Help the Aged officers to talk over management problems with a Greater London Council visitor. Supervisors meeting in the canteen afterwards at which I gave them my assessment of our prospects. Not very cheerful either, tho' the meeting went quite well.

❦

2 February, Tuesday

Incensed to discover, quite by chance, that after getting me involved in the planning of a new Hindi grammar, and leading me into buying new matrices and casing a large fount of Deranagri last May, the CP (that is, Chester) had quietly given the book to Stephen Austin. I wrote a sharp note to Davin, and enclosed with it an invoice for £196. No wonder old JJ used to feel savage about the way he was treated. Later in the day I had an apology from Bruno for the sarcastic note written by his (very keen) paper buyer, which left me feeling a little less sore than I had been earlier in the day.

Works Advisory Cttee at 3.30. Good tempered, usual harangues from Fulton, who is trying hard to get the Safety Cttee chair for a chapel member, no doubt himself. I said no, and to most of the other points he argued. But the change in tone is noticeable, and after I had described the trading difficulties we are up against I felt there was a more cautious attitude in those who are pressing for more of everything. This may have been stimulated by the news of another 40 or so redundancies at Hazells.

At long last JH was able to report success over our stereotyper problem. The new man, Kibbey, sounds a winner, and should make a useful successor to Scroggs, who will be leaving at the end of June.

A brief meeting with CHR on the annual report, new Delegates and how to introduce them, and on the possibilities and savings of converting our oil-fired boilers to gas. How times have changed that we can even think of such a thing. Apparently the Mill, a great fuel user, can save about £18,000 a year at current prices.

3 February, Wednesday

A very nice and characteristic letter from Charles Broadhurst on my CBE. He said that his impression over the years he had known me was that I tried to extract the maximum pleasure and interest from everything I did. This is not really so, at least not these days, but it was curious to get such a comment from someone not too close.

As the postal strike still drags on, very little is coming in apart from bits and pieces from CP and London. We are managing to get a few invoices distributed in the London area but of course not many invoices are coming to me, which helps the cash position for the time being.

Lunched with Sam Wright, JH and RR at the Berni next to the Scala. Sam is doing a lot of work at Bedford Row on manpower needs for the industry and came to talk to John about labour movement to and from the Press. We had a useful talk on the use of computers and the NGA. He says that the executive is faced with a policy dilemma on how far to go in pressing their claims for control, and part of their problem is controlling their own militants, who don't understand the niceties of the situation and don't want to. On our side of things, he is attending meetings of an informal group, Roderick Boyd, Gilbert Smith, and John Jarrold, who are trying to work towards some sort of policy

I left the lunch early to go to a college meeting. Much longer than it need be. Dear Kelly[102] believes in giving the meeting its head. He never imparts any pace. At dinner later Graham Midgley[103] commented on my 'amazing patience' in sitting through it all; but on the whole I find it interesting even tho' little of the business touches me directly.

Picked up A from the 9.25 and another day's decorating at Fentiman Road. Head dusty but unbowed. I'm now reading Cairns's splendid edition of Berlioz's *Memoirs*.

---

102 Canon John Kelly (1909-1997) was Principal of St Edmund Hall 1951-79, transforming it into a constituent college of the university.
103 Graham Midgley (1923-1999) was a much-admired tutor in English at St Edmund Hall, where he was Dean (1956-78) and Chaplain (1978-85). His books include *University Life in Eighteenth-Century Oxford* (1996).

❦

4 February, Thursday

Jane's birthday, that most sacred day. It always brings to my mind the snow-covered parade ground at West Kirby (*in the Wirral, where VR was training as an RAF wireless operator in 1941*), when the telegram with the news was brought to me. Apart from the snow, the weather this morning, with the clear blue sky, is not unlike that day.

I left just before noon for the Oxford Motel, where I was to take the chair at the Industrial Society's 'presentation', with a buffet lunch thrown in. The lunch was nothing much, with a rather sickly sherry, and one of those bright yellow white wines that have no particular taste. About 40 people turned up, including Basil Blackwell and Dr Lloyd,[104] director of the Polytechnic. The presentation was quite good and included a show of slides which gave a little variety. The aim of these things is to recruit more members.

We finished punctually at 2.45. On my way back I looked in at Jordan Hill, mainly to go into the airdome which now contains most of our *OED* stocks. The interior is impressive – vast, and surprisingly light. Air pressure (2 lb per sq in) is held by two fans pumping air in at one end. At the other, an oil heater and fan blows in a pleasant stream of warm air, which keeps the interior at a very comfortable temperature. I walked around with Thompson, the admirable floor supervisor under O'Dogherty: he seemed enthusiastic about the dome and with the long stretches of new Dexion racking now being installed in the main warehouse.

Back at the Press I rang Batey at the Chest to find out what is likely to happen to the University's contract with Shell and BP, and the consequences if most of the University users go over to natural gas, as the Mill is now doing. The contract ends in 1972 but already Shell are cutting the rebate because of the Mill conversion. Batey did not think

---

104 Dr Brian Lloyd (1920-2010) was founding director of Oxford Polytechnic (now Oxford Brookes University), a post he held for the next ten years. A nutritionist, he became Chairman of the Health Education Council in 1983.

that the Chest would be able to negotiate a cut price with the Gas Board, but I said that I would open talks with them and keep him informed.

Jane and the chicks were at Stanley Road when I got back: the latter, stimulated by J's birthday, had been wrapping up innumerable small toys from the toy boxes as 'presents'. These covered the sofa and when they had gone and peace reigned once more A & I had the laborious job of unwrapping all the toys again and putting them away. We listened to, and taped, Anne's interview with Peter Shingleton on Oxford Radio. Children a bit puzzled that A's voice, so life-like on our radio, should be there and separated from her.

❦

5 February, Friday

Met Slight and Wilkinson of PA, with RR, to discuss their final report on Bindery production control. Slight is doing a good job and they now want to sell me another 8 weeks of consultancy in getting the scheme going. I said I was shocked by the amount of time they said they needed. After some haggling W said he would go away and reconsider the schedule. If he can cut it to 6 weeks I shall accept, because it would certainly be an advantage to have Slight here when we make the changes he has proposed.

Before our meeting I saw briefly the other deputation from PA on printer/publisher relations. Marsh had brought down the two men from their 'Corporate Strategy Division', who will be working on the project with help from Turner and Slight. I can't say I took to either of them at first glance but they may improve when we see more of them. They hope to start work on Monday week.

Very little in the post. Fortunately another volume in the Victoria County History got to us from Pugh (*The general editor of the VCH 1949-77*). We can do with it because the keyboards are still fairly light.

Axford is now home and should be back in a few weeks.

꙳

6-7 *February*

To Bristol with Jane & Rolf to stay at Brecon Road with Ben, and to see him in his Polish opera *The Haunted Manor*. Ben rather low, because he fears he has strained his voice; but in the evening he sang well before an enthusiastic audience in the Victoria Rooms. The singing, particularly the choristers, was more professional and animated than the orchestra, or at least the string section of it, and Ben's excellent enunciation helped him to get his words over quite a sound-barrier at times. We had a word with him afterwards, backstage, where speeches and presents were being dished out generously, and did not meet again until the next morning.

The Oxford party visited Brunel's *Great Britain* in the old dry dock, walked on Brandon Hill, and then met Ben and his Cambridge friend Rachel and *her* boyfriend for lunch at a Chinese restaurant in Whiteladies Road. We left at 2.30 and were back in Oxford by 4.30.

꙳

8 *February, Monday*

Not much in the box from London or CP. Reprint lists now looking very thin as the departments rapidly overtake the meagre input. At our CP meeting CHR accepted my invoice for McGregor without demur – indeed the lapse was so obvious that there was nothing to argue about. He also told me that DMD would now instruct Chester in writing that no more books were to be placed with The Alden Press after my complaint (the second incidentally). We had a brief word or two on the forthcoming PA assignment. I noted that he had more or less the same reservations about the chosen investigators. I reported their impending descent on us to the managers during the afternoon meeting. As for work generally, things could be worse, taking the plant as a whole. If the strike lasts much longer we may find it harder to keep going in the Composing Rooms. Perhaps a greater problem will be the influx of proofs now held by authors and editors, quite apart from the surge of delayed post.

At 5 I went along to the Playhouse for a directors' meeting. Financial state bad. Frank now singing a new siren song about the virtues of becoming primarily a touring company. I am sceptical, particularly as in the same voice he sang of the virtues of taking over the New Theatre and leaving the Playhouse. I said that it seemed strange to me, in the light of what he had said about touring, to think of going into that vast place, even if it can be turned into a 1000-seater (as he claims), when we can't fill the present 600-seater with the kind of play we want to put on. It was a typical Frank performance. I didn't get much help from Merlyn Thomas or Dorn, my two fellow directors, tho' Bamborough in the chair was much more cautious. We also deferred consideration of an educational project put up by the public relations officer, a rather vague project, we felt.

❦

9 February, Tuesday

Anguished letter from Walter Oakeshott[105] about proofs of an article he had written for *The Library* in 1968! I managed to sort it out for him, tho' he seemed to have been in a great muddle, partly because he had been forced to rewrite most of it after showing the proofs to the formidable Graham Pollard. Toured part of the Works during the morning, mainly the Folding Room and engineers. I had some talk with our splendid engineers' storekeeper, Joyce. He is, alas, going to retire in November, when he is 65, and his going will be a real loss. His organization of the Stores has been remarkable, transforming a confused muddle into an orderly, clearly labelled, scheme. We shall probably need two men to do what he does unless we are lucky.

Lunch with our consultants and their regional manager, Ashworth. The underlying purpose was to persuade me to accept the 8-week implementation scheme. I did, because they managed to convince me,

---

105 Sir Walter Oakeshott (1903-1987), headmaster successively of St Paul's School, London, and Winchester College, was Vice-Chancellor of Oxford University 1962-64. A scholar of medieval literature, he discovered the Winchester Manuscript of Sir Thomas Malory's *Le Morte d'Arthur*.

and RR, that they couldn't do it properly in less time. After lunch we had a quick look at the airdome.

Help the Aged policy meeting in Jack Lankester's pleasant office at 5. A & I dined at Lady Margaret Hall as guests of Kate Lea.[106] Menu – duck, which is what I had chosen at lunch time! Home in time to see Apollo 14 crew safely down.

☙

10 February, Wednesday

Very little in post from publishers, tho' a fair amount of proof back from the CP. Talked with JH on future of Stores when Joyce goes: he made the sensible point that as we may soon have some good people on our hands because of the run-down of orders, we should wait for a few months and then perhaps offer the job to someone like Stevens in the Machine Room. He has served us well in a number of different places as an assistant and seems to have the orderly mind needed. But he is no Joyce.

Halsey reported on his visit to the BM at the 10 o'clock meeting. Jacob is active and gave H some useful work to bring back. The Society of Antiquaries also has plenty of manuscripts in hand. This again reinforces my feeling that composition won't be a major worry this year.

JH reported that Cyril Foster had been taken ill in his caravan home (after a night out!) and was in the Radcliffe. Not thought to be in any danger.

Sandwich and cup of tea at my desk before catching the lunchtime train for the Book Section Meeting at Bedford Row. Surprisingly large number there. Henry Arrowsmith Brown in the chair. He let the meeting flounder along far too readily. Sat next to Brooke, who seemed in good spirits. Charles Alister told me afterwards that the trade was very quiet, even Jarrold had several large machines standing and was getting concerned about the immediate future.

---

106 Kate Lea (1903-1995), Tutor in English and Vice-Principal of Lady Margaret Hall 1947-71, had a particular love of English poetry and Italian literature. During wartime tutorials in her college room, she provided her pupils with blankets and stone hot-water bottles.

❦

11 February, Thursday

Longish meeting with JH to talk over what we might have to do if work falls very low in the Litho Department. We can ease things by bringing back into the Composing Rooms, where we have a steady flow of work, some of the comps we trained for film make-up, putting some of the surplus litho men in their place. This assumes no resistance from the chapels, but my hand is a strong one when they consider the alternatives.

Cox, the Readers' Room representative, asked to see me. We had just invited a few of the graduate classical readers to work overtime, and this prompted Cox to appeal to me (for the third time) to put the non-graduate readers on the staff and off the clock. I refused again, using or repeating my earlier arguments, and he retired with as good grace as he could muster.

KS Thompson and Sidney Street came down from London. I gave them lunch next door, and we talked over general business problems. KST is still in a depressed state, and I can't help but think that his London seniors are handling him badly. He is not told of certain important matters affecting production, & somehow hasn't got it in him to bang on the table. He talks of retiring in two years' time.

Attended first-aid class taken by Sister Westley in the canteen. Useful.

Bartók Quartet at the Town Hall – Mozart, Bartók, Beethoven…

❦

12 February, Friday

No talks yet between the postal factions, in spite of the Wilberforce report. Looks as tho' Govt determined to sit it out.

Forgot to note that yesterday an Old Bristolian called Zisman phoned to ask whether I would become president of the OB Society for one year.[107] No duties to speak of, so agreed. March '72 for office.

Rang Publisher, who goes abroad on Monday, to warn him that many of our machines may be at a standstill by the end of the month. He was

---

107 VR had been at Bristol Grammar School as a boy.

sympathetic enough but I am following up by sending RR to see Philip Chester next Wednesday. One more cheerful item was a request for an estimate for a *Companion to Sport*, to be edited by John Arlott. The aim is to publish in the autumn of '72, which seems wildly optimistic if the *Art* volume is anything to go by. I am to estimate for the first printings of 25,000 and 50,000; it could sell in v large numbers if it is good enough.

Looked in on Jakeman in his reading box. He looked better and says he is better. Also called on Harold Boyce and Cyril Foster in the Radcliffe: HB may go home on Sunday and CF tomorrow.

After lunch an Indonesian, Sakri, was brought in by a British Council representative to ask questions on the setting-up of a University Press. As usual, he was mixed up about functions and shd have been talking to a publisher, but I was able to help him a little. He is to take charge in Bandung (Indonesia). The scheme is being supported by the Dutch govt, and they have given him a Rotaprint of all things, to get him started.

Polytechnic governors' meeting at 4.30. Dennis Willson standing in for the chairman – he is very good. Lloyd is better as director than he was as chairman of governors, and I think he may do rather better than I thought he might. Great distress at having the budget cut by the City Council from £89,000 to £40,000. It doesn't grieve me at all, knowing what can be wasted on 'research', but there were several noisy speeches in apocalyptic terms from members of the Academic Board, and even an impassioned one from Jumbo Dawson. Mrs Young spoke excellently in reply. Finished at 6.15.

❦

13-14 February

Strike still on, tho' there are now to be talks on 'productivity', that favourite face-saver. To St Mary's on Sunday evening to see a lavish and splendid presentation of one of the mediaeval 'Coventry' plays. Graham Midgley looked and sounded magnificent as God the Father. We had not bought seats in advance and all good ones had been sold by the time we arrived. But K Ross (*stalwart of St Mary's*) angelically got us

into the front row of the gallery – the last shall be first... We came out
at 10.40 to be met by an unwelcome rainstorm.

☙

15 February, Monday

D day. No great complications here so far. In spite of fresh talks, no sign
of an end to the strike.

At 8.15 JH brought in the new stereotyper, Kibbey. He gives every
appearance of being a winner – young, keen, clean, etc – everything to
delight a boss's eye and heart. He had tried to make a living on the US
West coast, in North Hollywood, but with the running-down of the aer-
ospace programme, there was very heavy unemployment and he decided
to come back to the UK. He should make a good successor to Scroggs.

Main topic at our CP meeting was the slipcase for the Microform
edition of *OED*. Another aspect was the increased demand for sets:
they now want 12,000 by the end of June, whereas the most we have
said we can produce by that time is 4000. I have since told GBT to
increase our output. With a lightening of the Bindery load, it would
be exasperating to see much of this excellent if heavy work go to other
binders. The trouble may be machinery.

Wrote to Cummings, secretary of the Oxford Locals delegacy to
propose new terms for their settlement of my account. They have been
owing me £46,000 since the end of September, in other words using
us as an interest-free bank. As they get paid in advance they have been
doing very nicely out of us.

Met Slight and RR to talk over S's plans for implementing his proposals. He is to hold a series of talks on production control throughout
his stay here, and wants me to attend the first and the last. JH had
already dealt with the personnel changes, so that all should be fairly
straightforward from now on.

Enjoyed seeing Eliz Bergner, Hugh Griffiths, and Rupert Davies
in Chekhov's *The Proposal* on TV. I hope the BBC will do all his short
comedies, they suit the medium so well.

❦

16 February, Tuesday

Apart from one or two useful reprints the post was reduced to almost nothing. The lack of it hasn't yet had any serious effect on production but it is obscuring the actual work flow situation. No one can say what is in the pipeline because it is choked, and all we can do is to play by ear from day to day. I spent a good deal of time around the Works, talking in particular with Chalmers about the problems of handling a greater quantity of the Microform *OED*. He thinks our sewing capacity can take it, and possibly our Singer sewing machines, which are used for reinforcing the first and last signatures to give extra strength. Casing-in may be a bigger problem, because of the size of the book; but we may be able to overcome that by starting shift work.

The Litho Department has now come to the end of its long runs. Coles thinks that his short-run work might last until the end of March, which isn't too bad. The profit record of the department is bound to take a hard knock.

Irritated to get a phone call from Elphick of PA to inform me that he and his colleague were coming down tomorrow, 'as the Secretary has no doubt told you'. I said 'with some asperity' that I hadn't heard a thing, and when did they expect to arrive and what did they want to do when they got here. They want to 'look around'. I said that they had better report to my secretary and I would take them around myself. And that was that.

RR brought in a new recruit to the computer section at Neasden, who is to be involved in our typesetting projects. Ex-ICL, bearded, lethargic, so much so that I began to feel bored with my own questions.

A bit of Fulton nonsense brewing up in the Bindery. The wretched chapel officials, Gibbons and Knight, are caught between Fulton and their own chaps on the folding machines, and are asking JH what they should do. His truthful reply should be 'to look after your own affairs and keep Fulton at a distance'; but he said tactfully that he would have to consult me...

❦

17 February, Wednesday

Messrs Elphick and Chadwick of PA arrived at 10.15. We had a preliminary talk and then I whipped them around the Press before setting off for Cambridge with A at noon. Still not impressed by E, who seems to me rather spivvy and uneducated. He seemed surprised that proofs went to the author and not to the publisher only.

Heavy rain on our way to Cambridge. Tea with dear Col in his comfortable room *very* high up in the hostel overlooking St Mary's. Then to the college chapel for the first part of the *St Matthew Passion*. Soloists good; choir (inc Col) ditto; orchestra less so – rather ragged. Self-served supper (also good) in hall, then back to the chapel for part 2, which ended at 10.30. Back for another half hour with C, then to the comfortable lodging house he had booked for us near Christ's Piece.

❦

18 February, Thursday

A stayed on in Cambridge for the morning. I caught the 9.35 for King's Cross to keep my appointment with Grieve and attend a Management Research Group lunchtime meeting. G pronounced my neck as much improved!

Oxford Street traffic absolutely gummed up by procession of postal workers on their way to a rally at Speaker's Corner. I stood watching for a few moments at Oxford Circus. I was wearing my Russian fur hat. One striker saw me and shouted 'That's the right hat, mate – revolution!' Laughter all round.

A met me off the 5.15 and our circuit was over.

❦

19 February, Friday

A meeting in the Typographic Library at 9, when David Slight addressed the senior managers on his production control scheme. His exposition was not as good as I had expected, but he made his points clearly. A little difficult to gauge what the managers thought of it, as they don't speak so freely when I am there. I gave a few words of exhortation on improving our delivery services, and then left for my usual 10 o'clock meeting. After this I spent some time in the factory, talking with various managers and supervisors, including Mrs Fulton. I was intrigued to hear Fulton's wife saying how lucky everyone was to have a job at this time – I warmly agreed, and added my two pennorth.

Allegri lecture at Holywell Music Room. Bartók no. 2.

❦

20-21 February

A to Fentiman Road. I had lunch at the King's Arms, after a talk with Julian Blackwell, who said the strike was now hitting their large mail order business very hard. Allegri concert in Town Hall: Haydn's *Emperor*; the Bartók; and Beethoven Op. 132.

At home on Sunday. Länges to lunch.

❦

22 February, Monday

Today we began a new arrangement, under Slight's scheme, in which RR takes a short meeting with the production manager and department managers at 9.30 three days a week. The purpose is to take a quick look at schedules and promises, and incidentally to try to solve the difficulty of Taylor's rather bull-at-a-gate personality, which does not endear him to every supervisor. RR has the formal authority, GBT can only cajole and advise – not his strong points.

At the CP meeting, in discussing the *OED* Microform edition the Sec announced that an acknowledgement to the American instigator of the idea, Boni, was to be inserted in the prelims. Chester pointed out that everything had now been printed and folded and binding orders had just been given out. No matter: the prelims will have to be reprinted. At any rate I can do with the work.

Later CHR asked my opinion of Elphick. I gave it. He then said he had spoken critically about E's approach to Marsh at PA; and added that we may part company. I can't see Elphick doing us any good whatsoever.

Jarrolds have phoned Richard to ask whether we can show about ten litho machine minders around the plant. They must be very short of work if they need to fill in time like this.

Roberts of the Bibliographical Society wrote about the Short Title Catalogue. This enormous and expensive project has been on the stocks for years. We did a revised specimen last June or thereabouts. Now he is calling for yet another revision, and when that has been agreed copy should be ready for us.

Practically no post in. One good manuscript from CP, little else. Still no sign of an end to the strike. At least the weather is good.

23 February, Tuesday

RR brought in Sabido, of the computer section at Neasden, with Tony Reeve. S is the systems expert (I trust) who is to examine our office and accounting methods to see how they might be adapted for the computer. He seems a competent and unassuming man who should get on quite well with the staff.

Chadwick of PA also came in to outline his plan of campaign. A relief that he should appear without Elphick. He ran through a questionnaire with me which he wishes to use when he is interviewing the senior managers and key people. I had to make clear to him the subtle distinctions between the University Press, the Clarendon Press, and the OUP, distinctions which he might have gathered from the Waldock Report, tho' I can hardly blame him that he hadn't.

Soon after twelve RR brought in Charles Birchall, the director of Clay's litho house in Norwich, Fletchers. He said that they were fairly busy, and extremely busy on paperbacks, tho' they too had been forced to reduce their shift working. Jarrolds, he said, also had several big web presses standing. This was confirmed by a phone call from Jarrolds' works manager to RR, as I recorded yesterday.

Birchall gave an amusing account of Dick Clay's differences with David Hale. Both are great talkers and at board meetings David would go on and on, asking whether all the facts had been taken into account etc etc, while the steam poured out of Dick's ears as he waited to get a word in. No wonder they parted. It would be hard to think of a less temperamentally suited pair, but Dick brought it on himself when he bought the Northumberland Press and David with it.

He also said that Dick had made Strachan and Henshaw take back the big rotary press they had built for him. It had never printed properly during the trials at Bungay, and fortunately for Clay's, Roderick Boyd had written a most detailed specification which the press failed to meet. Dick also got £20,000 as an out of court settlement for the disruption caused, and it was for that reason that the S&H manager got the sack. Timson is now building the press for Clays.

A to London to see Ben and to attend the Frank Cass[108] party for Tambimuttu.[109] I dined in Hall, a small group on a non-guest night.

❦

24 February, Wednesday

Practically nothing in the post boxes this morning. Halsey reported at some length on his visits to the Br Museum and the Br Academy. Not much reprint work about, tho' plenty of learned new work in preparation. He had also called at Fabers, hoping to see the new production manager, Phillips, but could only see Brian Rooney, who is leaving at the end of the week. From what he heard it looks as though the two large books I quoted for last year, one on Chinese ceramics and the other a collection of letters, will be coming here before long.

The Keyboard Room load has improved. The Filmsetting Section is heavily loaded and Harris is going to train another operator, Roberts,

---

108 Book publisher taken over by Taylor & Francis in 2003.
109 Tambimuttu (1915-1983) was a Tamil poet, editor and publisher, whose *Poetry London* magazine and Editions Poetry London publishing house issued the works of many notable writers including Lawrence Durrell, Kathleen Raine, W H Auden, Jack Kerouac, Keith Douglas, Henry Miller and Vladimir Nabokov. He published AR's second volume of poetry in 1941, her verse play *Cain* in 1943, and *The Jesse Tree* in 1972.

one of our own men, as a reserve. Mansfield is also hard-pressed; his load doesn't stretch far into the future, but what he has in hand is all wanted quickly. He has four minders still away, which is making things difficult.

Slight came in to say that he has now been asked to help in the PA policy assignment, mainly in gathering facts, and so should be with us until the end of June. This should be a great help in getting our Bindery production control scheme under way. I had a word with the young man we have put in charge of the marshalling area, David Brown. We all think he is the right man for the job – he is certainly enthusiastic enough at the moment.

JH had some delicate staff moves to make arising out of this new scheme. He shunted Thomas, a warehouseman who would have liked Brown's new job but has no cutting edge, to Jordan Hill, and made redundant one of the Bindery office staff, Carlton, an odd character of 64, who is well looked after by two sons and seemed quite pleased to be going. JH still has to deal with a lame duck in that office, Cox, an ex-guillotine operator who is frightened of going back on to the shop floor since he had trouble with his hands and wrists. If he can't go back – and he now lacks all self-confidence – JH is thinking of turning him into a messenger and putting our active messenger on to the cleaning staff. Quite a problem.

❦

25 February, Thursday

A few reprints in the box this morning, and all the galley proofs of Morison's Lyell Lectures – six weeks late. With these came extracts from a letter of Nicolas Barker's congratulating us, rather patronizingly, for the high standard of setting and reading. I showed these proofs to Slight, to give him an idea of what our readers do for authors. The point I wanted to make was that if the book had gone to an outside printer on grounds of urgency (as it nearly did) no doubt the printer would have rattled through it at a great pace, but none of the queries raised by my reader to help the editor would have been raised. In other words, like is not being compared with like. Slight got the point, very firmly.

Skelly came in to report on his London visit. Not many reprints about but we shall be asked to quote for more Overseas Dept booklets, which could help the Litho Department. Otherwise rather quiet at Ely House.

Frost brought in the monthly accounts for January. They show that we have already exceeded the budgeted profit for the year, but the volume indices now show signs of moving downwards. One particularly good point is that the work-in-progress figure has been substantially reduced, the result of the blitz on the departments to get outstanding orders closed.

CHR rang down late in the evening to ask me whether I thought that the reduced *OED*, now to be called at N York's pleading the 'Compact' *OED*, should be described as being 'microphotographically reduced'. I thought not, as we had not used microscopic equipment on our cameras to do the job. Later, after I had consulted *OED* itself, I suggested 'reproduced micrographically from the original pages', as being more accurate.

Did my stint on Richard Gray's brains trust at the English Speaking Union in the evening. RG gave the Team – Janet Young, Jessup, a Canadian solicitor by the name of Fergusson, and me – a steak and kidney ESU dinner beforehand. I quite enjoyed the evening, mainly because the questions weren't too inane. A kindly picked me up after her Subscription Concert in the Sheldonian with Mary Wilkinson.[110] George W joined us at home soon after we had got back and I Spiro-Agnewed[111] to Mary's views on this Govt and its sins for a few minutes before we got on to family affairs.

26 February, Friday

Looked in at Jordan Hill. Rows of new racking now in place, looking

---

110 Mary and George Wilkinson were close friends of A and V. Mary had been at Downe House School with A, and was the niece of Olive Willis, founder of Downe House School.
111 Spiro Agnew (1918-1996), Vice-President of the United States 1969-73, was a right-wing Republican deputy to President Richard Nixon until forced to resign for taking bribes.

very neat and orderly. I had a word with Thomas, the w'houseman we moved from Walton Street. He seemed quite happy and Thompson, the foreman, told me that he had settled in very well. Thompson is a good man to have up there: he could run the place probably rather better than O'Dogherty in fact.

In the afternoon I said farewell to three men, each of them with over 50 years service. The first to come in, Colmer, was a caster 'operative' (vile word), a simple, solid fellow who told me that a secure job was far better than big money and insecurity. His hobby is woodwork, chiefly toys: he makes dolls' houses and farmyards to order, and intends to do more of it in his retirement.

The next was Hall, from the cleaning staff, a tiny, bent, chap, with warts, gappy brown teeth and a cheerful smile. He wants to do a little part-time work tho' he doesn't know what.

The last was Holloway, a machine assistant who had been in the Letterpress Machine Room all his life. He has a contented smile, and even seems contented, in spite of the £5 a week rent he has to pay for his maisonette overlooking the river near the old gas works. He *may* look for something to do, but not at the moment. Rather sad to see such stolid men depart, but I suppose we have plenty more being slowly processed into stolidity.

With A to see a praised Western, *Monte Walsh,* with Lee Marvin and Jack Palance. Very disappointing. Good scenes wasted by weak direction, and spasms of fine photography didn't compensate.

☙

27-28 February

Man up from Horns to check gramophone stylus sold me by the amiable but sluggish David Dillon. Dud, said man. Lunched at King's Arms with A, then to Walters to hire my CBE clobber. Staggered by the sight of myself in grey topper, the first I have ever worn. All to be ready next Saturday. Bought new gas cooker with self-cleaning oven at SGB, Bartók qrt (1+2) record for Col, and investigated second-hand pianos at Taphouse. A tempted by reconditioned model at £165 and only slightly put off by the speckled oak finish. Decided to consult Jane. Looked at curtain material for dining room in Ellistons. Home in time to greet Horns man, back with a new stylus.

On Sunday I went to the Town Hall for the Harmonic Society's performance of Berlioz's *Faust*, with Philip Langridge in the name part (v good). Attendance about 350. Richard Silk conducting. A and the Länges to Philippa's for tea. A to hear Dick Southern[112] talk at St Mary's, then back to pore over maps of Sicily and to discuss holiday plans.

No sign of an end to the postal strike.

March 1971

🦌

1 March, Monday

To London on the 9.20, to pick up the investiture tickets at Buckingham Gate, and make some inquiries at the 'Discovering' travel agency about our projected holiday in Sicily, before going on to the BFMP special finance meeting at Bedford Row. This was called to discuss the raising of the subscription and also to confirm that group subscriptions be abolished. The abolition, which was agreed to, will hit firms like Robinsons fairly hard, because they have many separate plants, each one of which will now have to stand on its own and be assessed accordingly. But they are not likely to complain, or so I was told. LEK (*Leonard Kenyon of BFMP*) was there, looking bronzed after a fortnight in Minorca. He told me that his impression was that book printers and binders were busier than most other sections of the trade. General colour printing looked pretty slack, also the carton sections. His news of Bernard Nicholls is not good. Apparently his condition is more serious than was first thought; and it sounds as though he may be paralyzed from the waist down.

---

112 Sir Richard Southern (1912-2001), Chichele Professor of Modern History at Oxford 1961-69, and President of St John's College, Oxford 1969-81, wrote the seminal study *The Making of the Middle Ages* (1953).

Travelled back with Howard Colvin,[113] who had some complaint of the way in which we had ignored instructions in the setting of the index for his book. It had been compiled by Hector, Harry Carter's friend at the Public Records Office, who had been meticulous in laying it out. No complaint had come my way, and so I was non-committal in my comment, tho' I did say that if we had been instructed to follow house style (as no doubt we were), that would override any marks on the copy itself. Apparently poor C had found himself pig-in-the-middle between the CP, who refused to alter the setting, and Hector, who refused to read the proofs unless it was altered. I made a few notes because I want to know just what did happen. C was gracious enough to say that the Press reader had been helpful.

❦

2 March, Tuesday

At Finance Cttee today, George Richardson,[114] an economist of St John's and a one-time member of the Oxford Management Club, attended for the first time. It was quite a relief to hear someone asking pertinent and searching questions on financial matters, particularly as we are going through a very difficult time. Sales to the US are still down, tho' total sales in money terms are steady. The postal strike is aggravating the cash shortage because although orders are getting through from the booksellers, money isn't. The outlook for the Mill is also more gloomy than ever. It is shut for this week, and after that there are sufficient orders to last until the end of the month, when it may have to shut again. Richardson asked several good questions and was referred to Henderson for the answers. Robert Blake[115] is also now a member of

---

113 Sir Howard Colvin (1919-2007) was a noted architectural historian and Fellow of St John's College (1948-2007), whose magisterial *Biographical Dictionary of British Architects, 1600-1840* is the standard work in its field.
114 George Richardson (1924-2019) succeeded Colin Roberts as Secretary to the Delegates in 1974 and, over the next 14 years in the post, transformed OUP both in terms of its organization and its finances.
115 Lord (Robert) Blake (1916-2003), Provost of The Queen's College, Oxford, 1968-87, was an eminent historian whose biography of *Benjamin Disraeli* and *The Conservative Party from Peel to Churchill* (now extended to John Major) are standard works.

FC, a real heavyweight who isn't afraid to give a forthright opinion, whether asked for or not. Hicks goes off at the end of the year.

I gave my usual report. My financial summary looks good, with profit to date well above budget. But I warned the Delegates that my management accounts were already showing a falling-off in volume in the two most profitable departments, the Letterpress and Litho. They seemed resigned to a cutback in profits.

3 March, Wednesday

Clifford, now retired from the Registry, brought in a leaflet he wants me to print – information for overseas students. He still looks after a few things of this sort for the University. In gossiping afterwards he said it would be a scandal if Campbell didn't succeed Sandford as Registrar when S retires next year. He thinks this would be the opinion of the University. When C applied for a post from Barclays Bank their only critical comment to Douglas Veale was that he was perhaps 'rather too forthright'. It may be that this quality has offended CHR, who is not one of his fans, as we in this business are.

Special meeting of Works Advisory Cttee in the canteen at 3.45. Purpose was to give up-to-date picture on present and future workload. As usual, the only person to speak when I had finished was Fulton, even tho' I appealed to other members for questions or comments. My statement was well received. Fulton asked whether I would do anything to help protect the earnings of those whose bonus opportunity was cut off through no fault of their own. I explained the difficulty but said that we would look at the problem sympathetically. The meeting ended fairly punctually at 4.30 – when the bell went!

4 March, Thursday

Began drafting my statement on the workload, future prospects etc, for distribution within the house, as agreed at yesterday's meeting. Ivor

Robinson and a fellow craftsman-binder, Philip Smith, came in to see me at 11am to bring the material for the binding exhibition catalogue sponsored by the V&A and the Pierpont Morgan Library. All meticulously laid out. Smith, who has designed the catalogue, struck me as a fussy man, and I begin to fear the worst. The catalogue is not wanted until November, so that we shan't have to rush it.

Drove over to the Swans[116] with Anne, almost in time for lunch. But we spent precious minutes wandering up and down the byways near Newbury so that we didn't find Cobwood until 1.25. Several of the locals *knew* Sir Kenneth or Lady S, *and* where they lived, but seemed quite incapable of directing us. One said something about a sewage works, and another more or less lived out the old joke of 'If I were going there I wouldn't start from here' – he found it *very* difficult, and we waited in vain while he thought and thought and muttered and puffed.

K is now 94 and Milly 91, both very frail but as kindly, courteous, and welcoming as ever. After an excellent lunch, complete with a good moselle, K took me to his study to hand over another collection of his verses that he wishes me to print for distribution to his family and friends, while A enjoyed the garden with M. We came away before tea, as I had to get back to the office for signing. Beautiful, cold weather, somehow a most fitting atmosphere for that gracious pair.

Jackson, leader of the postal workers, getting it in the neck from his furious members as he announced a settlement of the strike. As they go back with no increase in the GPO offer their rage is understandable. Badly led, alas.

5 March, Friday

Another talk with Chadwick at 9.30, mainly on charging principles. He has now seen quite a number of people here, and at Ely House. Then

---

116 Sir Kenneth Swan (1877-1973) was a QC, acknowledged authority on patent law, and AR's godfather. His father, Sir Joseph Wilson Swan (1828-1914), invented the incandescent light bulb in 1878, a year before Thomas Edison.

Stallabrass looked in to discuss some Help the Aged business.

Miss Cox duplicated my statement on the work prospects for distribution in the house, and sent the copies over to JH. Lunched at the Club next door – a small gathering, including John Ashton with his neck in a large plastic collar. Just like a Beatrix Potter frog.

Toured the Press during the afternoon, inquiring, and heartening my rather despondent troops. Mrs Fulton seems v happy in her work, despite shortages and absences.

Skelly in late in the afternoon to talk about the bad impression our errors in Bindery invoices is making on Sidney Street. Immediately after this I went over the ground with Frost, to impress on him how seriously I took such reports. He is to investigate on Monday.

*

6-7 March

Picked up my investiture clobber from Walters. Neil Jenkins, the ex-King's tenor, to stay overnight for the *St Matthew Passion*. Attended the second half, then on to Teddy Hall to read the lesson at evensong. Housepainting in between. Now postal strike is over I am hoping we shall soon get in a useful load of orders at the Press.

*

8 March, Monday

Usual meetings, no particular matters discussed, except the outcome of JH's first talk with Fulton on the subject of waiting time if work gets very low. Indeterminate, but F was to call a meeting of the chapels committee to discuss our proposals, after which he was to meet JH again on the Tuesday night.

Had a rather sharp (and exasperating) exchange with Mansfield at the managers' meeting on the workload of his department. His continued cry is that there is no work ahead, what is he to do with the men at the end of the month... and so on. And yet, as Taylor says, dates are always having to be revised because Mansfield is hard pressed. In fact he *is* busy, but can't bear not having six to nine months' work ahead of him. It will be interesting to see what happens in six weeks' time: the exam peak will have passed but holidays will have begun.

☙

9 March, Tuesday

To London for the investiture at the Palace. Jane came to stay the night with us. Church came at 7.45 and by making an early start and taking the Western Avenue route we were at Marble Arch by 9.30. Time for a coffee in fact. Everything well organized within the Palace, as it should be with the dozens of equerries & flunkeys floating around. The Queen stood on the dais in the gilt and white ballroom for over an hour, going through the wearisome job of shaking hands and giving out decoration almost as though she enjoyed it. I was told that she would probably say 'What is your work?' and she did. When I had been 'processed' I came back to the ballroom from the other side, and had to sit for another 40 minutes while the others were done. Kate had met Anne and Jane beforehand, and they were sitting on the raised seats behind me, so that I didn't see them while the ceremony was going on. The three looked v smart, all with floppy, rather county-looking large felt hats. Jane was in borrowed plume of purple, Kate in a handsome leather jacket and skirt, also purple or mauve – a present from the Wilsons. The band in the gallery did its best to relieve the boredom and its noise allowed some conversation to take place without insult to our gracious sov.

A Westminster Press photographer took a group shot in the quadrangle when all was over. Then we drove to Fentiman Road for lunch with Tim, who was busy decorating alongside Mr Donaldson, their next-door neighbour and professional decorator. We had Valerie Eliot's bottle of champagne to celebrate with and even persuaded the reluctant Mr D to take a glass with us.

After lunch, and after a tour of inspection (gratifying) we left the Wilsons to struggle on and travelled along to Peter's base in Donald

Reeves's vicarage at Morden, to see his paintings and murals.[117] All very exciting, and commissions, if not cheques, seem to be coming in fast. We had tea and a brief word with Donald after a close look at the paintings, said goodbye and were back home by 6.45.

❧

10 March, Wednesday

Post now coming in well, tho' not yet bringing much new work. JH has had no success with his flexibility proposals in return for waiting time payments. Not altogether surprising. A lot of price cutting now seems to be going on. I am having to lower some of my prices in order to keep the work at a time when we badly need it – not encouraging for the future. Fortunately my capital expenditure for the coming financial year should be pretty light. My main problem will be to decide whether to commit us to £100,000 on the new web press in 2 years' time.

Further talks with Frost on charging policy and the difficulties of simplifying it.

Visited Miss Cook in her pleasant upholsterer's workshop alongside Lucy's in Walton Well Road, to choose the material for doing up our old armchair. A place one can trust, I felt.

Clarissa Melville and her (very) young man to High Tea. They are playing for the ballet at the New Theatre.

❧

11 March, Thursday

A light post again, with only a few orders, none of them substantial. Went round the Works. Comps and small machine rooms nicely busy, the Litho and Bindery ticking over. Litho now printing the maps for Lord Salisbury's Roxburghe book, and making a good job of it. The *Rossetti* plates volume is now finished and also looks very handsome in its red buckram binding. The reproduction of the drawings has turned out well – it will be interesting to see whether it draws any favourable

---

117 Peter Pelz had painted the Stations of the Cross in St Peter's Church, Morden.

comment from John Nicoll, the CP editor who has been nursing it along.

John Lord of Ely House took sherry with me later. He is having to cut back his budget for promotion expenditure and is not at all hopeful about sales over the next twelve months.

Wrote a note to Leslie Taylor, of the CP Education Department, who retires today. He has always been most helpful and friendly to the business and we shall miss him.

Chadwick brought in the head of PA's Corporate Strategy Division, Lawson. We had quite a useful talk on the relationship of the businesses. I can tell from what he says that PA realizes they have taken on an extremely difficult assignment and are a little anxious about their progress.

A party was held in my library for Leslie Taylor. CHR made an excellent speech. LT, overcome, did not reply. Thomas Norrington[118] and his wife were there and invited us to dinner on Monday week. She is the widow of a Waterlow and we were soon on to the subject of 'The Man Who Stole Portugal'.[119]

Michael Shanks was our Management Club guest at Pressed Steel. I there learnt that Jenkins had died – a great surprise because no one had told me he had been ill. Shanks is now employed by British Leyland. I wonder for how long. Dick Conch has been retired, so Garne told me. Jumbo Dawson has retired himself – at 60 – and seemed very happy with himself. He and his wife are also travelling to Bristol tomorrow evening to hear Berlioz's *Requiem*. Their elder daughter is playing in it.

---

118 Sir Thomas (ALP) Norrington (1899-1982) was OUP's Secretary to the Delegates 1948-54, President of Trinity College, Oxford 1954-70, and Vice-Chancellor of the University 1960-62. He devised the so-called Norrington Table for ranking the results of Oxford colleges in final examinations. AR at one time sang madrigals at his house, and was asked by Norrington in the late 1960s to join him (and Peter Spicer and Roger Mynors) in his study at Trinity, in order to make the final checks of the Old Testament *NEB* translation.
119 In an extraordinarily brazen fraud, a criminal called Alves dos Reis in a complex series of manoeuvres persuaded the British printer Waterlows to produce 200,000 unauthorized National Bank of Portugal banknotes in 1925, worth almost 1% of Portugal's GDP at the time. When the fraud was eventually discovered, the National Bank successfully sued Waterlows, winning £610,000 in damages, from which the printer never fully recovered. The episode destabilized Portugal's economy, leading to a political dictatorship that lasted till 1974.

☙

12 March, Friday

Finished *Resurrection* at breakfast this morning, and sorry to have done so.

Had a letter from Davin, pointing out an error of 100 pages in a cast-off[120] we had done for a German anthology. As he had already asked the editor to cut his text on the basis of our cast-off, this error had thrown everything into confusion. Finding a way round this one is going to be difficult.

Called in at Bodley after lunch to see Miss Briggs and Michael Turner about production of the catalogue for the exhibition on the John Johnson Collection. The text is complete, and Turner has found an amusing 19th-century cartoon showing a bill poster and a tramp with the caption 'I want all the scraps I can get', which should make an attractive cover. I said that we would make a cast-off so that Turner would be able to see how much space he has for some illustrations.

Left for Bristol with A at 4.45 to hear the Bristol University Music Society do Berlioz's *Requiem* in the Colston Hall. Reached Ben before 7, had supper with him, and found he had booked us v good seats. Interesting to hear the effect of orchestra, chorus, and the four brass bands in the Dies Irae, which can never be reproduced satisfactorily on tape or disc. Thrilling. Ben subdued, because he still has to rest his voice, tho' it is improving.

☙

13-14 March

Left Brecon Road, Ben with us, in the late morning. Had snack lunch in the Bull at Fairford. Enjoyed the wonderful glass in the church. Sunday was a lovely, spring-like day with all crocuses on parade. Pottered and gardened while the little girls enjoyed themselves dressing up and making complicated sand 'salads'!

---

120 Term used for an estimate of the number of typeset pages a manuscript will make in a certain typeface at a certain size of type.

❦

15 March, Monday

A heavy post this morning, tho' not much of substance and very few reprints. Talked over possible retirements and redundancies to be faced in the Bindery if work does fall off badly: at the managers' meeting Chalmers said he had a fair load for April at least, and so we must go on, planning from week to week and trying to adjust the labour force as we go.

RR brought up, with Frost, the question of the budget utilization indices and what I wanted them to be set at for the next financial year. I said that in one sense it made no practical difference as to what we did: if we kept them the same as for the current year and utilization dropped badly, we showed the loss in the period accounts. If we lowered the indices to what could be a more realistic level we should then be pushing our cost rates up, but given the state of the market I shouldn't be able to put my charges up to correspond, so that the loss would simply appear in a rather different form. In the end we decided to make a minor reduction in the departments affected.

Signed two indentures for Bindery apprentices. Housing Society meeting at 5.

Nice letter from Batey, who had only just learnt of my award from the Members Circular. But the poor man has to face an operation (the 10th!) for the removal of his gall bladder.

Farewell party in the Old Library at St Mary's for Philip Martin (*Vicar of St Mary's*) and his wife Mollie. Good crowd there, including, of all people, John Sparrow![121] Many speeches, one good one from the curate.

❦

16 March, Tuesday

Chadwick in to see me. I sense that he is still floundering with all the

---

121 John Sparrow (1906-1992), Warden of All Souls 1953-77, was a well-known book collector and bibliophile, who wrote books and essays on epigraphy, painting, Latin and English poetry as well as other topics.

contradictory points and policies he is unearthing. I shall be surprised indeed if PA can produce anything really helpful and constructive. I don't think they can have met our peculiar type of animal before. One comment of his intrigued me: he said that Tim Chester thinks that because my litho prices are so competitive I must be clobbering CP in other areas in order to make the annual profit I do. Chadwick realizes the reverse is true and asked me whether I could fully explain the high profitability of the Litho Department. I said it was partly the high volume of work coupled with shift working. Then I asked him a question: could he explain why outside litho printers were charging more than me? He couldn't, of course.

Art Advisory committee at Polytechnic. Grimshaw, Saugman,[122] & Ruari (*McLean*) were all absent, so Tom Colverson took the chair. Good discussion on the proposed new publishing course syllabus and on the poor 'liberal studies' response.

Ben still with us. He goes back to Bristol, alas, tomorrow.

RR, JH, away – with Fulton! – on a one-day seminar in Bristol.

❦

17 March, Wednesday

BFMP meetings in London. Travelled up with Taylor, on his way to Ely House. He was not expecting a difficult day because most of the delays are now on their side.

Lunched with Eric Dixon at the useful pub in Theobald's Road. Back on 5.15. Ben had gone back to Bristol. Our new (for natural gas) cooker was in situ when I got home, with one piece missing and another piece broken...

❦

18 March, Thursday

Had Halsey in to give me an account of his London visit. He had called in on an earlier customer of ours, Crosby Lockwood, and it is just possible

---

122 Per Saugman (1925-2005), head of Blackwell Scientific Publications.

that they may like to print with us again. The BM doesn't appear to be short of funds. Jacob has a number of new projects and reprints in the pipeline which we should benefit from eventually.

Help the Aged meetings from 11 to 3.46, with 20 minutes for lunch.

Dined at the Robertses. That delightful man, George Richardson, was there, also Anthony Quinton[123] – larger than life and very entertaining – and his German-Russian wife, whom Colin thought was American. Also Peter Sutcliffe (*CP editor*) and Laura Salt. A very good evening. Surprised to learn from Alison R that they are exchanging houses in May with the Kitsons, who live in an old, and larger, house at Appleton.

❦

19 March, Friday

Quiet day. Not much new work in the post, which otherwise was large enough. Toured the departments – sad to see the Bindery so empty of work stacks, but we are going along reasonably well there. The last litho machine on shift comes off on Monday: we are getting through the remaining work rapidly now, tho' one brighter area is the web-offset, where we hope to start up again next week on a Bible order. This should help to boost morale in Litho.

Gillman sent in part of the mss for the history of Barclays Bank, which will allow us to get the format settled and set a specimen. This book should give us a useful amount of composition when we get the all-clear.

Aubrey Owen, a good comp who left in the early '50s to take over his parents' tobacconist business on Headington roundabout, has sold up and wants to come back to us. JH is hoping to make him into an estimator and he seems interested altho' he has had no experience of estimating. But we are hard pressed in that section, and a man with comping experience should be more useful to us than someone outside the trade.

---

123 Lord Anthony Quinton (1925-2010), President of Trinity College, Oxford, 1978-87, was a renowned political and moral philosopher who reached a national audience as presenter of BBC Radio 4's *Round Britain Quiz.*

❧

20-21 March

Piscatorial Society dinner at the Victoria Arms, Marston. I took old Fred Taylor, who keeps an anglers shop off the Cowley Road, along so that he could respond to a toast. A pleasant sing-song afterwards.

Colin back from Paris when I got home. A fine bristly chin, presaging a beard, he says. Länges up as usual for Sunday lunch and onwards. Colin given his birthday presents, mainly of books and records.

❧

22 March, Monday

At our meeting this morning CHR said that in order to get a pre-tax return of 10% on capital employed the publishing department have to cut production by between 15 and 20%. This is already having a significant effect on us, even in the Composing Rooms; and we may have to cut overheads more dramatically than I had hoped a month or two ago.

Ella Oelrich[124] is now in Oxford and came to see me in the afternoon. She is fairly cheerful on the subject of N Y Bible sales but gave me details of closures and changes in the US production scene that surprised me. Riverside taken over by Rand McNally with Morgan Smith, Dean Hocking and Charles Rean all gone or retired. Van Rees closing their composing rooms because of the last wage settlement in N Y of 15%. World Book has closed and American Book–Stratford reported in difficulties. This has tended to ease both competition on the Bible front and Bible production.

A back safely from Coventry. Still reading 'The Hunting Sketches'.

❧

23 March, Tuesday

To the Crematorium at 10.30 for the funeral of Harry Gardner, an assistant in the Bindery, who died suddenly last week. A pathetically

---

124 VR first met Oelrich on a two-month trip to North America in 1951. He had visited many of the printers she now reported as having closed.

small number of mourners, but the service was taken with great feeling and dignity by a young priest, no doubt from the parish.

Elphick of PA came in at noon to ask a lot more questions. I still get the impression that they are floundering desperately.

Wrote a short paper for Finance Committee on the proposed investment of £100,000 in a new web-press. I am anxious to get the publishing side more involved in such decisions than they have wanted to be in the past. I don't know whether I shall succeed but PA may be able to help me in this area.

Dinner party for Ella Oelrich in St Edmund Hall. We – Anne, RR, JH, GBT, Carol and Agnes – met in the Hearne Room. It was raining, which prevented us from wandering around the quadrangles beforehand; but the manciple and Cyril provided excellent food and drink. We parted at 10 o'clock, and I managed to see the ITV 'trial' of the Industrial Relations Bill presided over by Lord Devlin. Most impressive witnesses were Geoffrey Howe (for) and Prof Wedderburn (against).

24 March, Wednesday

Still very little new work coming in. Before very long the Keyboard Room will be running dry. I can switch operators into the main room but even there we may run out of work when the exam season is over and another ten men are available for bookwork.

Attended the AGM and lecture of the Oxford Bibliographical Society. This year it was held in the Massie Room at Balliol, a room far too small to accommodate us and the two projectors and screens needed by the lecturer. Subject: Books of Hours. The paper was rather too thickly clotted with learning to be followed at all easily. Tea in the Bodleian Canteen afterwards. Talked mainly with Mrs Simmons about Tolstoy and Turgenev. She told me a curious story. Apparently Turgenev's cruel mother had an affair when she was in her 50s and produced a daughter. The father was Dr Behrs. I wonder whether Tolstoy knew of this.

Looked in on Jane and Rolf and their new small piano, now installed in the sitting room. It takes up surprisingly little room. Colin was also there, enjoying an enormous plate of spaghetti and tomatoes.

Went on to the Motel, where the managers had laid on a dinner for me to mark my CBE. I had vaguely thought of the 4 senior managers plus John and Richard, but it turned out to be a much larger gathering, including Boswell and Eaglestone. I hadn't gone prepared to make a speech, but during the course of the very good meal John got up and read a most charming, generous and semi-fictional discourse on my manifold and great virtues. Of course I had to reply with something more than a smile and a thank-you. In fact I think I did it rather well, and managed to keep my speech short, even after the gin and french I had taken earlier.

We stayed on talking until 10.45, when I slipped away. The others seemed all set to continue. Very touched by it all.

☙

25 March, Thursday

Post late and full of circulars and invoices – little work or returned proof. No fixed engagements today, for a change. After visiting some of the departments I had the Blanche Henrey illustrations brought into my room so that I could see what she had chosen. She has sent along a vast number, far more than I thought we had agreed to, and we may have to get her down here if we are to make any progress. Skelly had had quite a good day at Ely House, tho' again there is not much about in the way of manuscript. At least the atmosphere is reasonable, as one would expect when the pressure is reversed.

Andrew Thomson, our most reliable layout man under Ken Stewart, came to ask whether I would act as a referee if he were to apply for a job with the Open University at Bletchley. He is a very good and conscientious man and I don't want to lose him, and so I took things gently and sounded him out. He doesn't really want to leave, but now that he lives in the country, some way from Witney, his wife, who has just had a child, feels rather lonely and wants to move. Bletchley of all places... Anyway, I have persuaded him to talk things over with John before he does anything more. I hope we shall be able to find a way of keeping him here.[125]

With A & C to see the film of Orton's *Loot*. Madly funny, most of the time.

❦

26 March, Friday

Long meeting with the chairman of the audio-visual committee of the University, Franklin, and a colleague, Band, to discuss my attitude if the University were to encourage, by advertising, a greater use of slides, microfilm, etc, so affecting the Bodley studio. Would I be ready to increase staff and equipment, for instance? I said that in principle I would be, but not until the pressure was seen to be there – I would not increase capacity simply on their assurance that the work was coming. I also said that any more of this kind should be cleared with the Librarian because his staff was also involved. The chairman was charming but delightfully vague. Band said little.

To London on 4.30 for the Galley Club dinner at the Saddle and Sirloin, Rood Land. Not an ancient hostelry but a Mecca establishment in the basement of a semi-skyscraper. Quite pleasant, but the table arrangement, because of the large pillars, meant that half the guests were behind me when I spoke. It went off well enough, but an odd feeling doing theatre-in-the-round without turning around.

David Hall presided. He surprised me with a new wife, which made me glad that I hadn't asked warmly after his first one, a woman much older than himself whom A and I had liked when we met them both at Eastbourne a few years ago. The new one has several children and his family is now 5. He is still out of a job after IPC closed his section down. He blames a lot of IPC's general muddle on Hugh Cudlipp,[126]

---

125 Thomson became a Baptist minister.
126 Hugh Cudlipp (1913-1998) was a seasoned Fleet Street editor, Chairman of the Mirror Group of newspapers 1963-67 and Chairman of the International Publishing Corporation 1968-73.

who, says DH, promised to stand down from the chair when Cecil King was pushed out after a year, and didn't. David also told me that he is in demand as a lecturer on video aids, cassettes and so on, unfortunately, mostly unpaid.

Hugh Williamson gave the vote of thanks in his usual ponderous and slightly embarrassing way. The poor fellow will *talk*. I caught the 11.15 and was home soon after 1.

☙

27 and 28 March

Kate and Tim arrived at lunchtime for the weekend. In the evening A and I to a dinner given by Elsa Booth at the Saraceno. Her daughter Janet (looking very charming) and Terry, her husband; the Swanzys; the Fletchers; and ourselves made up the party. We sat around one of those large circular tables and had an excellent meal. Towards the end I got talking with Kay Swanzy, who told me that when Eric Ravilious's wife, Tirzah Garwood (whom I had commissioned to do work for *Contact* in 1947), died in 1951 they had taken over the three children. John, the middle one, who suffers from leukaemia, is now married to Caroline Whistler.[127] It was like fitting a jigsaw together: her brother-in-law, Henry Swanzy, shared a flat after the war with George Weidenfeld, and I remembered that HS had also written for the early issues of *Contact (for which VR was designer in 1946-47)*. No doubt that's how I met Tirzah G.

☙

29 March, Monday

Last Friday I had written to Dan crying out for composition. I said that my turning away exam work last summer had been singularly ill-timed

---

127 In fact it was James, not John, who married Caroline Whistler; he had been treated for lymphoma. Tirzah, his mother, had been taught wood-engraving by Eric Ravilious at Eastbourne School of Art and they married in 1930. In 1942, as a war-artist, Eric flew over Iceland in a small plane that never returned. Tirzah married Henry Swanzy in 1946, but when she died in 1951 his brother John and sister-in-law Kay took on the Ravilious children.

if now that we had the capacity very little new work was to be put our way. The response this morning was helpful: 5 new mss will be down this week. Colin rather surprised me by saying that he hadn't realized we might be short of composition. I shall now keep the pressure up to get a good load before the exam work falls off in a few weeks' time. So far we have given the CP about 3000 pages more than this time last year. They haven't got much to complain about.

Elphick of PA sat in on my afternoon meeting with the managers. I still have very little confidence in him.

Frost brought in the financial summary for tomorrow's FC. Profit well above budget, but this is now history, alas, and the volume indices again show a further decline. I shall be hard put to it to make much of a profit during the coming financial year.

A paper from CHR for FC puts forward a proposal for combining two of the three sections – at Oxford and Ely House – now concerned with 'educational books' (mainly school books) into one department at Oxford. The third 'English Language Teaching' is to continue its separate existence at Ely House, no doubt after strong resistance from Nugent, who runs it. A pity, but I very much welcome the merger. It will give us a closer liaison with this part of the business, and we must reconcile ourselves to the fact that most of the design work will move over to CP. It may mean a slight reduction in our design section over the next year or so. All this, I think, as a rather belated response to the Longman/Penguin threat.

I also had copies of the publishing department budget. No real increase in sales forecast, and possibilities of price resistance from the public may slow things down even more. We shall face an acute shortage of cash by the autumn. It will be interesting to see whether the bank will be resisting an increase in our overdraft by that time.

More paper mills closing down, it was announced this morning. This *may* do Wolvercote some good, but most of them seem to be craft paper mills, a field W is not concerned with.

Help the Aged meeting at 5. Left at 7.15. Long day.

❧

30 March, Tuesday

Beautiful spring-like morning for Budget day. Many meetings during the morning – Chadwick, Lady Wheare – pursuing me on behalf of charity with her usual energy; and to lunch with a PA crowd, including their so-called printing expert, a most terrible bore who pontificated not only in our car going out to the Dog House at Frilford but throughout the meal. I pootered in stony silence while he went on. O dear. Back in good time for FC. The Vice-Chancellor and the new senior proctor attended. The educational book reorganization went through without dissent or even much questioning. The report on the Mill caused more discussion. The situation is now very serious and unless business does pick up over the next six months, I fear the Delegates will have to face closing it. As the V-C pointed out in his usual blunt manner, there is the political impact to be faced, because there is little hope of gaining anything from a forced sale, and it is University money – all this quite apart from the effect of putting 230-odd out of work. Unfortunately I had to leave for the Double Crown Club meeting before FC ended so that I missed discussion on Jordan Hill & its further extension.

A large gathering at Kettners to welcome Harold Hugo.[128] I sat next to Herbert Spencer with one of the young Harrisons, Hugh, on my left. Berthold had brought his son Paul, broken-nosed and with Margaret's looks. Hugo was well received. He showed about 80 slides, mainly of the beautiful books he has done for American museums. Chester Kerr of Yale also present: we had a drink over the road afterwards.

❧

31 March, Wednesday

Norman Bratt to lunch. Ebullient as ever, and more or less reconciled to working with us via Ely House and Sidney Street. I took him around

---

128 Harold Hugo (1910-1985), President of the Meriden Gravure Company in Meriden, Connecticut, whose work producing high-quality illustrated books on art and design history VR very much admired. VR had visited Hugo at Meriden on his US trips in 1951 and 1960.

the plant and showed him that work was being done in the film section on his illustrated Bible. He is one of the few people I know who is not particularly worried by rising costs, mainly I suppose because of the subsidies the Bible Society can give to its editions. He hopes to let me have another reprint for the Nonpareil Bible before the end of the year.

April 1971

🌱

1 April, Thursday

Much telephoning in the morning. At last I have managed to fix up a farewell dinner for John Simmons at Teddy Hall. I have also had to arrange another dinner party for Harold Hugo next Monday evening.

Left for London at 10.30. MRG meeting at Charing Cross Hotel, where I stayed the night. British Academy dinner at Senate House in the evening. John Brown also there. Mrs Thatcher and Lord Trevelyan[129] principal guests. The latter made a long dull speech about the future plans for the British Museum, a striking contrast to Ken Wheare's[130] sparkling presidential toast. Trevelyan made the unusual mistake at the end of his reply in proposing a toast to the Academy, which took everyone by surprise. Sat next to Francis Watson[131] and Prof Kane, with Robert Shackleton[132] and Kenneth Muir[133] (rather shy, or at least silent) opposite. Managed a few minutes afterwards with Nicholas Hammond,[134] who seems very happy at Bristol University.

---

129 Lord (Humphrey) Trevelyan (1905-1985), British diplomat who was Chairman of the Trustees of the British Museum.
130 Sir Kenneth Wheare (1907-1979) was Rector of Exeter College, Oxford 1956-72, Vice-Chancellor of Oxford University 1964-66, and President of the British Academy 1967-70.
131 Francis Watson (1907-1988) was a biographer of Gandhi and historian of India.
132 Robert Shackleton (1919-1986) was Bodley's Librarian 1966-79 and the author of the standard biography of Montesquieu.
133 Kenneth Muir (1907-1996), a great Shakespeare scholar, was Professor of English Literature at the University of Liverpool 1952-74.
134 N G L Hammond (1907-2001), Classical scholar, was Headmaster of Clifton College 1954-62 and Professor of Greek at Bristol University 1962-73. For his exploits in Greece and Crete during World War II he was awarded the DSO. He was AR's cousin.

❦

2 April, Friday

At Monotype House in the morning for an up-to-date demonstration of the Monophoto 600 given by Albert Goldthrop and Laver. Quite impressive. I shall have to look at this project again.

IPEX (*International Print Exhibition*) lunch at the Savoy. A strange mixture – Herbert Newman, Leonard Kenyon (*BMFP director*) etc, alongside Peter du Sautoy (*Faber Vice-Chairman*), John Carter (*bibliophile*) and a bunch of machine manufacturers. Jack Matson (*head of Monotype*) in the chair. A good meal at any rate.

Church picked me up at 3.20 and we were back at the Press by 5. Richard came in and reported some good and some bad news of the day – the usual mixture. At least the weather is glorious.

❦

3-4 April

Col back from Fentiman Road on Sunday evening, otherwise no great activity at Stanley Road. Sun trying to break through, overcast & drizzle.

❦

5 April, Monday

Rather acrimonious discussion at CP meeting on the degree of responsibility for a book that had to be reprinted at a cost of £5000. I think that right is mainly on our side, tho' I wish we had proceeded more cautiously in our attempt to get the job through on time after many frustrations, not of our making. One of those cases when hindsight would have helped more than goodwill.

Picked up Harold Hugo from the 14.20 train. We had a short time here, then I took him home for tea with Anne and, later, with Colin who had been down at the Bodleian. H in good form, tho' he now has the use of only one eye, and that is not perfect.

In the evening I drove him out to the Old Swan at Minster Lovell, for a dinner with Richard, Coles, and Carter. Meal not bad – rather pricey – but surroundings pleasant enough, and H enjoyed himself. We had a cross-country run to Kingston Bagpuize afterwards, to get Harry home. He enjoyed himself too.

For me the day was rather overshadowed by the prospect of redundancies in the Litho Dept, which is coming ominously close. GBT reckons that the dept will be virtually out of general bookwork by the end of next week, and there is little prospect of anything substantial ahead to fill it up again, even on daywork. The other departments are holding on, and holidays will help, but the outlook is not at all good.

❦

6 April, Tuesday

H Hugo here at 10. After a brief talk I handed him over to Jim Coles and the Litho Department until 11.30, when I took him on to Bodley and Ian Philip. We looked into the Johnson Collection and the Bibliography Room with Michael Turner until lunchtime. Then Philip took us to the Saraceno for an excellent lunch. H was looking a bit worn afterwards so we said our farewells at the Randolph entrance and he then retired within to sleep it off.

At 4 Richard brought in the successor to Miller, the present Clerk of the Schools, another ex-policeman by the name of Barnes. Miller did most of the talking so that I had no real opportunity of assessing Barnes; but from the few words he did let drop I guess he should do the job well enough.

Talked again with R & J about the work situation in the Litho. Earlier I had gone over my budget for the coming year with Frost and decided that we had better budget for no profit at all, on the grounds that as I want to hold on to my skilled men as long as possible the cost of doing so might be heavy enough to wipe out a modest profit pretty rapidly. I may have second thoughts because FC may be less likely to press me to get rid of people if my budget shows *some* profit, however unattainable. The total number in the Litho, including management, is 55.

❦

7 April, Wednesday

Rather neglected this diary over Easter. Thompson & Street down from Ely House. We lunched together and had a useful discussion on invoicing and charging. Thompson came to my room on his own afterwards and confirmed what he had told Skelly last week: that he would be retiring at the end of the year. So Bruno and his officers have got their way. It may not be to our advantage because KST has been a supporter of ours, unstable tho' he may be. He says that they now intend to go for 'someone big', and it will be interesting, at the least, to see who they pick.

❦

8 April, Thursday

A letter from Monty Shaw,[135] giving details of his new publishing venture. His list, all in limited editions, will cover typography, music and musicology, and late 19th-c English literature. If his finances are sound this could be an agreeable connection for our Litho Department. He is coming down with Berthold, who is advising and lending pieces from his collection for reproduction, next Friday.

A tiresome 'confidential' letter from Simon Nugent of the English Language Teaching section at Ely House, complaining of our unhelpfulness over the *Progressive English Dictionary* specimen, as compared with Oliver Burridge (of all people!). He *is* a cold fish, and very difficult to deal with. RR composed a long answer which I thought much too detailed and a short one has now gone off saying that I should be getting in touch with his boss, Philip Chester, early next week. I hope to have calmed down a bit by then, and I may call at Ely House to talk or thrash it out.

---

135 Montague Shaw was a publisher and typographer who ran the small Merrion Press with his wife Susan Shaw (1932-2020). Among the books they later published was *Selected Poems of George Darley* (1979) edited by Anne Ridler. Sue Shaw founded the Type Archive in 1992 in South London, which is a unique repository of now redundant machinery and matrices for hot-metal letterpress printing, especially Monotype.

🍂

9–12 April, Easter Holiday

A full house from Saturday, as Kate & Tim came over from Bath. Ben still struggling with his voice trouble, poor fellow, and very different from his usual ebullient self. Coldish winds until the Monday, when we had a really warm, spring day. Trespassed in Wychwood Forest during the afternoon – no keeper in sight, fortunately. Ran into long queue of cars at Yarnton on the way back, so turned off and came home via Eynsham and Botley. TV news said congestion on roads had been 'hell'.

🍂

13 April, Tuesday

Back from the holiday. Another beautiful if rather cool day. Everything calm on the labour front at the moment. Little new work in the post although plenty of returned proof. This even included Valerie Eliot's proof of her Introduction which we have been waiting for with decreasing hope. Many corrections in it but I didn't have time to see what they were.

Drafted and redrafted a letter to Philip Chester on *PED*. I had tried to get him on the phone. He came through at the end of the day, so I read out what I had written   calm and statesmanlike (I hope!) after my first fury   and we agreed that I should call at Ely House next Tuesday after my BFMP meeting. Nugent will be there and I should be able to straighten things out for everybody.

Called in Aubrey Owen, who rejoined us as an estimator after leaving us as a compositor almost exactly ten years ago to run his parents' tobacconists shop at Headington roundabout. He is a good man and John took him on to strengthen our estimating section which is soon to be weakened by retirements.

Also saw Gerard Frost. He had been given a rough time over Easter because of his father's illness; but death came on Monday evening, mercifully for all the family, who have been under great strain for the past 6 months.

Began drafting a letter to CHR on the Junior Mathematics mishap.

Important to get something on paper when we are wrongly accused of negligence, particularly when the accusation is so misplaced.

☙

14 April, Wednesday

One-and-a-half-hour session with Elphick in the afternoon. One of his conclusions, after a week at Ely House, is that a good part of our troubles lies in the distance between Ely House and Oxford, which I can believe. His suggestion that we may have to do more lunching of their production men would make old JJ revolve pretty briskly. The sad thing is he may be right. He also confirmed what I have often said to my people: that no agreement about work coming to Oxford between the principals can prevent individual editors and production managers from putting work with outside printers when it suits them, however short we may be. It is a difficult situation, partly to be overcome by better or more high-powered liaison. This latest trouble with Nugent and ELT over the dictionary is a good example of the misunderstandings that can arise. In the morning I phoned Jack Matson of Monotype to ask him to do all he could to get the dictionary equipment to us by the end of the month. He phoned back to say that he had been on to the works, they were clearing the decks and Duncan Avery, the man in charge, would be letting me know tomorrow what they can do.

An ominous sign: Harris has had to take two keyboard operators from their room and put them on to compositors' work. Certainly v little new ms has been coming in, and we do need a lot of it.

Ella Oelrich's thank-you letter brought news of the bankruptcy of the best trade typesetting house in the US, Westcott and Thompson. The firm had done a lot of work for Oxford NY; fortunately they had nothing in hand when the crash came.

Wrote a letter to CHR, refuting on paper the charges levelled against us at the last Monday meeting of negligence in running the Junior Maths books. Although I feel strongly about the episode I kept my resentment in check, not without an effort.

❦

15 April, Thursday

Again very little new work in. Toured the Works, which still has quite
a busy feel about it, tho' the Bindery floor, usually packed out with
work in various stages, looks bare. Chatted with Fulton, who seems
cheerful, perhaps because he is plotting some fresh villainy against us.
I emphasized that we would have a poor year, just to make sure the
point is getting home.

❦

16 April, Friday

Went through my final budget figures with Frost. If we make no more
profit than £50,000, which is quite likely, we shall end this year with
an overdraft of about £125,000, another severe strain on our finances.

Monty Shaw and Berthold lunched with Butler and me, to discuss
their first two books. The first title Shaw wishes to publish is a German
alphabet book (*see plate 13*). This is really a sequence of architectural
plans designed in the shape of letters, and apart from a mild curiosity
value not something I would have thought of great interest. But he
feels confident of his market, and as long as he has the cash to pay for
the production I am happy enough to print it for him. Berthold also
brought with him Moran's book on the printing machine which Faber
would like me to print. It looks good at a brief glance.

With A to *The Valkyrie* at 5.30. Ended at 10.40. Splendid but *long*.

❦

17-18 April

Lunch with A at the White Horse, next to Blackwells. Visited the
Sidney Nolan exhibition at the Ashmolean – mainly paintings inspired
by Shakespeare's sonnets and v exciting. Gardening, removing bluebells
mainly. A did the Parish breakfast at St Mary's. Watched Britten's *Burning
Fiery Furnace*, then to the Playhouse for a Bach Festival evening of
Greek drama extracts, a Harrison Birtwhistle piece on a Greek Theme,

conducted by him, and Stravinsky's *Soldier's Tale*. Announced by Alvar Liddell. Rather too much Greek dialogue, as it was done in Greek by members of the Nat Greek Theatre, but we were glad to have stayed the course which many of the audience, including Sternfeld, didn't.

Back in time to see part of the Cartier-Bresson programme, *and* the final sequence of Gene Kelly's remarkable if kitsch cartoon section of 'Invitation to the Dance', *Sinbad the Sailor*. A Kultural weekend.

❦

19 April, Monday

Quite an amiable discussion at the CP meeting on a rather ill-phrased letter from a young man in their production department. We had offered to set an Atlas Gazetteer in 4 weeks, under pressure, the understanding being that we would both set and print. The CP letter said that we *may* be given the printing if my estimate was satisfactory. At the meeting I said this wasn't good enough. Either we did both or neither because I couldn't turn the place into a trade setting house when I had departments other than the Composing Rooms to keep going. In the end this was agreed. Davin on his own, or Kit Bourne of Cartographic for that matter, would have sent us the whole job anyway, but the production boys are now, in a buyer's market, indulging themselves with plum-picking, and I must resist it as best I can. So we start setting on Wednesday. Several new manuscripts announced, and the production manager of Cassells wrote, sending a large batch of copy, to say that he was pressing Croft, the author of *English Autograph Manuscripts*, to complete his part by the end of July so that the book can be published next spring.

Another monster reared his head. Hassall, Lord Leicester's librarian, phoned and wrote to say that his Lordship now wants his Roxburghe Club copies numbered. As they are all bound and packed, I wrote him a rather firm letter on this suggestion. I'm not sure I got the tone right, as I don't know him well, but it is worth a try to stop him. Hassall can't really cope, which is one of the troubles.

Went over my budget for the year with CHR, emphasizing its

speculative content. Also showed him my draft for FC on the new web press. He supports its purchase, which should help to get it through. My real purpose is to get FC to take actual responsibility for the decision on a detailed knowledge of the facts, so that if the publishing dept don't supply the work to keep it going I shall not be left to fight alone.

That strange but nice fellow Leslie White came to lunch with me. He has now retired from the insurance world, tho' he still has a directorship that takes him abroad occasionally. He, a lifelong bachelor, spoke of getting married 'for companionship'. I asked him whether he had anyone in mind and he replied 'Well, Mary Bland[136] is very charming'! I can't see *that* happening. He also told me that Eric White had had a spastic son who died at 21.

☙

20 April, Tuesday

Just before I left to catch my train Miss Cox brought a message to say that Fulton had resigned his offices of House and Machine Room Father. Interesting news, and it will be even more interesting to see who is elected in his place. It may be the result of some discussion between his union and SOGAT.

Lunched at Ely House with CHR, Bruno, Philip Chester, and the newly elected British Council officer for India. Colin and Bruno were going on to Bentley House for a *NEB* meeting, and Dykes drove me on to Bedford Row for the special President's meeting to discuss the succession to Leonard Kenyon and Charles Alister. Those present beside the President and Vice-President and LEK were Elliott Vincy,[137] Lord Ebbisham, Max Bemrose,[138] Stanley Clarke, Herbert Newman, and myself. The group fairly quickly resolved itself into two factions – rather too strong a word for it – one group wanting to have the jobs

136 David Bland's widow, who was a bookseller.

137 Elliott Viney (1913-2002) was a director of British Printing Corporation and Hazell, Watson & Viney.

138 Sir Max Bemrose (1904-1986) was Chairman of the eponymous printing company 1953-78, and twice President of the British Federation of Master Printers (1967-68 and 1971-72).

'specified' and advertised (Bemrose, Ebbisham, Viney); the other in favour of appointing Henry Kendall as director and Sam Wright as head of industrial relations. I spoke forcibly in favour of the second course, and, I believe, swayed a few waverers. The upshot was that the second view prevailed and the President was to say to the Alliance presidents at his annual meeting with them next Monday that this was our recommendation to Council. I don't think there will be much opposition, certainly not over Wright.

After this meeting I went back to Ely House to sort out Simon Nugent. I managed to do so effectively, but I was struck at the end of our quite long talk by the fact that altho' he admitted misunderstanding completely what had been our main problem with his dictionary specimen, he gave no hint of apology or regret for what he had written or for bringing me up to London. A cold fish indeed. Philip Chester was charming and helpful and did his best to 'chair' our meeting. Then to the Connaught Rooms for a dinner meeting of the Purchase Tax Joint Standing Committee of the Paper, Printing, and Stationery Trades, mainly to meet and to hear the new Commissioner of Customs and Excise, Christopherson, on the Value Added Tax. He struck me as a most able man (ex-Treasury) and gave us a clear account of what has to be done if the Tax is to come in during 1973. Several awkward problems for our industry. I expect this will be one of the main concerns of our Legislation Committee next year.

❦

21 April, Wednesday

Lunch in the office, then over to Denham in time for the AGM of Help the Aged. The meeting was held in the attractive common room of the association's first project, Courtney House. I presented the accounts, and afterwards we talked with some of the residents and visited their flats. They all seemed remarkably happy and grateful, and no wonder, because their living conditions are enviable. We took tea together and I then managed to slip away and drive back to Oxford in the glorious sunshine. A rather dull Management Club dinner meeting at Hertford, tho' I enjoyed sitting between Brian Lloyd and Gordon Dick. I felt so tired after our speaker, the professor of economics, had finished that I slipped away and went home – the first time in 23 years I can remember doing so.

☙

22 April, Thursday

Disaster! I forgot to tell Church to collect Anne for her 10.13 train to Coventry. When she rang at 10 I was aghast. After a flurry of searching, Pat Cox managed to get hold of Church, and I told him to drive A there. So that was that, but I felt the wormiest of worms.

Had Fulton in at 9.45 for a chat about his resignation. I didn't really get much out of him as to his real motives for throwing in his hand, but he said that the work had grown so rapidly that it was taking more of his time than he wished to spare. He has been involved heavily with the *Oxford Mail* and their new web-offset installation. All on his side, he said, had been staggered to learn of the rates that the *Mail* is already paying its men – they had no idea such money was being paid in the Oxford area. He finally presented me with a copy of the NGA's new occasional and lavish journal, which I gracefully accepted.

Then I had in Harris and the FOC Philip Walker, with another keyboard operator, Compton, to bang on the table about their recent behaviour in banning overtime on a job which I had only got with difficulty. They *can* be dim, the dear, wretched fellows.

Hugh Tempest-Radford, production director of Longmans, and Nicholas Russell (RR's brother), who looks after one of their nine production sections, came to lunch. The talk turned to printing in the Far East. T-R said that Longmans did all their books intended for the European market in the UK, and only books for the Far East and Africa from Hong Kong and Singapore. We may in time develop quite a useful relationship with Longmans, tho' I can't see it turning into anything large scale.

CHR rang through to say that the third web press had been mentioned at a meeting of the Joint Management Committee, and unanimously supported, tho' Philip Chester had again said that he was anxious to be given some idea of costs. I don't want to be drawn into giving precise figures at this stage, but I told CHR that I would make some comment at FC on Tuesday. He felt this would be necessary, and even decisive, for the Delegates, but that is probably putting it too strongly. I discussed this afterwards with Richard, and we agreed to brood on a suitable formula over the weekend.

Halsey came in to say that he had had a phone call from my book-seller-publishing acquaintance in Paris, who was delighted with my quotation for one of his science books. It amounts to almost £10,000, and we both felt after that we might have added another £1000. Of course French costs are notoriously high. I told GJH to check with Ely House on their financial soundness.

❦

23 April, Friday

At Bedford Row in the morning for a legislation sub-committee to consider another draft of the Standard Conditions. The cttee consisted of Tony Fisher, Eric Dixon and his assistant Smyth, and me. We got through in just under the hour, so I spent a few minutes with Kenyon discussing the outcome of Tuesday's special meeting. He now wants me to attend the President's dinner with the Alliance presidents on Monday evening, and I agreed. He seems very anxious that I should be there to put my point of view as forcibly as at the Tuesday meeting. I am attending in the rather transparent guise of stand-in for Blackmore, the SW Alliance president.

Met John Hall at the Connaught Rooms for a special all-group lunch of Management Research Groups to which Robert Carr[139] had been

---

139 Robert Carr (1916-2012) was a Conservative MP who introduced the Industrial Relations Act in 1971 and was Home Secretary 1972-74. He became a life peer in 1976. Labour replaced the Act with their own modified version in 1974 when they returned to power.

invited as guest of honour. He is quietly impressive, but I was disappointed in his speech because it was simply a repetition of the speeches he has given many times before. Question time was more lively, tho' like all politicians he didn't really answer many of the pointed questions put to him. Tom Morland, Donald Mothersill, and Geoffrey Tillotson (the MRG president-elect) were also there. Caught the 4.15 back, in readiness for the Simmons dinner I have arranged at Teddy Hall in the evening.

❦

24–25 April

Uneventful weekend. A back from Coventry on Saturday.

❦

26 April, Monday

Preparing for discussion in FC on new web press. CHR wants me to give some idea of comparative costs. Difficult but necessary. He showed me a tiresome (partly) letter from Bruno asking whether there should not have been a committee to go into size, specification, etc! He didn't seem to realize that the whole thing had been flogged through the production manager committee about five times, and the new size agreed.

To London for BFMP finance and president's dinner at the Bath Club to tell the Alliance presidents about the planned succession to Kenyon and Alister. Some of the usual rather wild comment from the Home Counties & London, but Stanley Clarke and Val Curtis spoke up and in the end everything went off calmly. Stayed at the Whitehall Hotel. Quite comfortable, but smelling of stale cooking oil which is rather depressing.

❦

27 April, Tuesday

Federation Council in morning. Long discussion on finance, but I managed to get my piece on legislation said and done by 12.15, in time for me to catch my train for our own FC.

Rex Richards[140] appeared for the first time as a new Delegate. Alan Bullock the V-C also present for most of the time. Main subject was the continuing strain on cash resources. I presented my budget which the chairman thought must be conservative and I told him firmly that it wasn't. Then my proposed investment of £100,000 on a new web press was debated, with a favourable outcome. I now have full backing for it, and the assurance from the publishing departments that most of the medium-size dictionary work will stay here and not go to the Far East.

CHR reported that Roderick Henderson was a sick man and because of recent incidents at the Mill had been put on indefinite sick leave. Mill still very short of work and its state still very worrying.

From the breakdown of the London Business sales budget I was surprised to see what large sums were allocated to categories such as medical books that we never get asked to quote for. I tackled Bruno on this afterwards and I shall have to press much harder if we are to get our proper share of what is going.

28 April, Wednesday

Cold, sunny day. One manuscript down from CP, otherwise a poor post. Keyboards, now lighter by four operators, keeping going; Letterpress Room quite busy; Litho slack; Bindery patchy.

At 4.10 I went along with Harris to the Keyboard Room to talk to the men about the present workload. They listened quietly, and asked several good questions which I was able to answer with some semblance of conviction (I hope). Then I hurried on to a junior supervisors meeting in the canteen which was uneventful.

---

140 Sir Rex Richards (1922-2019), a member of the Waldock Committee (see Introduction) and a highly distinguished scientist, was, amongst other appointments, Warden of Merton College, Oxford, 1969-84, Vice-Chancellor of Oxford University 1977-81, and President of the Royal Society of Chemistry 1990-92. VR met him on 8 June 1971 (see below).

🦌

29 April, Thursday

Very light post again. The Monotype Corporation more than lived up to their promise for the Monophoto special equipment and phoned last evening to say that it would be ready for collection in London this morning. As Church was taking Prof. McHardy to Ely House he was able to get it here by lunchtime. Nugent was away when I phoned but I was able to speak to the *PED* editor, a pleasant-sounding young woman who was delighted to get the news. I promised the final specimen early next week.

Had a card from Batey to say that he goes into hospital for his operation next Tuesday. He seemed cheerful, but it will be quite an ordeal for both of them. Wrote a note to Henderson.

The first Works Advisory Committee for about 12 years without Fulton. Philip Walker has taken his place as House Father, and one of the benefits at our meeting was that several members spoke up for themselves and did not leave everything to Walker. I spoke at fair length on the state of work, tho' my report was not all that different from the last. I also mentioned the new web-offset press and its ultimate effect on the other departments. Quite a useful meeting in fact.

With Λ to the Playhouse to see Peter Hall's RSC production of Pinter's new play *Old Times* before it goes to the Aldwych. The usual hypnotic, vaguely menacing stuff, well acted, but thin on substance when stretched out to make two hours. Difficult to decide whether Pinter is a genius or just very talented. He has certainly created a world of his own that audiences seem eager to accept. The theatre was packed.

🦌

30 April, Friday

Elphick of PA came in at 11.30. He made a slightly better impression on me this time, tho' I still find a feeling of dissatisfaction left at the end of our meetings. He is now planning a one-day seminar of those connected with production, mainly because they are finding many of the problems apparently deep-seated emotional ones. We discussed whether I should attend and decided against on the grounds that the others would speak more freely (!) with no senior officer present. I should dearly like to hear what is to be said, all the same. My team will be Russell, Halsey, Harris, and Taylor, tho' Elphick reports strong animosity to Taylor. CP will send Cordy, Jonathan Price, and Tim Chester; and London Simon Nugent, McFarlane, and Sains. Elphick and Chadwick as leaders.

A survey of Slight's Bindery assignment with him, Wilkinson of PA, and Richard. It seems to be going well, tho' I wish that the workload were putting greater pressure on the new system while Slight is still here.

Farewells over a cup of tea to Miss Padden of the Bindery, and to Jack Clifford, who has been Maths Ship clicker for many years. Miss Padden, in talking about conditions in the outside world, said that 'you can see the writing on the wall'. I thought she was using the phrase as a cliché, but she went on to say that it was all in the Bible and what was happening was exactly as prophesied. I did not ask her where Hugh Scanlon and Jack Jones[141] fitted in the picture.

To supper in the evening at the Spicers, then on to Gosford Hill School (PJS is a governor) for a performance by their 'A Capella Choir', and very good it was.

May 1971

☙

1 and 2 May

To Cambridge in the morning, first to a lunch party given for Chester Kerr by Brooke Crutchley at Trinity Hall, then to stay with Colin at his hostel. We enjoyed the party: the Davids, the Kerrs, the Colmans, the Finleys, Ronald Mansbridge (*former manager of CUP in New York*) and his successor – Schulmann (*not* very attractive) – and Kingsford

---

141 Hugh Scanlon (1913-2004) and Jack Jones (1913-2009) were leaders respectively of the Amalgamated Engineering Union (AEU) and Transport and General Workers Union (TGWU) in the late 1960s and 1970s. They were known as the 'Terrible Twins' for opposing union reform during both Labour and Conservative periods in office.

(*Secretary to the Syndics, CUP, 1948-63, whom Dick David succeeded*). I sat between the Davids and tended to talk shop, A sat by Brooke, with Moses Finley[142] as her neighbour. She said after that he couldn't have been less interested in discourse, which surprised me because he had been very voluble with me when we were drinking Pyms no 1 beforehand.

Lovely day, cold wind. Took Col to Ely, then to a dullish Bresson film, *Une Femme Douce*, in the evening. A & I to King's Chapel for matins, then to the Plough at Fen Ditton for a pub lunch. Crowded but pleasant by the river. Left dear Col at about 3.30 and made for home. Wonderful weather, Cambridge looking marvellous.

🦌

3 May, Monday

Another lovely day, sunny and cool. Usual meetings, usual topics, no matters of great moment. CP announced two more manuscripts, which we badly need. RR pointed out to Davin that two tight programmes had been broken by them. Duly noted. I collected a couple of galley proofs of the *PED* specimen. They look satisfactory and I phoned Nugent to say that we should get the specimen away tomorrow or Wednesday.

🦌

4 May, Tuesday

Very quiet. Henderson came down for lunch and told me of his recent troubles. He has now given up drinking, which was their chief cause, and he seems to mean it. He thinks that a one-machine can still be run profitably in this country, provided the Scandinavian problem can be licked. There isn't much sign of that just now. I thought he showed little sign of strain in the conventional sense, but I suppose the effort of trying to sell the Mill, so doing away with his own job, and keeping it

---

142 Sir Moses Finley (1912-1986), Professor of Ancient History at Cambridge 1970-79 and Master of Darwin College 1976-82, was a Classical scholar whose books *The World of Odysseus* and *The Ancient Economy* proved both influential and controversial. He had been prosecuted in the early 1950s during the anti-Communist trials in his native USA.

running at the same time, has taxed him pretty hard. He doesn't know when his period of 'sick leave' is to end. He also speaks well of his new man, Nuttall.

Wrote to Bruno in response to a note from him telling me the number of London books now with me. I want many more, particularly straightforward ones.

Had Hemmings of PA in for coffee. He is devilling for Elphick & Chadwick mainly in the Composing Rooms. In talking I gathered that he also is puzzled by the LB production people's attitude and suggested, as Elphick had done earlier, that we ought perhaps to do more wining and dining of the production managers. A sad thought, particularly as he is probably right.

Asked Frost to make a discounted cash flow assessment of the web-offset press.

Met A from the 8.22 from B'ham, where she had been giving a reading. Peter Pelz arrived at 10.30 to begin making studies in Oxford for the mural he is going to paint at the top of our stairs.

🕯

5 May, Wednesday

Fon Boardman from the NY office came to lunch. I took him to the Tudor Cottage at Iffley, where we found the food and service good, and modestly priced. We also found a large car park, which I noted for the future.

Boardman did not have anything new to tell me. NY is still very much taken up with the problem of 'buying around' practised on a large scale by Blackwell and others. The result has been a damaging fall in NY direct sales, with no immediate prospect of an effective answer to the threat. I don't think there *can* be a really effective answer, because if a buyer in the States can buy more cheaply by going direct to an English bookseller than he can from NY, he will do so, particularly when his own funds may be restricted. Brett-Smith is very upset and clamours for action, but no one has yet suggested anything positive.

Toured the Works. Litho v low, with several machines standing. Film Room, on the other hand, now v busy, and likely to be even busier when the *PED* specimen has been approved.

JH ran a showing of a BBC TV schools film, most of which had been shot here last year. Well done, but trying to compress so much about book production into 20 minutes made it v obscure in places.

☙

6 May, Thursday

Another quiet day of talks and plans. Met Lankester & Stallabrass in my room during the afternoon to consider the future structure of the office and management. No firm conclusions but S said it had been helpful. He pushes forward at such speed and with such determination that I'm not surprised his management problems are growing rapidly.

☙

7 May, Friday

To QB Printers at Colchester with John Walker and James of Harris Intertype. Purpose was to see a cheap computer-typesetter − £6500. Basil Loven, the technical manager, looked after us. QB print weekly newspapers by web offset a vast number of them and run a 3 shift system. The place must be profitable. Equipment quite impressive, tho' I'm not at all sure that Walker's idea of harnessing the typesetter to our computer at Neasden so that we can give customers a typeset proof rather than computer print-out is likely to make economic sense. I have asked him to put his ideas on paper. On the way back he told me that he was leaning more and more towards taking the job he has been offered at Bristol University. He now knows so much about computer typesetting equipment that he would be quite a loss, but I see no chance in the short term of keeping him busy on our affairs, and we shall have to make other plans.

☙

8-9 May

Fine weekend. Audrey Wheeler[143] and Ben to stay. Gardening, talk, and not much else, but all delightful. Länges up as usual for Sunday lunch.

☙

10 May, Monday

Davin reported three more manuscripts on their way. Otherwise the workload is getting steadily worse. Most of the Litho Machine Room is now standing idle, the Letterpress ditto is rapidly getting on top of what is available, and the Bindery is also looking for more work to keep all sections going. Booth, one of our most experienced web-letterpress minders, has given his notice. For many years now he has been associated with a cycle business, and he now intends to make it whole-time. Rather a doubtful moment to change, but he is fairly shrewd and probably knows what he is doing.

Elphick of PA came in at 12.15 to discuss representation on next Wednesday's seminar. I told him I wanted Taylor to be present and he at last got the point. He told me of his visit to Clowes, which seems to have impressed him, particularly their estimating and production control sections.

Later in the day I had another PA meeting, this time with Wilkinson, Slight, RR and JH. This was to discuss possible ways of revising or refurbishing the incentive scheme. From his work on Bindery control, Slight reckons there should be another 30% increase in productivity to be got and he could be right. The upshot of an hour's talk was that Wilkie is to make a *free* appraisal of the alternatives and put forward some proposals.

At the end of the day Butler came in to report the outcome of a meeting he had just had with one John Weal, representing a body called Colmiri Holdings. He had telephoned the day before, saying rather mysteriously that he didn't want his inquiry 'to get about the trade'. He

---

143 Childhood friend of AR, and godmother to Colin, living in St Mawes in Cornwall.

was asking us to print and bind 100,000 copies of a 3-vol biography of the N. Korean leader Kim Il Sung – 300,000 copies in all. Not to be sniffed at, but dear Butler seemed quite unaware that what we were dealing with was rabid anti-American extreme left propaganda. I spoke to Colin about it, who seemed to be in the same two minds as I was: what a marvellous job for the business, and what a political hot potato for the OUP. He said he would inquire about Weal at St John's, and possibly get in touch with the Vice-Chancellor.

※

11 May, Tuesday

The V-C thought that I shouldn't touch the N Korean job, tho' Jack Thompson had been rather in favour. That decided the matter, and I drafted a note for Butler to sign, turning it down. A sad blow in one way, giving up a chance of producing 300,000 bound books, and printing them by litho too. Still, I think the decision is wise.

Called on Michael Turner at the Bodleian to choose a poster for a trial experiment. If it sells when the JJ exhibition is on, that will be an encouragement to go ahead with a series, which could build up into a useful amount of interesting work for the Litho Department. Turner suggested a most beautiful poster by Bonnard, done in 1894, but I felt the reproduction would be too difficult and costly for our first experiment. Instead we chose two mid 19th-century posters which can be done quite simply and quickly in black only.

After lunch met with JH and RR to discuss the problem posed by Walker's departure on 1 August. In the end decided to discuss with Reeve of Neasden before considering a successor in case R thinks we can get by for the time being by using his new man on a part-time basis. JH reported at the end of the day that Reeve had been here, they had talked, and we could therefore avoid a replacement, at least until next year. And so we shall leave it at that. We also discussed the problems of the Work Study Section. Eaglestone is a rapidly declining force, and Chatting, admirable fellow as he is, is a number two and not the weight to run the whole section. JH suggested we might think of shifting Sinclair, assistant manager in the Litho Department and quite a tough Scot, to run it. It has some attraction, and Sinclair is ambitious and might go off before he comes to succeed Coles, but there are disadvantages, and we came to no definite decision.

To Eltons for dinner.

☙

12 May, Thursday

BFMP Legislation Cttee at Bedford Row. Long agenda, mainly taken up with problems related to the impending VAT, and revision of our Standard Conditions. I couldn't get the meeting over until 12.30 but I caught the 1.15 comfortably and had lunch on the train with John Alden, who seems v worried just now with the prices other printers are quoting against him. He had also lost a job to a Spanish printer in Tenerife, a job he had been doing for many years. His price was £5000 inclusive, the Spaniard's £2000 delivered to Southampton. His is our Hong Kong problem over again.

Another Elphick session in the afternoon, mainly on arrangements for next week's seminar, which he now proposes to hold at Weston Manor. He told me that he was now working on three reports, financial, production control, and a short one on his visit to Clowes. I am very curious to see what they turn out to be like. I still can't place this man and his reports might help me to do that at least.

Wrote a rather difficult letter to Chester on changes when we have the new web-offset press. I have been putting this off because there are so many imponderables that I don't want to commit myself at this early stage, but I have now done my best for him.

Oxford Association AGM and dinner at the Upper Reaches Hotel, Abingdon. Blackmore, Alliance president, gave a prolonged and boring harangue at the meeting. Jack Thomas gave a fair speech in proposing the Association and John Alden conducted the whole evening easily and with some good witticisms to keep everyone happy.

❦

13 May, Thursday

Two more manuscripts down from CP, and other reprint & binding orders also, giving me the perhaps illusory impression that 'things are looking up'. Skelly had a good reception at Ely House yesterday and brought back the second Weizmann typescript that we have been waiting for so anxiously.

Frank Hauser had invited me to lunch at the Saraceno, mainly to discuss the possibility of issuing another Meadow Players souvenir programme, covering the whole of his 15-year regime. He said that the Arts Council doesn't know whether it is coming or going financially, and had embarrassed us very much by delaying payment of the grant already agreed. He is now going to translate another Sartre play, has written the musical numbers and the music for a panto (for which he would like to get Ronnie Barker), and was also planning to edit the late Harold Lang's mass of papers and produce some sort of a book from them.[144] He reckons HL had the keenest theatrical mind 'in world theatre'. May be a typical FH enthusiasm, of course, but it makes me curious to see some of his mss. I suggested he try Bodley Head as the most receptive publisher for this type of book. He also said that Judi Dench had had an unhappy love affair with 'that scoundrel, and he *is* a scoundrel, Leonard Rossiter' before finding and marrying Michael Williams. One curious thing was that Rossiter and Williams, who both came late to acting, started their working lives not only in the same insurance company but in the same room.

Frank was also full of satisfaction that Meadow Players has now taken over the old fire station which means that all other rented offices and workshops can be given up. Only snag is a net increase in our rent of £3000 pa. He seemed to take this quite calmly. Wonder whether we shall at our meeting tomorrow.

---

144 Harold Lang (1923-1970) was a British character actor who appeared in numerous B-films of the 1950s. As a stage actor and director he was a devotee of the pre-war Russian theatre director Stanislavski's training and rehearsal methods.

❦

14 May, Friday

I held a short meeting with those who will be representing the business at the PA seminar next Wednesday, emphasizing the general attitude and line I wished them to adopt. This was followed by my final meeting with Slight and Wilkinson to sum up their assignment in the Bindery. By all accounts S has done a v good job, practical, realistic, and without relying on too many fixed procedures.

George Richardson came to lunch. If I judge him rightly, he will turn out to be one of our most valuable Delegates. We had quite a talk on the duties of a Delegate in FC, which was useful from my point of view. Afterwards I showed him over the new buildings, which he said impressed him, particularly by their cleanliness.

Meadow Players directors meeting at the Playhouse. Gloom – heavily in debt, bad season, everything now depending on an increased grant from the Arts Council, which I'm not at all sure will be forthcoming. Frank decided to remain silent during our discussion, so that we had none of his bewildering arguments proving black is white that usually hearten our darkest hours. Difficult to see *how* we can carry on, but I expect we shall. Allegri seminar in Holywell Music Room in evening.

❦

15-23 May

On holiday. Allegri concert on Sat night – Haydn, Britten, Mozart. At the Sheldonian on Sun afternoon for *The Sea Symphony*, and *The Spring Symphony*. Britten's first TV opera *Owen Wingrave* in the evening.

To Radnor on Monday morning. Glorious week of almost continuous sunshine. Rain on the Sunday we returned to Oxford. Found that Hinkins & Frewin had finished the terrace extension and v nice it looks.

❦

24 May, Monday

Not too heavy an in-tray and no great disasters reported. I spent an hour with RR catechising him on the Wednesday seminar. He had left me a useful list of points and comments. Now we await PA's report. I was taken out for lunch at the Trout by Elphick, Chadwick, and Hemmings, at which we had a general discussion on the seminar and the lines of future action. I still get the impression that the more they delve into the problem the more difficult it seems, but several of the suggestions that came up in conversation sounded to me as though they could be helpful, particularly one on the simplification of the innumerable lists we use.

At the afternoon managers' meeting I learnt more about the state of work. No great change during the past week but we now have quite a useful pile of manuscripts to go into production. All departments still too lightly loaded, apart from the Composing Rooms, and yet I sense that things are a little more encouraging, and at the CP meeting earlier several more manuscripts were announced as being ready for us. The great lack is still of reprints, and there is no sign of a change for the better here.

My experimental poster reprints from the JJ Collection which I am doing for sale at the exhibition have been proofed and look v well on their tinted papers. I have suggested to Michael Turner that they should be sold at 25p at least to start with. The galleys of the exhibition catalogue are now with him so that he can select his illustrations.

Glyn Robbins of Meadow Players came in to discuss their souvenir programme. I have given him a firm deadline – 1 July – for everything, as with our holiday season in full swing at that time the eight weeks we shall have for production is none too long.

Elphick's report on his visit to Clowes appeared suddenly on my desk. Quite interesting, and no unfair comparisons made with us. What it does show is the difficulty of making comparison when the two houses, tho' producing books, are really faced with different problems. Of course his visit had been quick and superficial, and what he got was only a series of impressions, but I was interested to read them.

Latest grotesquerie in our new web-offset press proposal: RR reported that when he saw Philip Chester in London last week P said they weren't sure now that they did want to change the size of Hornby's *Advanced Learner's Dictionary*. What a crowd!

25 May, Tuesday

Catching up on correspondence in the morning, FC in the afternoon. Before the meeting Bruno came in to see me and I was able to tell him how exasperated I was getting at the shilly-shallying going on over the size of the new edition of *Hornby*. I also find it extremely irritating that he tends to adopt the attitude more of a college head – primus inter pares – towards his subordinates than of someone in command. I said I would put something on paper again, and he said he would talk to Philip Chester... He is a curiously elusive character.

A short FC meeting, well-attended. The one item that gave it any length was Wolvercote Mill and the treatment of Henderson. I can't think that Colin has really handled the situation sensibly, but the upshot is that H is to remain on 'sick-leave' with full-pay until 1 October; his contract will terminate at the end of the year, and from 1 October he won't go back in charge of the Mill but be retained on some sort of consultancy basis, yet to be defined. The V-C questioned all this in his usual blunt and vigorous way, but it went through, with his acceptance, on the line that as the future of the Mill is in such doubt it would not be sensible to think of advertising for or appointing a successor. The Mill is therefore going to be looked after by a committee, with CHR as chairman. Meanwhile, what H does with himself until October was not made clear, and this will not improve matters because his doctor was reported as saying that it would be best for him to get back to work and knowing H I'm sure he is right. It all seems an unholy muddle but none of the other officers present, as well as myself, felt that this was a matter they should comment on, and it was left to the Delegate members to debate.

Valerie Eliot came to Stanley Road for the evening, her arm still in a sling. Lots of chat and interesting stuff about Ezra Pound, Wyndham

Lewis and Stravinsky, and of course of Tom and Fabers. I hadn't realized that Fabers had been in such serious financial troubles. That is why, says V, de la Mare was forced by the banks to give up the chairmanship and become president. The old liquidity problem again.

❦

26 May, Wednesday

To Bedford Row for General Services and Organization meetings. Snack lunch with Eric Dixon. Farewell dinner at the Club next door for Ken Scroggs in the evening. He retires on Friday, and plans a four-month tour of the continent in his magnificent new Volkswagen caravan. He gave us a long and amusing account of his working life. Apprenticed here, then other jobs as a stereotyper with Brendons of Plymouth. Worked as a dilutee engineer with Lever Bros most of the war – he said that Vim, Glitto and Panshine all came from the same vats, and that Gibbs's Dentifrice was made from the same material with peppermint flavour and soap added. He was called up v late in the war – by mistake – and seems to have had a splendid time getting lost in Italy and Greece. We broke up at 9.30 and walked round to the car park to inspect the Volkswagen. We shall miss old Ken in some ways, in spite of his slow and sleepy manner. I am now combining the management of the Foundry with that of the Letterpress Department under Mansfield.

❦

27 May, Thursday

I had to give some time this morning to a distinguished Mexican whom the Govt wish to make much of because he can influence the sales of British books in his country. He had been in the Mexican government and for a time their ambassador in Washington. He was accompanied by Miss Bossy from our International Rights Department at Ely House, a female from the COI (*Central Office of Information*) with green-tinted eyelids, and a silent, chubby, smiling colleague who said nothing. The great man himself was also chubby of cheek, and eager to learn. I had to spend part of the short time we had in explaining that I was responsible for printing and not for publishing and – more difficult – that tho' belonging to the University we were not on the same footing as other University departments. As soon as I had handed the party over to O'Reilly I had to see one of my Composing Room apprentices to hand over the books he had chosen for his John Johnson award. Then I had to prepare a few words to say to those assembled in the Library for the presentation of a farewell cheque to Ken Scroggs.

After lunch and further short meetings I caught the 3.35 for London to attend, in full evening togs, the commemoration dinner of the Grocers' Company to which Elliott Viney had invited me. The old hall had been burnt down about 3 years ago and recently rebuilt on a solid and lavish scale. The occasion was a 'splendid' one. I sat between the Lord Crowther[145] and Bernard Shore,[146] so that I was able to talk political economy on one side and music on the other. I was thankful that I had refused Elliott's request to reply for the guests because his own speech was one of the very best I have heard, and it would have been extremely difficult to follow. Not that Sir John Wolfenden,[147] who did reply, spoke badly: he did well, but E's was the kind of speech that should be left to stand on its own.

Crowther is v pro-Common Market, mainly on the grounds that inflation is psychological and going in may at last bring home the connection between cause and effect. He agreed that no one yet had any kind of satisfactory solution. He also told me that when he was editing the *Economist*, the closer he was to a deadline the easier he found it to write a leader. He usually wrote them at home on the Wednesday night. He is now in his third year as chairman of the Royal Commission on the British Constitution. He hopes to report next year.

---

145 Lord (Geoffrey) Crowther (1907-1972) was a transformative editor of the *Economist* 1938-56, later becoming Chairman, and Foundation Chancellor of the Open University from 1960.
146 Bernard Shore (1896-1985) was a distinguished viola player, as well as a composer and author.
147 Sir John Wolfenden (1906-1985), Director of the British Museum 1969-73, chaired the Committee whose Wolfenden Report of 1957 recommended the decriminalization of homosexual acts between consenting adults in private.

Bernard Shore gave his opinion of conductors. Barbirolli and Sargent – out. Beecham and Boult – in. Younger conductors not much good. A great admirer of Boult.

Leonard Kenyon drove me back to the Whitehall Hotel and we agreed that plans for his and Alister's succession were going well. Sam Wright has accepted Alister's succession and I don't think he will now be tempted away.

❦

28 May, Friday

Ben's birthday. I met him, A, and Peter at Schmidt's in Charlotte Street for a birthday lunch which went very well. After lunch we went on to the Book Bang at Bedford Square, where A was to meet Charles Monteith and give a reading of her poems at 3.30. She gave a splendid performance before a good audience seated on beer crates in a plywood tent. Outside noises were a distraction but she made herself heard through it all. The annoying thing was to have no copies of her poetry books in print and on sale. The audience had to be content with Monteith's announcement of her next book next year. Feliks Topolski[148] was doing portraits outside at £3 a time and had quite a queue of patient sitters alongside him. I hope the whole thing is successful but an entrance fee of 50p for adults is something of a deterrent.

❦

29 May-31 May

Whitsun bank holiday. Sat v wet so Tim, A & I went to see Frankenheimer's *The Fixer*, which was being shown with the Marx Bros *Circus* at the Moulin Rouge. Sunday also wet, Monday much better and devoted mainly to the garden.

---

148 Feliks Topolski (1907-1989), Polish-born expressionist painter who came to Britain in 1935, was an Official War Artist during World War II and depicted Queen Elizabeth II's coronation in 14 friezes. He painted portraits of HG Wells, Graham Greene, Harold Macmillan, Aneurin Bevan and many others.

June 1971

❦

1 June, Tuesday

Pat Cox now on holiday in Scotland. The weather is settled again, and she should be luckier than those who chose last week.

Rang up Mrs Batey. To my surprise Charles came to the phone. He is quite well again and feeling on top of the world. A real Mother Hubbard's dog.

Workload in Keyboards now better than it was, partly because we have moved two operators up into the Filmsetting Rooms to use the new Datek keyboards we have put in to punch the Crockford tapes for the Neasden computer. Elsewhere we are still only ticking over. On the other hand the estimators are hard pressed, which is a good sign for the future.

Poor old Arthur Foster, whose son died suddenly last year, is in the Radcliffe after some form of heart attack. I went to see him in Lichfield Ward. He looks well enough but told me that he had had three very painful attacks that really knocked him back. As he was to retire at the end of this month we shall not see him at work again, I fear.

Looked in on the Filmsetting Section. Beckley now hard at work clearing up *The Waste Land* pages in time for Valerie's visit on the 15th. The JJ exhibition catalogue is also going well.

Had Bridgewater, our alcoholic night porter, in to say goodbye on his retirement last Friday. He came to us as a machine feeder in 1923 and according to him spent 'many happy hours' here. He is easily made garrulous by the bottle but as this was 5 o'clock our meeting passed off fairly quickly and quietly.

Peter Pelz arrived at Stanley Road in order to work on our new mural.

❦

2 June, Wednesday

A fairly quiet morning. Cornell University wrote further about their plan to follow the 5-volume *Malpighi* which we produced for them a few years ago with the *Correspondence* which may be even longer. But they want to know how long it will take – one of those useless questions publishers will ask, either to comfort themselves or the author. We also had instructions to proceed with an Islamic Diary, quite useful for the Litho Department, when they get it. In fact we are now getting some sizeable orders, particularly for the reference books: Scholes *Companion to Music*, *COD*, and Hornby *ALDCE*.

Help the Aged board meeting in the afternoon. Not too drawn out, and over by 4.15. Dined at St Edmund Hall, many guests, including Hume-Rothery's widow. Lively evening.

3 June, Thursday

Four manuscripts in this morning, one of them the history of Barclays Bank – a useful piece of straightforward setting. I called in on Michael Turner at Bodley. The proof posters are now on sale at 25p and are going at the rate of 4 or 5 a day. As they are not at all well displayed in their book and postcard area in the Divinity Schools this is quite encouraging and I am hoping to persuade Shackleton to do many more.

Ben was at home when I got back for lunch, and v lively & cheerful. Peter painting furiously up in Colin's room. We have kept out of the way and so have no idea as to what our mural will look like.

Toured the Works after lunch. Even the Litho is not despondent, and Sinclair, who is in charge while Coles is on holiday, is quite cheerful about the slight improvement. Mansfield is also away and Tyrell in his place is also 'in good heart' with the workload.

Later I saw briefly one of the members of our Nigerian branch in Ibadan. They want me next year to take on the printing of some of their schoolbooks – editions of perhaps 300,000 in two colours – because the local printer is swamped now that conditions are more settled and educational plans are in full swing. This is encouraging, and just the sort of work we need for the Litho Department.

I heard that Cyril Piper, now 77, was back in the Radcliffe with some form of internal bleeding. I went to see him in Bever Ward. Amazingly lively and cheerful, but the poor man is practically a skeleton. They have been giving him pills and he hopes to be back home again in a few days.

Wilkinson of PA has now produced a draft of his proposals for overhauling and simplifying our incentive scheme. He wants to make a start in the Bindery, at a cost of some £10,000. We meet next week but I plan to go over his proposals with RR and JH at our lunch meeting in the Club tomorrow.

❦

4 June, Friday

The lunch meeting was useful. We discussed the size of our present labour force; possible changes in London representation; the management succession in the Letterpress Dept; and the latest PA proposals for revising our incentive scheme. The last took up a good part of our time, partly because we are all rather dubious about some of the points made so blithely by the PA supervisor, Wilkinson. However, we are meeting him with other PA brass on Monday afternoon, when we shall be able to cross-question them and judge from their reaction how strongly they believe in their ideas.

❦

5–6 June

To Cofton Pumps on Sat morning to meet the Pennants. V cold northeast wind with overcast marred the outing, altho' the old house and beam engine, and the people restoring and running it, were interesting enough. A splendid old boy in the rear yard was stoking up a model traction engine he had made. He told us it had taken him about 3000 hours and we could well believe it.

Peter Pelz had completed our mural on Sat evening – v exciting and it delights us.[149] A great struggle to hoist it into place on Sunday, but we managed it in the end. Donald Reeves, who came in the afternoon to pick up Peter, was also enthusiastic, and it certainly looks v fine, glowing away at the top of the stairs.

☙

7 June, Monday

Pat Cox's second week of holiday. Rang Mary Bland to arrange a meeting for next Thursday.

We have now had in so many manuscripts from the CP that at our meeting this morning I had reluctantly to turn away two more, one of them a science book, because of the 5 offered 3 of them had to come to me. I think we are rapidly approaching our earlier state in the Composing Rooms – great pressure and delays – which will be a pity. Elphick has now produced his report on the seminar. It tries to tackle the Comp Room problem and we must certainly experiment on the lines he suggests; but I can't see any miraculous cure for what is in effect a more-or-less permanent shortage of skilled men. On the reprint side, of course, our situation is still fairly grim, with no sign of improvement. CHR himself is gloomy about prospects: the CP has suffered a substantial loss for the last financial year, and simply increasing our selling prices doesn't do us much good when most of our main customers have restricted funds.

Met the other PA group at 4. Went through Wilkinson's survey of our incentive scheme with JH and RR. We would like to revise the Bindery scheme to start with, but although politically to do so at a time when we are in trading difficulties might help, any sudden increase in productivity – W speaks of 25% – would be hard to cope with unless we were to make nearly 60 people redundant. At the end I was non-committal and told Ashworth and Wilkinson that I would consider the proposal again when they had submitted their complete survey.

---

149 The large painted panel depicts various elements of Oxford architecture in an impressionistic style, arranged around the central image of the pear tree in V and A's garden, with the Cherwell river and someone punting flowing into the middle of it.

Gardner and his charging and estimating people have now moved into the Counting House extension and seem very pleased with the move. The area had last been used as an overflow white paper warehouse, but with the changes at Jordan Hill we no longer need the space.

A & I to the Woodwards in the evening, to talk Sicily. V kind and helpful. Mrs W, née Bryant, had been taken on by John Johnson in 1930 to help Bill Collett soon after JJ had reorganized the office.

❦

8 June, Tuesday

Perishing cold in the office, dull and overcast outside, as it has been for some days. Clamour from the departments for heat, and Ashby had to raise steam.

RR away at Kettering with Coles and others to discuss the final details of the web-offset press with Timsons. Still no confirmation from Chester or Bruno in London of the size we propose. Davin confirmed within a few days of my letter.

Elphick brought in his report on our financial control, with proposals for its improvement. At first glance they appear helpful, although his approach is entirely commercial, and I shall now have to study it carefully with Frost and RR. Elphick seems happier in dealing with figures than with general policies or people, and his suggestions in this area of the business could be valuable. They are certainly expensive.

Had another new Delegate, Rex Richards, in for lunch and a quick look at the new buildings. He was a member of the Waldock Committee and a most able and likeable man. He showed particular interest in the Filmsetting Section, where we are fortunately very busy.

Later I called in Ken Stewart to discuss the younger members of his section. I am not satisfied that they are getting all the guidance from him that they should have, and seem to be spending far more time in the careful finishing of layout than is necessary for our purposes. He puts the responsibility for this on Garland upstairs, who has been demanding this sort of high finish. I told Stewart what I wanted him

232

to do, that I didn't want to increase the staff of his section while we are cutting down in other parts of the business, and that I would talk to Davin about their requirements. The cost of CP bookjackets to the CP must have increased enormously since Garland (now working part-time, I'm told) took over.

☙

9 June, Wednesday

A day clear of fixed engagements. Quite heavy rain, and still v cool. Drafted a piece on 'The Printer's Task' for James Moran's piece in *The Times*. Hope to see Brooke Crutchley with it at the Meynell lunch tomorrow.

Butler reported on his London visit which seems to have gone well. He brought back some useful reprints for estimate – small booklets, really, used overseas and formerly printed by people like Butler & Tanner, Mackays, etc, so they can't be feeling too happy at seeing this work going back to Oxford.

The John Johnson catalogue proofs are all back and being corrected for machine. I sent Turner an estimate for reproducing the Bonnard poster: it should allow Bodley to sell it at about £1 a copy, and at that sort of price I think it should go fairly quickly. I told him that I could begin machining at once if he wanted copies in time for the exhibition, tho' they couldn't be ready in time for the opening.

Management Club AGM and dinner at the Management Centre, that hideous building in the wooded hillside above the Kennington Road. Good attendance, excellent dinner, amiable chairmanship by John Allen, no set talk. The Club seems rather healthier than I was beginning to think, but that may have been the effect of the dinner. Norman Leyland acted as host in the absence of his successor at the centre, Tricker. Leyland said at dinner, talking of hi-fi and his own equipment, that he had all Bang & Olufsen with 32 loudspeakers. I wondered how interested he is in music.

❦

10 June, Thursday

More rain. To London with A, Harry and Ella Carter for the lunch at
Nash House in honour of Francis Meynell's 80th birthday. He himself
looks frailer than when I last saw him at the Curwen dinner, tho' he
seemed lively enough. Other guests included the Botley Simons, John
Carters, Stones,[150] Milner Gray,[151] Cleverdon,[152] Tony Bell, John Dreyfus,
and Dick de la Mare. No speeches, but a few words from Bobby Simon
and Milner Gray. FM said thank you, and as the atmosphere then began
to thicken slightly with English constraint I told a brief story about a
book I had bought years ago that had FM's signature on the end paper.

After lunch A & I went along to the new Faber offices in Queen's
Square. Charles Monteith met us there and showed us over its several
floors. Valerie Eliot had been rather disparaging of the place but we
both thought that it looked well. We saw Dick de la Mare's penthouse
office – the presidential office – and were surprised to see the repulsive
colour scheme, peppered green walls and yellow ceiling, he had chosen
as a setting for the large book and china cabinets brought over from
his old and handsome room in Russell Square. We found him hard at
work in Giles's office, which he is sharing until the penthouse is ready.
Also had a delightful few minutes with Alan Pringle (*Faber editor*), who
disclosed that Larry Durrell[153] was over here and signing copies. I was
glad to be introduced to Phillips, their new production manager, and we
saw Peter du Sautoy (*Faber Vice-Chairman*) briefly before we came away.

---

150 Reynolds Stone (1909-1979) was a renowned wood engraver, typographer and painter. His
daughter Phillida Gili is a well-known book illustrator.

151 Milner Gray (1899-1997) helped establish industrial design as a recognized profession in
Britain. He wrote *Lettering for Architects and Designers* and in 1964 advised British Railways on
its new corporate identity.

152 Douglas Cleverdon (1903-1987) was a distinguished bibliophile, bookseller and radio producer. He commissioned Eric Gill to design the fascia lettering for his bookshop in Bristol in the
early 1930s, which formed the prototype for the Gill Sans typeface. It was here that VR met Gill,
whose Perpetua typeface of 1929 inspired the name of the Perpetua Press.

153 AR had, while at Faber, formed a close friendship with Durrell (1912-1990) when the firm
was considering for publication his avant-garde prose work *The Black Book*. He pronounced her
poetry 'the real egg'.

11 June, Friday

A busy morning getting through correspondence and taking the usual 10 o'clock meeting before getting away to Eastbourne and the Federation Congress. I sent off my draft piece for Moran to Brooke and managed to have a fairly full talk with RR on his visit to Timsons at Kettering. All his party seem to have been impressed by the improvements T have made in the design and engineering of their web presses since we put in our last in 1963. They have in their factory at present a new web letterpress machine, delivering 2x48s, destined for Richard Clay. As it is intended to print the standard size paperbacks it offers no competition to ours – assuming we go ahead with it, because I have still not had any confirmation from London.

I travelled to Eastbourne by train, via Victoria. I reached the Grand Hotel at 6.15, in blazing sunshine – a change after a morning of steady rain in Oxford, to be greeted by that good man Wyndham-Smith, who is acting as one of the stewards. My room is quite pleasant, tho' it doesn't face on to the sea front. But at least it has TV and radio! I dined with Alistair and Jean Stewart, still sunburnt from their Sicilian holiday; and later, at the reception (Derys Knill-Jones did *not* ask 'where's Anne', which was tactful of her!) I chatted for a time with George Wood of Harris-Intertype. While I was standing in the centre of the floor, trying to grab a glass of champagne among the milling throng, a feminine arm encircled my waist from behind. I was about to imprint it with a kiss, at the risk of breaking my neck, when I managed to swivel round to find the redoubtable Mrs Val Curtis beaming upon me. I managed to extricate myself with some dignity and made for Ron Hudson whom I'd spotted in the distance. Receptions can be hazardous.

I got to bed quite early, 11.15 in fact, only to find I'd left my pyjamas behind and so had to join that band of cads remarked on by Peter Sellers who sleep in their vests.

❧

12 June, Saturday

Overcast again but not too cold. I skipped breakfast and got to the opening of the business sessions punctually at 9.15. The second of the three speakers, Philip Sadler, director of the Ashridge Management College, gave a first-rate talk on 'Business Environment 1980'. The other two were fair and poor respectively. But the morning can be counted a success.

After lunch I strolled into the centre of the town, mainly to buy a pair of pyjamas and a new pair of black shoes. The shopping centre seemed almost totally made up of shoe shops, and in the end I more or less spun a coin and bought some at Manfields.

On the coach out to the Royal Pavilion I sat with Colonel Lockwood. He told me that he retired completely a month ago but he still hopes to attend the annual congress. At the Pavilion we had a pleasant past-presidents' dinner in the Adelaide Room, one of the suite of rooms on the upper floor which has now been fully redecorated. In fact all redecoration has been finished. The dancing in the Music Room made a fine scene, tho' I can't think that the Prince would have been much impressed by the would-be pop group of what seemed to be Burmese players. I strolled around and chatted with Michael Smith of the Institute of Printing, Roy Fullick, who was being catty about William David, editor of *Punch* (RF prints it), and I got away at 11.15, which wasn't too bad. Not as bad as the caterer's wine dished out to the multitude.

❧

13 June, Sunday

Sunny and warm, with a few clouds in the sky. The church service at All Saints was taken by its vicar, PM Renouf, a youngish man who gave a refreshingly lively and direct talk, well suited to his special congregation. My heart warmed to him particularly when he referred to A's prayer for printers as 'that wonderful prayer'. Everyone spoke appreciatively of the way in which he conducted the service. It was slightly marred by some scrannel-shrieking from the middle-aged ladies who made up the choir.

Cocktails and lunch with the President. I sat opposite tomorrow's speaker, Joe Hennage, an entertaining and wealthy printer from the US. He let fall that he had recently laid in 3000 bottles of French wine. No wonder the prices go up and up.

At the Congress Theatre in the evening we were entertained with a remarkable piano recital by John Lill, who played two Beethoven sonatas in the first half and a selection from Chopin for the second. Very powerful, 'brilliant' playing.

Finally to a party given by the East Anglian Alliance. I managed to have a good talk with Wyndham-Smith, and shorter ones later with David Ensor and Charles Birchall. We had all been rather disappointed with John Jarrold's talk on web and sheet offset at the afternoon's business session. Birchall's view was that John played things close to his chest as he didn't want to give anything away.[154] It was certainly uncontroversial. I tried to get some argument going but it soon faded out, and the large audience moved off placidly to tea.

❧

14 June, Monday

Wind and rain. Usual tedium of the AGM. But Joe Hennage livened things up with an excellent and intriguing talk on business, and his business, in the States, and particularly in Washington DC. He also presented us with a full-colour portrait of Ben Franklin.[155]

After the coffee break we ended with a panel session which included Joe H, and also Peter Robinson, now managing director of BPC. He impressed, mainly because he packed good sense into a few words. As panel sessions go, it wasn't bad. I lunched with the Ashridge speakers, Sadler and Barry. Conversation didn't flow too easily, and I found myself working hard to keep things going.

Quite heavy rain all afternoon, which I spent in reading *Dead Souls*

---

154 John Jarrold ran the eponymous printing firm in Norwich (now closed).
155 Benjamin Franklin (1706-1790), one of the Founding Fathers of the United States, and an extraordinary polymath – writer, inventor, diplomat, philosopher, politician – was also a renowned printer and newspaper man.

and in listening to an intriguing piece by Stockhausen. Then preparations for the reception and banquet. The chief guest, Chris Chataway, was held in Parliament by a 3-line whip for a vote on children's milk, and so we had to make do with a substitute from his office. He started quite well with a good story but then followed it with an account of the GPO and its troubles etc etc. Harry Knill-Jones got through his presidential toast in his usual workmanlike way, but we had rather more speech-making than I thought was necessary at the badging ceremony. Fulsome praises were sung by practically everyone,[156] and my head began to spin with 'I cannot let this occasion pass'... 'you would not wish me to...' 'it gives me great (enormous, sincere) pleasure', and all the desultory clapping that had to follow.

The meal was good, the wines poor. I sat between Lady Ebbisham, a straightforward, Downe House type, and Henry Davy's wife, a lass from S Shields whom I thought a honey. She taught domestic science at Ledbury and she now takes a hand with a repertory company near Newcastle. We had enough to talk about to keep us going comfortably until the speeches.

After all this I discreetly retired to my room for a rest. I emerged half an hour later to watch Derys Knill-Jones giving away the sports prizes, drink two glasses of orange, take tea with Eric Dixon and his wife, before returning to bed at 12.15. So I had a fairly quiet evening of it.

❦

15 June, Tuesday

Still raining hard tho' better weather is promised. Caught the 10.03 from Eastbourne. Found A & C having lunch on the terrace. C with a fine-looking red beard. Stopped for coffee before going down to the Press. Not too many problems to deal with. Maddening and shillyshal-lying letter from Philip Chester about the new web-press – I can't make out *what* they are up to in London. Saw a sheet of the JJ exhibition catalogue – we have made a beautiful job of it. Miss Briggs rang from

---

156 For VR's year as BFMP President 1968-69.

Bodley to order 1000 copies of the two posters, which was good news. Valerie Eliot due here tomorrow, when I shall be in London, to pass final proofs of *The Waste Land*. I had a quick look through them with Butler and they appear to be in good order. Poor Simmons has died at last. Funeral Thursday.

🦌

16 June, Wednesday

As Chairman of Legislation Cttee I met the President of the Publishers Association and his officers, with Eric Dixon and Harry Lott, to concert action on VAT. Useful, short meeting. Rayner Unwin[157] agreed to write to the minister to emphasize importance to publishers of zero-rating.

Then on to Design Centre to inspect plans and texts for the printing design exhibition which is to open next month. Met John Branch, in the absence of Fellowes, and with the designer and script writer Sally Jay went over what they have prepared. Later we saw the exhibition itself being constructed in the Design Centre. John Shepherd was with me, and we agreed over a pub lunch around the corner that it should be a great success, especially with the general public.

With A & C to *Amphitryon 38* at the New Theatre. Rather fussy production, good ensemble acting by Christopher Plummer and Geraldine McEwan. Production by Olivier was hampered by the vast number of pillars used in Malcolm Pride's elaborate set.

🦌

17 June, Thursday

Frantically busy day. Maddening letter from Philip Chester in reply to mine pressing for confirmation of the web machine size. He said that he was now going on holiday and so had asked Nugent to speak to Bruno...

Saw Hemmings and Slight at 10 to discuss their radical proposals

---

157 Rayner Unwin (1925-2000), Chairman of the publisher Allen & Unwin, and Publishers Association President in 1971. As a child aged 10 in 1936, he wrote a report for his father, Stanley Unwin (founder of the firm), recommending publication of JRR Tolkien's *The Hobbit*. In 1951 he took on *The Lord of the Rings* for the firm.

for the revision of our production control system. At a hasty reading it seems good in parts, though I think they are far too sanguine about the possibilities of forward planning. Had to break off at 10.45 to slip round to Help the Aged for a review of the annual accounts. I got away within the hour, back in time to see Geoffrey Keynes. He said he was delighted with our work on *Blake Studies*, and with the Godine book. His main purpose was to leave a copy of his Donne Bibliography with me as a style pattern for the new edition now with the CP. I wish he would leave such things with them, but he likes to do things in this way and I am quite happy to humour him. He is an astonishingly vigorous 84.

Simmons' funeral at Botley after lunch. I felt very sorry for that splendid widow of his. A small group at the church, tho' plenty of relatives, fortunately. Chalmers came with me and there were several representatives of the St John Ambulance division.

Miss Pantzer, redoubtable editor of the BM Short Title Catalogue, is over on a business visit from Harvard, and came to see me. We had a useful talk about the final specimen, which I criticized on several counts. But the committee seems to have set its heart on keeping the revision I deplore, and she has also.

I gave her tea, and we met again for the opening of the JJ exhibition by the V-C at Bodley. He made an excellent and appropriate opening speech, and I was relieved to see the hundred advance copies of the catalogue ready by the entrance. The Librarian amused me by saying that the way to make sure the catalogues of an exhibition were ready on time was to invite the printer to the opening. I urged on him and on several curators the idea of reproducing & selling more pieces from the collection. I hope it may have some effect.

❦

18 June, Friday

As I had few visitors I managed to get through a fair amount of correspondence, including a letter to Elphick commenting on his seminar report. He is now anxious to arrange a meeting of the senior officers.

Valerie Eliot has been in the front library the whole week. She assured me as I passed by her table that her corrections were only minor, but all this delay means reducing our already tight schedule for positives by three days. And now I hear that the Litho Department is full up with work for the whole of July – so quickly can the scene change! Readers Digest want 40,000 copies of their 3-volume *Encyclopaedic Dictionary* by mid-August – which means getting all the big machines back on to double-shift – and we also have several large orders from or via Ely House for Nigeria. Our Filmsetting Section is hard-pressed, and if much more work comes into the house for the Composing Rooms we shall have trouble in keeping our dates. So the outlook is more cheerful than I dared to hope two months ago.

The most tricky problems at the moment relate to prices. As the market is still depressed, very tight prices are being quoted, and I am continually getting reports that many of my prices are too high. I have already tightened several of them, and it looks as though I am to be squeezed even more if I want to get the volume we need. I still have some elbow room for this sort of thing, and I'm certainly not going to let good work pass us by, but I have less scope than I had twelve months back.

To Aldens for dinner, v pleasant. Hughes, the head of Ruskin, was there with his charming Scottish wife, and two other guests. The house is vast, with a fine view. It must be draining dear John pretty severely.

19-20 June

A to Bristol to fetch Ben. A & V to concert on Sunday evening in honour of Jack Westrup[158] at Holywell Music Room. Marion Milford and Peter Reynolds were singing in an interminable piece by Locke that went on for 1½ hours. We left at the interval and so missed *King Thamos* by Mozart, but we felt we had taken as much as we could manage.

---

158 Sir Jack Westrup (1904-1975), musicologist, writer, conductor and composer, was Heather Professor of Music at Wadham College, Oxford, and deeply involved in musical life in the city, conducting variously the Opera Club, University Orchestra and the Bach Choir. He wrote books on Purcell, Handel, Liszt, Bach and Schubert.

In the afternoon A & V went over to Standlake to look at the cedar-wood shed V wants. They are on display in a large area by the roadside, run by Cotswold Building Co.

❧

21 June, Monday

Still cold and overcast, but no rain. Must be the coldest June ever. Not much of importance in the post. The deputy education officer of Hertford wanted to know something about our rule for 'ize' and 'ise' endings, otherwise it was simply a matter of bits and pieces. Davin is away and we met the Secretary and Tim Chester only at the 11 o'clock meeting. Two more manuscripts reported as on their way, and possibly a few reprints.

I gave CHR a copy of an article from *Management Today*, 'How to plan survival'. I had read it some months ago and felt it had some lessons for us in it. I shall be interested to have his comments.

Letterpress Rooms still light, says Mansfield. The other managers are now well loaded for the next 4 weeks, the filmsetters overloaded.

❧

22 June, Thursday

A rang to say that Colin had got a II.i! Great excitement.

At last – sunshine and warmth. A quiet day, and I was able to make good use of it by studying more closely the PA reports and recommendations. I made a series of notes on them, and decided how I wanted Richard to deal with the next stage of the report on production control. This report cannot just be issued to all those affected by it because it recommends the merging of two sections and the appointment of a senior 'overlord'. To let this recommendation go out to Halsey or Taylor would only create uncertainty, and so I revised the PA paper, omitting all references to the senior appointment. Fortunately this could be done without weakening the main items.

I had Mrs Salmon in for some coffee. She doesn't look all that well, although she says she is very much better than she was. She mentioned Ian O'Reilly, whom John Hall is grooming as a possible successor. She wonders, as indeed I do, whether he has it in him to develop the weight required for the job. He is now 24, remarkably good academically and with paper, but he seems rather too much of a backroom boy at present. It is always difficult to know how someone like that will respond to greater challenges. I hope he does justify John's faith in him, but I was interested to get Mrs Salmon's opinion, as she herself works quite closely with him.

A man from Radio Oxford called in at 4. He wanted to talk with someone who knew John Johnson, and Michael Turner has put him on to me. He did not stay long and the interview went off smoothly enough, altho' I found it a little distracting to have the microphone thrust in front of my face with gleaming eyes and a beard in close support.

To the *Merchant* at Stratford with A & Colin. Lovely run in the early evening sunshine. Splendid and ingenious settings by Timothy O'Brien; good performances by Emrys James and Judi Dench. In spite of our remembrance of earlier reviews we thought it a success.

❦

23 June, Wednesday

Another quiet day. I decided not to go to the Encaenia or the garden party in the afternoon, which left me more time to study the PA reports and work out a provisional plan of action.

Harold Hugo, with his usual generosity, has sent me another parcel of superb specimens, including the Dürer catalogue that he had mentioned when he was here, and *Zen Paintings & Calligraphy*, a most beautiful piece of typography and printing.

I toured part of the Works later in the afternoon, the Bindery in particular, where I came upon a stack of bad work and wrote a scathing note to Chalmers about it when I got back to my desk.

Not very much in the post, but a few reprint enquiries should be useful if anything comes of them.

❦

24 June, Thursday

Midsummer Day, and still sunny and warm. Another quiet day for me, leaving me time to catch up with several matters I had been forced to put on one side. Talked with Boyce about the possibilities of using our graduate readers on copy preparation, and found rather to my surprise that he was strongly in favour of trying it. I had to break off our talk in order to meet Reeve, our computer expert at Neasden, with Richard and Frost, to discuss progress or the lack of it on the various projects he has in hand. We all think that more drive should be put into the experimental computer-assisted-composition program, particularly in view of what Cambridge are said to be doing; and I said that I would write to the Secretary and the Publisher on this because I should be on holiday when the next committee meeting is to be held.

Kelly came in to report on his London visit. There is definitely more work about, and one welcome piece of news was an inquiry about a possible reprint of the Jubilee Bible, which most of us thought had been killed off by the RSV version. It could be for 25,000 or 50,000. When I signed the estimate I was appalled to see that our charge is now one third more than it had been in 1967. Also saw Boswell and told him in confidence that Henderson had resigned as Controller of the Mill and would become Resident Consultant from 1 July. I did not enlarge on this change, but left him to draw his own conclusions, which he is quite capable of doing.

The CP accounts have just been circulated to members of Finance Committee. They make very gloomy reading – sales down, and a loss of £195,000 on the year's trading. There are a few bright patches but we are obviously in for a difficult time unless there is some dramatic improvement in our overseas sales.

I also spent some time with Frost in going through Elphick's proposals in financial control. He, Frost, has not yet finished his detailed study of them, but broadly speaking he thinks they are useful and can be accepted.

Eltons to dinner. A nice party, with Ben and Colin to entertain and help us.

❦

25 June, Friday

Two more good manuscripts down from CP this morning, and several interesting enquiries from London. GBT reported on his meeting with the production managers, and they seem to have resolved a few at least of our outstanding problems with forecasting shortages, reading procedures, etc.

Ron Harris came in at 9.45, and over a cup of coffee told me that he wanted to take a week of his holiday next week. His reason was that he was still 'tensed up' because of the dispute he had had with Boyce a few weeks ago. The underlying trouble between these two excellent men is that Boyce is jealous of his position as head reader and resents being classed as just another of Harris's subordinates. He thinks that he should be answerable direct to the Printer, and in fact I do often consult him directly on reading matters. But I have always regarded Harris as being in charge of the whole composing side, and that includes reading. I must now make this quite clear to Boyce. I don't think this would be necessary if it had not been first for his wife's illness and then his own. He has grown more moody during the last year, and the other supervisors in the Composing Rooms find him difficult to deal with. It is an interesting problem and I hope to resolve it, at least partly, when I see Boyce on Monday morning. I then hope to see both of them together when Harris is back.

Monty Shaw came to lunch, bringing with him the material for the first publication of the reincarnated Merrion Press. I shall have to give him a revised estimate but most of the material is straightforward enough. He jumped at my suggestion that he might issue a book on our wooden alphabets. I had offered it to John Ryder but nothing has come of it, so that I felt free to offer it to Monty. I also said that Anne might like to edit something for him, and he has asked me for suggestions.

❦

26–27 June

Christopher Bradshaw called in at 11.30 on the Sat morning to talk about the training of designers. He is a tremendous talker but not a bore or insensitive and we had quite a useful discussion, although I don't think the shortage or quality of training is all that serious.

Kate arrived for a short weekend. Michael Milford also turned up, and reminded me that he had written to ask me for a copy of *Hart's Rules* some years ago. He had also tried to cadge a copy from Richard Russell when they met by chance in Scotland.

Showery, April-like weather. Managed to get my concrete edge strip laid along the kitchen-garden path, rather to A's disgust. I have assured her that grass and the passing of time should almost obscure it.

I took Ben to the station on Sat morning to start him on the first leg of his holiday in Austria. He looked like a hermit crab with his enormous knapsack and his guitar fastened to it. He is staying in London until Wednesday, when his little party motors down to Dover for the crossing that night. He was very cheerful tho' his voice is still not right.

Wrote to a Mr Pardoe, who had mistaken me for WH Ridler.[159] He is a librarian and amateur printer and had sent me an example of his work.

❦

28 June, Monday

I started keeping these notes a year ago today, and I shall stop on Wednesday, the last day of the month.

At 9 am I had Boyce down to talk over his side of the quarrel with Harris. He is obviously deeply hurt by the personal remarks made by H in his fury and frustration; and I can't help being intensely irritated that RR, who was in charge of the meeting, allowed them both to behave like that, with no attempt to control. I did my best to talk about reconciliation and what was necessary for it; but at the same time I had to spell out quite clearly that Harris *is* in charge of all the Composing

---

159 WH Ridler had a shop on the High Street in Oxford selling antiques.

Rooms, including the Reading Department. Boyce would like to be answerable only to me, and feels his job to be unique. He also feels that he is guardian of our 'purity' in the eyes of the world, and again I had to explain to him, tactfully, that this is my responsibility and not his. We were together for a good three-quarters of an hour, as I wanted to feel my way into the situation gently. The passing of time will do a lot, but I suggested to him that when Harris comes back next Monday (I gave him H's reason for going), the three of us should meet.

Another four manuscripts announced at the 11 o'clock CP meeting. Dan Davin is now recuperating from an operation on his arthritic foot and may be absent for another week. Not much else of moment came up at the meeting tho' CHR irritated me by giving as a reason for not using the text paper I recommended for Morison's Lyell Lectures that the editor (in this case the young John Nicoll) 'thought the illustrations would look better on the chosen paper' which is whiter. This is what always baffles me about Colin. He professes occasionally to want my advice yet invariably goes by what his own young people say as tho' they had all the experience in the world.

Lunch meeting to discuss the PA reports. We were in broad agreement on our attitude to the main recommendations, and I now wait on Elphick to make the next move. We also agreed that if the £10,000 odd can be found we would ask PA to revise the incentive scheme in the Bindery.

Uneventful managers' meeting in the afternoon. Mansfield gloomy about his workload, the others quite cheerful. I reported that Henderson had resigned as Mill Controller from 1 July and would henceforth act as Resident Consultant. Earlier CHR had told me the Mill prospects were increasingly gloomy and the Mill may have to close in the autumn. This is extremely depressing, because I'm in no position to take on more than a very few of its 300 employees, and there may not be many other jobs going in this district. A surprising number of the smaller mills have already been closed or merged with others since the beginning of the year, and the state of the paper trade generally is still depressed.

After this meeting I had in two apprentices, each with a parent to act as a witness in the rather elaborate signing-of-indenture ceremony established by Batey. One of the boys is a West Indian who is said by Mansfield to be doing very well. He was accompanied by his mother, quite a lively woman who smiled at everything I said, irrespective of its import. As it mainly concerned the weather there was little to smile about, but it at least helped to cheer us up.

❦

29 June, Tuesday

Had Fissenden, our chemist, in for a talk at coffee-time. I don't think we are working him hard enough which is a pity because he is quite an earnest fellow. RR thinks he could make an adequate successor to Boswell as paper buyer, and he may be right.

At 10.15 I was aroused to fury by Colin ringing through to ask me whether I had seen a letter from Bruno about my new web press. When I said no, he said he would come down with it. I really blew up when I read its contents, tho' my rage was compounded by the fact that he hadn't written direct to me in the first place. He is saying in effect that they can't decide on changing the size of *Hornby* without a great deal of research, they may want to print abroad etc, there was nothing in the new machine for them, and I shouldn't count on the dictionary for the new machine.[160] All this when my work on the project was started by London. I told Colin that there seemed to be complete lack of control at Ely House. He was by way of blaming Thompson, Bruno's production manager, but I cut that one short pretty quickly by pointing out that the pm's minutes all went to their seniors and the discussion had been minuted several times. And Bruno had said nothing against the project when I put it to FC. Colin retired baffled and said he would speak to Bruno at lunch...

---

160 Nevertheless the new web-offset press was eventually ordered for Hornby's *Advanced Learner's Dictionary* so that the Works at Walton Street could print the book in its new demy 8vo size. The machine was installed in 1973 and was capable of printing at a speed of 18,000 impressions an hour. It was used to produce a variety of Oxford reference books.

Spent the rest of the morning cooling down, working on my FC papers for the afternoon meeting, and preparing a new estimate for the new edition of *SOED*.

FC after lunch. Very long and heavy agenda, and mostly gloomy, with losses, losses all the way – the CP, Cartographic, New York, the Mill. My own report sounded quite cheerful. George Richardson spoke up well, as usual, so did the new 'outside' merchant banker, whose name escapes me as I write. Bruno made no mention of his letter, in fact we exchanged not a word, and he went off immediately after the meeting. Funk probably.

The chairman remarked that for this financial year they could only rely on London and the Printer to make any profit. This is probably true, unless my costs go up steeply in the next 6 months or work falls off again. I think one of our troubles just now is that we have no new big moneymaking books about, unless the *Compact OED* at £28 a time does the trick.

☙

30 June, Wednesday

More good work in for both Composing and Litho, and not all of it wanted in a rush. At 11 o'clock I walked over to St John's with CHR for the Sales Conference and lunch. On the way I told him again what I thought of London's extraordinary behaviour over the web press and how put out I was that Bruno had written to him and not to me. He said that *he* had been surprised at the last, and also that he 'got the impression' (tactful phrase) that delegation at Ely House was not all it might be.

The Sales Conference was held in the JCR, with CHR, Bruno and myself occupying a rather too lofty platform in an annex at one side. The travellers were more cheerful than I had expected, but not all the staggering price increases on the more recent books have seeped through to them as yet. There was some talk of cheaper printing for the very low-sale but important monographs of the simpler kind, which I took part in. The university bookseller at Leicester gave a not v stimulating talk on trials of a bookseller faced with ever-increasing costs. We then went over to the Hall for lunch and I came away immediately afterwards.

Sidney Street, our Bible manager, came in with Skelly at 4.15. He too seemed v cheerful, and if all his present plans go through we shall have a mass of setting and printing to do next year, if not before.

In the evening went with A to see Burt Lancaster in an indifferent Western called *Lawman*.

This now ends my year's stint as a diarist. I have not re-read any of it while I was writing and I expect that it is full of repetition and non-sequiturs. But at least it may give some idea of the sort of problem one has to deal with, and of the people one meets. I can't really tell whether it does or not until I have read it right through, and even then I shan't know how much I may have left out that would have given a more complete picture.

I can't resist recording a remark made to me this afternoon (1 July) by Harry Carter. We were having lunch with Charles Batey, RR and JH before the pensioners' party. I told the company that Arnold Prosser would not be coming because he had been knocked off his bicycle. There was a pause, and then Harry said, in his quiet, deliberate way, 'I'm sorry he's been knocked off his bicycle, and I'm glad he's not coming'...

6pm FINIS 1 July 1971

MY LAST YEAR AS PRINTER
1977-1978

2 October, 1977

s my last year in office has now begun, I think it may be worthwhile to make a few notes of what takes place as I go along. My successor, Eric Buckley, has been designated. He is to take over not only the Printing Division but the Publishing Production Division, or section, as well. George Richardson, the Secretary, has always been anxious to draw the printing and publishing parts of OUP more closely together. The intention is good, and Buckley should be in a strong position to bring it about, because he is already in charge of the publishing production. The publishers are disgruntled because they feel that they are being downgraded. My people, from what I hear indirectly, feel that the same thing is happening to them; but my directors are quite ready to accept EJB, although I think several seniors expected Richard Russell to be given the post. This is what I would have preferred, but knowing the views of the Delegates on the Finance Committee, I thought it better to support EJB's nomination rather than an outsider because he is already in his late fifties. When he retires RR should have a good chance of succeeding. He will be that much older, and I have asked both the chairman of the Finance Committee and the Secretary to consider him favourably when the time comes. Much will depend of course on EJB's own assessment of him. They are friendly enough, and I doubt whether EJB will have any reason to stand in his way. RR himself was disappointed, naturally. But I had told him earlier that because of the consultants' adverse report on him a few years back, he would have to prepare himself for a disappointment. He has taken the news well, as I knew he would. The trouble with EJB is that he says very little unless pressed, and not very much then. His experience is mainly in Publishing, which could help the Printing Division to get more OUP work. He is also calm in judgement and not easily ruffled. His memoranda, rare through they are, are usually well thought out and expressed. On balance I think the Works will come to accept him fairly quickly, whatever current attitudes may be.

❦

10 October, 1978

As this date shows, I failed miserably with my intention to record my last twelve months as they passed, and I must now try to put down some of the main events as they occur to me. This year, of course, is our so-called Quincentenary Year.[161] A committee was formed, chaired very well by Elizabeth Knight, who had recently become Robert Burchfield's[162] second wife; and far too many projects were put in hand. Those mainly affecting me and my Division were the two histories. One, a catalogue of sorts to go with a travelling exhibition, was done by Nicolas Barker, and heavily illustrated;[163] the other, a short history written by our residing cynic, Peter Sutcliffe.[164] Barker, running true to form, drove me to distraction with the casual and intermittent way he went about things. What he wrote was, as always, very good, but everything was done to suit his convenience, not ours. In the end, producing the books developed into a mad rush, with New York panicking for copies in time for the exhibition opening at the Pierpont Morgan Library in March.

---

161 Strictly speaking the 500th anniversary of the first book to be printed in Oxford, not of Oxford University Press itself, which dates back to 1585.
162 Robert Burchfield (1923-2004) was Chief Editor of the *Oxford English Dictionary* 1971-86.
163 Published as *The Oxford University Press and the Spread of Learning* (1978).
164 Published as *The Oxford University Press: An Informal History* (1978).

Nicolas was supposed to have organized the exhibition itself for his £5000 fee plus expenses; but if I hadn't called in aid Roy Bowditch, who immediately got to grips with the problems of packing, transport, and security, nothing would have been ready on time. By contrast, Sutcliffe's book went through quite smoothly.

One minor typographical point concerning the Sutcliffe book is just worth recording. I was asked to plan it on the basis of a very long manuscript. I therefore decided on Monophoto Times – which can pack a lot into the page in a relatively small size of type – a fairly long line, and fairly tight margins. The manuscript came in piecemeal, and we started to set. When the final sections arrived it became obvious that the extent would be less than half we had been told to expect. I could have gone to a much more open, lavish, and elegant-looking page if I had known this beforehand. Another maddening thing happened which also made me very cross. Unbeknown to me, the Filmsetting Section decided to set the text on our latest Monophoto keyboard and setter, which is equipped with a version of Times for use in setting mathematics. This contains what to my eye are degraded sorts designed primarily as symbols. The result to the connoisseur is a mealy-looking page which I found depressing. If time had allowed I would have reset, but we had gone too far. But it means that I can't now open that book with any pleasure.

For a final spree, I took Anne to New York for the opening of the exhibition.[165] After all, it was supposed to be celebrating Oxford printing and I felt strongly that I should be there to represent my lot among the bevy of publishers. Harold Hugo had very kindly arranged for us to stay at the Yale Club, which was comfortable as well as conveniently placed for the Library and the NY office. George Richardson stayed at the Harvard Club on the other side of 5th Avenue. NY had gone to town with their publicity. I could only hope that the vast expense sold a few more books, but I doubt it. For the Press show the public relations boys had produced an enormous cake with 501 candles aboard,

---

165 See 'A Letter from New York' that follows this last Diary entry.

designed more or less to look like the Walton Street buildings. Robert Blake, Byron Hollinshead, and GBR had the formidable job of blowing out the candles, which after a good deal of huffing and puffing they did. Peter Jay attended the evening reception and dinner in his role as British Ambassador, and made a short and pertinent speech which was well received.

Eric Buckley joined me, as arranged, on 1 April. I had cleared out, or partly cleared out, the first-floor room in the North House which looks out on to the Quad to serve as his office and that of his secretary, Mrs Susan Adams. Her arrival caused some upset among my staff because it quickly became known that her salary, at Neasden, was considerably higher than that of our secretaries including my own. A further aggravation was that she had been briefly employed in our Personnel Office by John Hall some years ago, and it was known that his opinion of her was not high. However, after the first ripple and gossip, no more was said or done.

I had arranged with EJB that he should concentrate mainly on Works matters in conjunction with Campling,[166] where he had most to pick up, and I would confine myself more to the sales side with Richard Russell. He began by going through the post with RR and myself, but after a few weeks he gave this up, perhaps because he felt it unnecessary. In fact he kept very much to himself, whether from shyness or for some other reason I cannot say. We had a few brief meetings, but he asked few questions and made few comments, which rather baffled me because, in spite of his taciturn but friendly nature, I had expected many more questions on the detailed running of the business. I came to the conclusion that he was really rather shy of me and would not attempt to begin making his number with the troops until I was out of the way. Such meetings as we had were usually heavy going for me because I had to make all the running. So much so that I tried an experiment. I had arranged for us to visit Fletchers, makers of our high-quality ultra-thin papers just outside

---

166 James Campling had joined as Production Director at the Printing House in 1972, when Richard Russell became Commercial Director.

Manchester. Church drove us and I decided not to start any conversation on my own account. Apart from a cheery exchange of good-mornings we travelled in silence – both there and back! Very odd. Of course he was still much preoccupied with Neasden and its problems, which were and remain considerable. He may have felt that he could not turn his mind to our affairs wholeheartedly until his responsibility for warehousing became nominal. He is more explicit and forthcoming on paper, and I was interested to learn on the grapevine that in the publishing offices he was known as 'Eric, or memo by memo'.[167]

Just after he joined me, a grand lunch – the great event of the quin-centenary celebrations – was held in the Codrington Library at All Souls. Harold Macmillan, the Chancellor, presided, and other guests included Callaghan, then Prime Minister, the United States Ambassador (*Kingman Brewster*), and Lord Davidson, Minister for the Arts. I was seated between these two, and was suddenly plunged into farce when HM rose and proposed the loyal toast. When I attempted to rise I found that Davidson's heavy chair was firmly planted on my gown. I attempted to straighten up: there was an ominous tearing sound. Rather than be stripped bare I therefore remained bowed low over the table, apparently to the casual onlooker searching Isaiah Berlin's shirt for soup stains, or to the television cameraman trying to suggest myself as the ideal man to play the hunchback of Notre Dame should the BBC decide to serialize it. Mac of course made a brilliant impression out of nothing very much plus perfect timing, and honest James Callaghan did his honest Jack bit with bluff overtones.[168]

167 A reference to an obscure novel by FW Farrar, *Eric, or Little by Little* (1858), popular in mid-Victorian Britain, about the moral decline of a boy at an English boarding school.
168 The national newspapers reported that Callaghan recalled Gladstone's observation when visiting the Clarendon Press: 'mechanically wonderful, but how much more so morally!'

A LETTER FROM NEW YORK

YALE CLUB

Fifty Vanderbilt Avenue at Forty-fourth Street

New York, N.Y. 10017   *Monday a.m. 6 March 78*

Dearest Col.,

Well, here we are, in this extraordinary city. The Club is comfortable, just the sort of thing we like. It was maddening to be shunted off to Washington on Friday, altho' Br. Airways looked after us quite well, and the cabby bringing us from Kennedy Airport on Sat. afternoon said that cars trying to get to the city on the Friday were stuck bumper to bumper for several hours, the weather was so bad.

We have already been to the Museum of Modern Art and intend to go again as soon as we can fit it in. Splendid examples of all the great figures, naturally, including several studies and drawings for Guernica, which has a room to itself. I was glad to see a fine Andrew Wyeth, and an extraordinary study of minute shells on a beach by Ben Shahn. The sculpture garden looked v. romantic under its covering of snow.

Yesterday afternoon we walked into Central Park. Skaters were out, but in the Zoo alongside the rink only one solitary polar bear was padding and swishing to and fro to remind us that the place was inhabited. I don't know what they do with the other creatures.

In a few minutes we are going to the office on Madison. There we shall learn what plans have been made for us, so that we can fit our own plans into the scheme. I gather that the exhibition has been safely assembled. The catalogue, thank goodness, has been much admired. Tomorrow we dine with Mrs Astor at the Colony Club – N.Y.'s poshest. There's glory!

Love & blessings,
Pa

LINES TO A RETIRING PRINTER[169]

White limestone chunks from Flamborough Head
Whose curious eyes – deserted homes
Of immemorial creatures – now
Wink at me from the flower bed,
Remind me that the ceaseless cry
And whirl and sweep around the headland,
Turmoil of gull and auk and gannet,
Still goes on, though I'm not by.

So think, on pearly summer mornings
Tasting your freedom, think how still
The whirl and sweep goes on without you.
Tired committees gasp for air
While the Chapels issue warnings –
And you not there, and you not there!

Anne Ridler

169 From Anne Ridler, *Collected Poems* (Carcanet Press 1994) by kind permission of the publisher and Michael Schmidt.

APPENDICES

Salutations by Vivian Ridler to Friends and Colleagues

Appendix 1

Foreword to John Ryder's *Printing for Pleasure*

For the revised edition of this charming little volume, published in 1976 by the Bodley Head, Vivian Ridler contributed a Foreword, giving a glimpse of his own early days in the world of print.

You may notice that this book first appeared in 1955. I wish it had appeared thirty years earlier, when, like many other schoolboys, I was tempted and then caught by those famous Adana advertisements that were published so regularly in the back pages of *The Magnet* – or was it *The Boy's Own Paper?* – offering me the power to print anything 'from a chemist's label to an illustrated magazine'. An illustrated magazine! What vistas that opened up in front of me, what emancipation from the jellygraph and the John Bull outfit. But alas, reality was sobering. Printing is an intricate subject. The basic facts that with years of hindsight now seem so obvious I found exceedingly difficult to pin down. What exactly was a *fount* of type? Why were some letters called Old Style and other, spikier-looking ones, called Modern? Why weren't they all the same? And *furniture* ... heavens, what was I letting myself in for? As for the niceties of typography, or its history, neither the school library nor the local bookshop had anything to offer me. *Printing Explained*, by Herbert Simon and Harry Carter, was not published until 1931. From then on, as the list of books and periodicals included in this book will show, the information one needed gradually became more accessible.

John Ryder would have soon put me on the rails. His book is compact, brief, and deals with essentials. By essentials I mean not only the techniques of printing, assembling the type and transferring ink from type to paper. If you are a beginner, it is just as essential to have some knowledge of the art of typography, and you will find it set down here with enviable concision. The right use of space, of course, only comes with experience, with the training of the eye; but at least this book will make you aware that such a skill needs to be acquired if really satisfying work is to be done.

It would be superfluous to repeat advice already given so clearly in the pages that follow. But it is perhaps worth emphasising to the beginner that this book is about printing for pleasure. Once you are equipped with a press, however humble, and a case or two of type, the temptation to print for profit is very great. Pleasure and profit can indeed be reconciled, but if you wish to explore to the full the possibilities for experiment suggested here, and your time is limited, you will be wise not to saddle yourself with the orders of importunate friends. Printing five hundred letterheads on a table platen is not the most agreeable of pastimes.

Instead, therefore, I would urge you to ponder chapter six, 'Developing a Taste for Experiment', where, as the author rightly says, 'it is a pity that few private presses have concerned themselves with experimental techniques since it is here on the amateur's workbench (a place from which the time-sheet and the wage-bill are absent), that experiments can be made and repeated without end and without fear of bankruptcy'.

And so be guided by Ryder. He will not let you down.

Appendix 2

Address at the Funeral Service for John Hall

As recorded in the Introduction, John Hall, the Printing House Personnel Manager (later Director) and my father Vivian Ridler's right-hand man, died suddenly on 21 November 1974. The Service of Thanksgiving was held in the University Church of St Mary's on 14 December 1974, conducted by the vicar, the Revd Ronald Gordon. The Address was given by the Printer:

We have come here today to honour the memory of John Hall, who until his death some three weeks ago had served the Press of this University for over twenty-seven years with rare and single-minded devotion.

Actions speak louder than words. This well-worn proverb, in some contexts so trite, sums up the man. He was not particularly at ease with words, whether in speech or on paper. But when it came to doing something, to solving a problem, breaking a deadlock, helping the sick, rebuking the transgressor, John would be there, and he would act. To be at hand when he was needed, that is how he saw himself: he would never turn away from any problem, however daunting, or refuse an appeal for help, however trivial; and his help would always be given without ostentation or self-advertisement.

Before the war, John had learned his trade in Oxford with the Church Army Press. After distinguished wartime service with the Royal Air Force he joined another printing house in Wales, but wishing to enlarge his experience he eventually wrote to my predecessor, Charles Batey, who had not long taken office and was then building up his staff. Batey, sensing his quality, made him his personal assistant, and it was in that role that I first knew him when I joined the Press some twelve months later, in the spring of 1948.

The intense concern shown by this rather shy, reserved man for the well-being of others made an immediate and deep impression on me, and I was not surprised when, in the autumn of 1948, he was appointed to a post new to the University Press, that of Personnel Manager.

John may not have been aware at the time of his appointment that the care and training of apprentices and other young people was to become one of his most rewarding interests. It was, I think, through Charles Batey's own involvement in establishing a national apprenticeship authority that this came about. At any rate John threw himself into this work with his characteristic tenacity, and very many young people must have passed through his hands during the seventeen years in which he served as secretary to our own local apprenticeship committee. His influence of course was far more than local: his advice was sought by our national Federation, by the Institute of Printing, and by technical colleges; and when the Training Board for the industry was formed in 1968 it seemed inevitable that he should serve upon it.

Perhaps I can best convey to you the impression he made in the educational world by quoting from a letter I received last week from the head of a college printing department. He wrote 'In all my contacts with training and personnel managers I have never known anyone who took such a deep personal interest in the development of young people undergoing their education in college and industry. John Hall was outstanding in his integrity and dedication, qualities which have been an inspiration to me.'

This tribute was well deserved, although I suspect John would have been embarrassed to read it. This brings me to another aspect of his character. With all his compassion and concern for others, there was no trace of sentimentality in his make-up. It is fair to say that John's essential kindliness persuaded him to suffer fools quietly, if not gladly; but he was a man of strong will, with a strong sense of what used to be called right and wrong; and if he was as harmless as the dove – as indeed he was – neither did he lack, if I may slightly misquote the scriptures in this place, the shrewdness of the serpent. It does so happen, however regrettably, that in the field of industrial relations voices are sometimes raised and tempers sometimes lost; and John, in his determination to be both firm and fair, could lose his temper with the best.

He was not given to the easy concession for the sake of peace and quiet. I well recall a doughty and disgruntled member of the Press, having as he said 'got nowhere with Mr Hall', coming to me no doubt on the sound trade-union principle of the higher the softer, and prefacing his case with the observation that 'the trouble with Mr Hall is that even when he opens his hand there's nothing but moss in it'. John enjoyed dining out on that story.

To his other duties as Personnel Manager, and later as Personnel Director, he brought the same seriousness of purpose and unceasing vigilance, whether it was to do with the Housing Association, the Athletics Clubs, or visiting the sick and the pensioners or their dependants. His inability to refuse any call for help, however remote, gave him little time for his own pursuits, particularly in later years. He enjoyed cricket and was sufficiently enthusiastic to become a member of the MCC. But perhaps his greatest love was choral music. As a boy he had been a diligent member of the choir of St Michael at the Northgate and throughout his life he seized the opportunity whenever he could of singing with a number of college choirs. He was, as many of you will know, a staunch member of this University Church, both as chorister and sidesman, and in this Service of Thanksgiving we are singing some of the music that he loved so much.

With the death of John Hall we have to reconcile ourselves to the loss of a fine man and a steadfast friend. He was proud to be in the service of the University Press, and we are proud of him and of the memory he leaves.

Appendix 3

Brooke Crutchley as Printer

A salutation from a book of tributes, compiled by Euan Phillips, on the occasion of Brooke Crutchley's retirement as Printer to Cambridge University Press in 1975. Typeset in Monotype Barbou, the volume is beautifully printed on handmade paper at the University Printing House, Cambridge. The piece has been shortened somewhat.

In a reciprocal salutation, writing at the time of VR's retirement in 1978, Crutchley remembered remarking, when the new Oxford Printer was appointed 20 years before, that 'he came nearer to the ideal man for the job than anyone I had known, and the respect in which Oxford printing is held today is proof of how right I was.'

Brooke Crutchley succeeded Walter Lewis as Printer in 1946. At that time we hardly knew each other, although we had a nodding acquaintance as members of the Double Crown Club. Then, in 1948, I went to Oxford. Not long after I had been there Charles Batey suggested that I visit Brooke to learn something of the 'payment-by-results' scheme he had recently introduced to the Printing House with the help of consultants.

That was for me the beginning of a close and lasting friendship. Looking back, I think the most telling impression he made on me at the time was the extreme openness and frankness with which he discussed his plans and the problems that beset him, coupled with a modesty of expression and an underlying conviction of the soundness of his views – a conviction of course not unknown among Cambridge men. None of the many meetings we have since enjoyed has done anything to modify that impression.

Incredible though it may now seem, in those days wage negotiations raged around the payment or non-payment of an extra five shillings a week, amid cries from one side that any concession whatsoever would cause the state to totter, and from the other that the masters – that notoriously hard-faced bunch – were intent only on holding down the living standards of the workers. A payment by results scheme acknowledged, in an admittedly rather rough and ready way, the interests of both parties. There were cynics and sceptics: if you could get an increase in output of a third or more, what on earth had the management been doing, and so on.

But slowly these schemes gained acceptance, not least because they also provided management with a clear and orderly presentation of costs and outputs, and their use in the printing industry is now widespread. That this is so can be ascribed, in large measure, to the foresight and initiative of Brooke Crutchley.

In 1948 Brooke became President of the East Anglian Alliance of the BFMP, which again gave him direct influence upon the industry's affairs. Then in 1951 he became chairman of the Federation Book Printers' Section. In its early days this body had been much stimulated by Richard Clay and Mark Clowes, who used their incomparable old-boy network as a means of knocking some sense into book publishers. To this arduous and daunting task Brooke was also well suited, and I well remember how the Section continued to flourish under his guidance. Some years later the Bookbinders' Section, partly because of a semi-theological argument on the alleged difficulty of separating a 'pure' binder from the more benighted sort, was combined with the printers' section to become the Book Production Section, to which Brooke continued to give his active support.

The Institute of Printing was launched in the autumn of 1961. Brooke was one of the founder members, and we both served for many years on its Education and Training Committee under Charles Batey's chairmanship. Brooke became vice-chairman, and eventually succeeded to the chair.

Those in charge of the two University Printing Houses are not, as their best friends so often assert, free from the onus of making money, although the confusion is understandable, because it is widely known that University Presses regard it as part of their duty to publish many unprofitable books. Nevertheless, it is true that University Printers are sometimes faced with problems where commercial constraints are not the first consideration.

It is partly for this reason that I used to value so highly the semi-formal meetings between the managements of the two Presses arranged by Brooke and Charles Batey during the 1950s. They are now on a more casual and less formal basis, although equally valuable; and I like to flatter myself that the close relationship established by Brooke and Batey – in marked contrast to that of earlier years – continues to this day.

University Printers, with their great weight of inherited tradition, tend perhaps to be more cautious than others in rejecting the old and embracing the new, although I think this obtains more in matters of style than equipment. Certainly as far as equipment is concerned Brooke has done his share of innovation. I recall the development of the flexible plate and the liaison with Dawson, Payne and Elliott in the design of their sheet-fed letterpress rotaries for use in conjunction with it. He established the first case-bindery at the Press; and was quick to see the advantages to be had from a computer-based accounting system. From the lively arguments I have had with him over the last few years I also know that he has been intrepid enough to push out patrols into the treacherous minefields of computer-assisted composition.

This last brings me back to the question of style. When I read Nicolas Barker's dazzling piece, *Printing's Second Revolution*, in a recent issue of the *Times Literary Supplement*, and came to a passage on computer-setting where he states bluntly that 'hyphenation is a waste of time: …if a break is inevitable the word should simply be broken as it stands. Now that words are legible letters and unabbreviated, the delay in comprehension is minimal: the "right place" to break is a useless concept', I could see some force in the argument, particularly as I have learnt so quickly when reading newspapers to discern the meaning through a forest of misprints and misplaced lines. And yet…I cannot of course speak for Brooke, but knowing him I doubt whether he would be any more eager than I am to tear up our rules and rush to embrace such a doctrine. In fact I think he would be more in sympathy with Kingsley Amis who recently described in *The Listener* his attempt to persuade *Teachers World* (*sic*) to use that 'handy and harmless speck of notation, the apostrophe', only to be told that 'modern design reasons' had made it out of date.

This is not the place for any detailed examination of the typographic subtleties introduced into so many Cambridge books printed under Brooke's direction. . . . For Brooke, as I understand him, design means far more than the simple enjoyment of what is, or can be made to be, visually attractive. It means a constant striving for the lucid, the rational, the orderly, something inextricably bound up with one's daily life, as it was for William Morris, something that directs and sharpens purpose.

Nowhere is this more clearly shown than in the new Printing House planned and built by Brooke and his colleagues in the early 1960s. As he himself wrote in the handsome gift book describing it,

> The building represents a protracted and closely reasoned effort to provide the best possible conditions for the production of learned printing, much of it complicated and all of it demanding a high degree of accuracy and finish...Installed here too are some of the Press's treasures from the past, notably the actual punches from which the type for Baskerville's folio bible was cast; typographical equipment of the great private presses of Kelmscott, Ashendene, Eragny and Cranach; drawings and layouts of many recent masters of typography; and examples of fine printing. Such reminders of past achievement provide the best possible stimulus for an exciting future.

If Brooke were a less modest man than he is, he might with justice demand of his successors that when he is no more they should cause to be inscribed in the entrance hall of his new building those splendid, laconic words, 'Si monumentum requiris, circumspice'.

But my purpose is panegyric, not lament. And so, as I push Brooke quietly but firmly towards the centre of the stage, Diana at his side, and supported by all his friends and admirers, I pronounce over them this gentle invocation:

> So alway, drawing homewards, ye shall tread
> Your valley parted by a rivulet
> Which day and night shall flow sedate and smooth.

He will know where it comes from.

Appendix 4

Hugh Williamson: A Tribute

A warm tribute, on the occasion of Williamson's death in 1992, published in the Printing Historical Society's Bulletin *34 (Spring 1993). The demerits of Williamson's character brought out in the Diary happily give way here to an appreciation of his virtues and accomplishments.*

Towards the end of September 1992, Hugh kindly drove my wife and me over to Cambridge, to take part in the celebration of Will Carter's eightieth birthday. He was his usual lively and informative self, and there was no hint at the time that we were unlikely to meet again. His sudden death three weeks later therefore came as a painful shock: at first I found it hard to believe, particularly as we were due to have one of our regular pub lunches with John Robson of Blackwell's Scientific, when Hugh would bring us up to date with the progress of his manuscript on Garamond, a subject which seemed to fill his waking hours.

His pertinacity reminded me of those years during which he was preparing his remarkable and comprehensive work, *Methods of Book Design*, published in 1956. He was working in London at the time, but came to Oxford fairly regularly, so that after the Printing House had closed for the day, we were able to sit quietly in my office going through his typescript. I should add that, as I remember it, my comments were nearly all concerned with minor technical matters and not at all with the general plan of the book, which Hugh already had firmly mapped out in his mind. He had decided, for example, that the chapter on the purpose of book design should come at the end and not at the beginning, where most authors would have put it; and that the index should not be set in the more or less standard Oxford style, but according to a plan of his own devising, in which the catchword would be set in italics. It certainly made for clarity and ease of use, though I don't recall that we used the style for any other book.

As Nicolas Barker said in his admirable obituary for the *Independent*:

'Hugh's unaffected modesty reflected a universal kindness.' He was, to quote a phrase of Eliot's, 'precise but not pedantic', and his orderly mind showed at its best when he took on the editorship of the Printing Historical Society *Bulletin*. In fact, one might say that he *was* the *Bulletin*. Certainly the bulk of it was written by him. As he himself put it: 'So far, I have found it best to rewrite some contributions in my own words, and I have shortened some of the pieces drastically, in order to cover as much ground as possible... The effect of drastic alterations should not appear to be the responsibility of contributors, so I have included or excluded their names as I believe they would prefer'. He knew how many words went to a column, and he prided himself on writing to fit. And his words did fit.

Hugh continued as editor until the summer of 1988, when Iain Bain (who as the first Secretary of the Society issued the first Newsletter, as it was then called, in 1964) again took over for the autumn issue, to be succeeded by Montague Shaw and later, Steven Tuohy.

In 1961 Hugh had been elected to the membership of the Double Crown Club. He became its secretary in 1980, a job he took to with typical thoroughness. '...the Double Crown still takes up so much time', he wrote. 'Putting together a proper account book, compiling a new edition of the Rules, and bringing the Minute Book up to date took much of the summer, and since then I've written out a new Record Book covering the last five years. It is all interesting and worth while, and I took it on because it needed to be done, but it hasn't left me many free evenings for some time.'

In the years before his retirement Hugh was a director of the Alden Press, where he compiled and arranged a handsome specimen book of types available in that house for photocomposition. The succinct introduction is a model of its kind; in fact the whole work again expresses the clarity of his mind and his skill in arranging often complicated material.

In his valediction Hugh wrote: 'I shall be seventy this year, and I have other projects in mind to enliven my next decade. The first of these will be to write a doctoral thesis on a printing-historical theme, for which purpose I have enrolled in New College and the Faculty of Modern History at Oxford University.' He had already written extensively on Jean Jannon, 'the man who was not Garamond', in several issues of the *Bulletin*, and his doctoral thesis was, as I remember, to be based on those articles. I believe there are plans for its publication.

Good writers on the art of printing are few. Hugh Williamson was one of them, and it is sad to realize that we shall have nothing more from his hand.

OXFORD APPRENTICE

by Richard Russell

It seems appropriate to include in this volume a reminiscence by Richard Russell – a prominent figure in the Diary – of his time at the Press. The full version was published in Matrix 34 (Summer 2016) *and extracts are reproduced here by kind permission of the author and the publisher John Rundle of the Whittington Press.*

I WAS not to know that, when I reported to the porter's lodge of the University Press, Oxford in September 1948 to start my three-year shop-floor training (with my compositor's apron) that, in exactly thirteen years, I would be reporting to start as Works Manager (but in a collar and tie).

Charles Batey, Printer to Oxford University 1948-58, was much involved in training and he kindly took me on as a management trainee when I had asked for help when a member of the Marlborough College Press. It was a wonderful practical training, and a great experience to have been on the shop-floor of this fine factory of 900 people. There was kindness, leg-pulling and personal instruction from people with the greatest of skills and dedication using a great variety of methods and machines.

Three years spent working in the different departments at the Printing House included acting as Vivian Ridler's 'dogsbody on Printing at Oxford 1478-1951, our contribution to the Festival of Britain. We had 1800 visitors in a fortnight, with a unique chance to see one of J. M. W. Turner's Oxford Almanacks next to the copper plate engraved from it, and a print.' Russell then spent five years gaining experience at a commercial litho printer, Chromoworks in Willesden, and a further five years as Works Manager at Balding & Mansell. He records the subsequent story:

I was thrilled when Vivian Ridler, who followed Batey as Printer, asked me back to the University Press as Works Manager in 1961. My first challenge was to plan and organise the building of a multi-storey extension of 100,000 sq. ft. so that the two main publishing arms of the Oxford University Press could take over most of the 1830 Printing House. Meanwhile the technical development of the Press from the 1950s was considerable. While new hot-metal faces, such as Fournier, Van Dijck and Ehrhardt were added, Monotype reached its peak in 1976; incredibly it had gone within ten years, the matrices and keyboarding equipment finding a new home at Whittington. The two Linotypes went in the 1970s when the University took over printing its administrative work. Monophoto came in 1960, with that elegant face Photina.

In the letterpress department, a pair of Italian Nebiolos came in 1960. The larger Miehles were replaced in 1960 with a pair of sheet-fed perfecting rotary letterpress machines, with plastic stereos and Dycril plates. These Dawson machines, from the same stable as the earlier Wharfedales, lasted barely twenty years, being superseded by faster and better litho perfectors. Meanwhile for Crown Octavo work we had a letterpress web-fed rotary, with gas drier, which produced folded sections. All letterpress had gone by the early 1980s.

Litho machining, with its higher speeds and ability to print type and tone simultaneously, steadily took over from the 1950s. Unlike many other book houses, we had a litho tradition going back to the 1890s. Latterly we had presses from George Mann and Roland. While sheet-fed offset was economical, we put in three Timson web-offset presses with driers, changing as publishers successively enlarged their formats. The bindery staff decreased through mechanisation. Chamber and Dexter folders were replaced by Stahls. Foil blocking, with automatic case-making and casing-in, was automated. Thread-sewing was mainly replaced, not by so called perfect binding, but by slotted binding.

I suggest that by 1968 the University Press, with its old and new skills, was at its peak. Thereafter it was a matter of too many skills, and with our variety of customers and responsibilities impossible to be economical in all of them. The many parts of the OUP became free to place their work anywhere in the world. The one market in which we served the world, and very economically with our variety of skills, was as confidential printers for examination authorities, but the profit base was too narrow.

We may have grandly celebrated the Quincentenary of Printing in Oxford in 1978, but the writing was on the wall. The terribly sad, but inevitable, closure came in 1989. This mirrored what was happening throughout Britain's book industry. In our case it resembled the abolition of a proud village for a new reservoir. It was heart-breaking to have been involved at the end but wonderful to have been part of this uniquely long tradition of producing worthwhile work of the highest quality. Bookshelves across the world preserve the record.

VIVIAN RIDLER'S DAY

by Richard Russell

A Vivian Ridler day in the 1970s was comparable with that of his predecessor, Horace Hart, Printer to the University of Oxford in the early 1900s, even if times were so different.

Ridler got to the Press at 7.30 a.m. and would start with a tour of the factory. He said that often he would ask how things were going only to wish he had not. He might start with the Stewart brothers, Ken and Freddy, in Layout and Copy Preparation. He tried to see the Departmental Managers, chat with anyone, and look at work on machine.

Meanwhile the Correspondence Office prepared the inward post for him to sort at 8.30, and add comments. I would be alongside and then to his office to discuss any points.

His secretary for forty years, Pat Cox, would have been asked to summon anyone he might want to ask about how they and things were at 9.45. At 10.00 he chaired a daily meeting of senior staff based on the post and production matters. I stayed on, and John Hall (Personnel Manager) joined us. On Mondays the Secretary to the Delegates (the OUP's CEO), the Chief Editor of the Clarendon Press and their production manager came downstairs to go through their work. The Secretary would stay on alone with the Printer. Ridler would then deal with his post and get on with the day.

His visitors might include University Officers like the Proctors; customers such as members of the lofty Roxburghe Club; learned societies for whom we worked like the British Academy; and general ones like the British & Foreign Bible Society. Then might come our architect; organisations like the Master Printers (of which he became President) and the trade unions (reminding them he had been a member); and our machinery suppliers (like Hart, he was a good technician: they had both served an apprenticeship).

Special visitors were always welcome such as Stanley Morison (on the great *John Fell, The University Press and The Fell Types*); Valerie Eliot (on the fine typographic facsimile of TSE's *The Waste Land*); or Henry Moore (on an exhibition of his sculpture).

He finished about 5.30 p.m.

1913   2 October Vivian Hughes Ridler born at 13 Ilton Road, Cardiff, son of Bertram Hughes Ridler and Elizabeth, née Best. VR's sister Mildred Hughes Ridler born there 12 September 1911.

Humphrey Milford succeeds Henry Frowde as London Publisher of Oxford University Press.

1915   Frederick Hall succeeds Horace Hart as Printer to the University, Oxford.

1918   Aged five, VR moves to Bristol where his father has been appointed Superintendent of Avonmouth Docks.

Attends Bristol Grammar School.

1920   R W Chapman succeeds Charles Cannan as OUP Secretary to the Delegates.

1925   John Johnson succeeds Frederick Hall as Printer to the University, Oxford.

1930   Together with David Bland, VR sets up a printing press in the basement of Bland Senior's vicarage in Cotham, Bristol. Title: The Cotham Amateur Printing Guild. They print the parish magazine.

1931   New name chosen, The Perpetua Press, after the typeface designed by Eric Gill whom VR had met at Douglas Cleverdon's bookshop. Their first booklet, a *Note on Henry Irving's association with the West Country*, printed for the Coleridge Bookshop, Bristol.

1931   VR begins a special apprenticeship at the packaging printer E S & A Robinson, based in Bristol, where he acquires a Typographical Association union card.

1933   David Bland graduates from Bristol University, allowing him to spend more time printing.

1934   20 April VR's father Bertram dies.

1935   Perpetua Press publishes *Fifteen Old Nursery Rhymes* in an edition of 150 copies, illustrated by Biddy Darlow and set by hand in 24pt

Perpetua; chosen by the First Editions Club as one of the Fifty Best Books of the Year.

1936   *The Little Chimney Sweep* by Eric Walter White published in an edition of 300 copies, illustrated by the filmmaker Lotte Reiniger and set in Baskerville.

1936   John Johnson, Printer to the University, Oxford, lectures in Bristol and invites VR and Bland to visit his collection of printed ephemera at OUP in Oxford. Subsequently VR and Bland travel to Furstenach in Frankfurt to meet Paul Koch, son of Rudolf Koch, the famous designer and type cutter.

1937   In March VR leaves Robinson's to join OUP in Oxford, invited by Johnson to assist Charles Batey, the Assistant Printer. Bland begins work in the production department of Faber & Faber in London.

30 July VR meets Anne Bradby, niece of OUP's London Publisher, Humphrey Milford, and assistant to T S Eliot at Faber in London. They become engaged in the early autumn. Hearing of this, Johnson – antipathetic towards Milford – gives VR three months' notice.

1938   VR becomes manager for Theodore Besterman of the Bunhill Press near Old Street tube station in London.

2 July Wedding of Vivian and Anne at Little Gaddesden in Hertfordshire. They move into Anne's rented flat at 15 Taviton Street, London WC1. (The first of their children, Jane, born in 1941, Alison Kate in 1943, Benedict in 1947 and Colin in 1952.)

1939   In September, at the outbreak of war, VR and Bland join the Auxiliary Fire Service, watching for enemy aircraft at night while continuing with their previous work during the day.

1940   In September air raids on London begin; a land mine drops near their flat, damaging it, forcing V and A to move to her parents' house in the country. David Bland begins training with the RAF.

1941   In January the Bunhill Press takes a direct hit; later that month VR begins training with the RAF, subsequently being posted to Kirkwall in Orkney to help protect the Royal Navy base at Scapa Flow.

1942   Kenneth Sisam succeeds R W Chapman as OUP Secretary to the Delegates.

In October VR sails from Blackpool bound for West Africa.

1943   Serves with the RAF in Nigeria, first with a Belgian mobile fighter squadron building an air strip at Ikeja near Lagos, where he develops bad jaundice; then from late May in Signals at Kano in the north. (Both Ikeja and Kano were staging posts on the so-called Takoradi Route ferrying planes up to the North African front where the Allies were fighting Rommel.) Keeps a daily diary of his experiences throughout the year (published in 2022 as *War Diary of an Airman*).

In August David Bland's bomber shot down over Germany; he is made a prisoner of war in Stalag Luft III.

1944   VR returns to Britain in May.

1945   Intelligence officer from the autumn, posted to Germany over the winter to supervise de-militarization in the Ruhr.

In September David Bland resumes work at Faber, now as Head of Production, after two years as a prisoner of war.

Geoffrey Cumberlege succeeds Humphrey Milford as OUP London Publisher.

1946   VR demobilized in June. Takes on freelance design work for Lund Humphries and George Weidenfeld's *Contact* magazine, also redesigns *The Burlington Magazine*; appointed, part-time, the first Lecturer in Typography at the Royal College of Art. The family live at 54 Southway, London NW11.

Charles Batey succeeds John Johnson as Printer to the University, Oxford.

1948   VR publishes article in *Alphabet and Image*, No. 6 (January 1948) on Victorian 'artistic' printing. On 1 April rejoins Oxford University Press as Works Manager, under Charles Batey as Printer. Moves with the family to 14 Stanley Road, Oxford.

A L P ('Thomas') Norrington succeeds Kenneth Sisam as OUP Secretary to the Delegates.

1949   21 June VR made Assistant Printer.

1951   Organizes exhibition *Printing at Oxford 1478-1951*, held at the University Press as part of the Festival of Britain.

8 September Sails to New York on *RMS Caronia* with Gordon Taylor, Press Production Manager; for nearly two months they

visit printers and publishers in New York, Boston, Cleveland, Chicago and Philadelphia. Meets Harold Hugo of Meriden Gravure Co. as well as John Begg and Ella Oelrich of OUP for first time. Keeps a diary. 27 October-1 November Returns home on the *Caronia*.

1953   Designs the Coronation Bible on which the Queen swears her oath in Westminster Abbey.

1954   Colin Roberts succeeds Thomas Norrington as OUP Secretary to the Delegates.

Harry Carter appointed OUP Archivist.

1955   30 November VR's mother Elizabeth dies.

1956   John Brown ('Bruno') succeeds Geoffrey Cumberlege as OUP London Publisher.

1958   VR succeeds Charles Batey as Printer to the University, Oxford; awarded the degree of MA by decree.

Faber publishes David Bland's magnum opus, *The History of Book Illustration*.

1959   National Printing Strike 19 June to 6 August.

1960   Monophoto machines introduced for filmsetting at the Press. First 12 Oxford Paperbacks published in the UK.

12 March VR flies to Toronto, where he meets Charles Johnson (son of John Johnson), head of OUP's Canadian branch, and over next month visits printers and publishers in Montreal, Cleveland, New York, Princeton, Philadelphia, and New Haven. 30 March Party held in his honour at Oxford Library, New York, with 45 printers, publishers, typographers, librarians, curators, authors, and journalists present. Keeps a diary. 6-11 April Sails to Southampton aboard the *Queen Mary*, as does Henry Fonda (though they don't meet).

1961   First letterpress web-offset printing machine installed at the Printing House. Publication of the New Testament of the *New English Bible*; 2 million sold in 2 months. The Library edition printed at the University Press, Cambridge, the Popular edition – designed by VR – at Oxford.

Richard Russell appointed Works Manager.

1962   Printing House working week reduced to 40 hours.

1963   First lithographic web-offset press installed.

1965   VR appointed Professorial Fellow of St Edmund Hall.

Output of exam papers reaches 12 million. OUP London Business moves from Amen House to Ely House. First computer installed at the Neasden Warehouse.

11 December Death of Mildred Ridler in Bristol. (During the war she had worked at Bletchley Park code-breaking centre, and at the BBC as a secretary to the young George Weidenfeld.)

1966-68   Construction of 100,000 square foot extension to the Printing House.

1967   Publication of Stanley Morison's *John Fell: The University Press and the Fell Types*, designed by VR. In May the Committee of Inquiry under Sir Humphrey Waldock appointed to 'investigate the function, organization, and operations of the University Press and its relationship to the University'.

1968   Annual production in the Bindery exceeds 4 million books.

Richard Russell appointed Assistant Printer.

In May VR elected President of the British Federation of Master Printers, to serve for one year.

Collotype Department closed. The John Johnson Collection (Constance Meade Collection) of Printed Ephemera transferred to the Bodleian Library.

1969   Annual BFMP conference held in June at the Imperial Hotel, Torquay, at the end of VR's term as President. A steam engine on the Dartmouth Light Railway during an outing carries a headboard naming it 'The Master Printer' in gold letters.

1970   19 January Death of David Bland.

New English Bible, now complete with the Old Testament, published; marked by a Service of Dedication in Westminster Abbey, attended by Anne Ridler as the only female member of the *NEB*'s Literary Panel.

Waldock Committee Report published in May. Dan Davin appointed Academic Publisher and Deputy Secretary to the Delegates.

29 June VR begins his Diary.

1971   1 January VR appointed CBE. Completes his year-long Diary on 30 June. In the same month, the John Johnson Collection of Printed Ephemera is displayed in a special exhibition that opens at the Bodleian Library.

Compact Oxford English Dictionary published in October.

1972   Printing Division created with its own Board: James Campling as Production Director, Richard Russell Commercial Director, John Hall Personnel Director and Gerard Frost Finance Director.

1973   Second lithographic web-offset press installed. Decision to close the London Business.

1974   George Richardson succeeds Colin Roberts as Secretary to the Delegates.

John Brown knighted. On 21 November John Hall collapses and dies at the entrance to the Press.

1975   Roger Elliott succeeds Jack Thompson as Chairman of the Finance Committee.

1976   London Business moves to OUP's newly expanded main office at Walton Street in Oxford. Harry Carter's *A History of the Oxford University Press*, Volume I published. VR publishes *Italian Prospect*, by Anne Ridler, at the Perpetua Press, handset in Bembo and printed on handmade paper in an edition of 75 copies.

1978   OUP Quincentenary celebrations: publication of Nicolas Barker's *The Oxford University Press and the Spread of Learning* and Peter Sutcliffe's *The Oxford University Press: An Informal History*; opening in March of a special exhibition at the Pierpont Morgan Library in New York; 5 April grand lunch in the Codrington Library, All Souls, attended by the Chancellor, Harold Macmillan, and the Prime Minister, James Callaghan; 11 May Quincentenary Service in Christ Church Cathedral; 23 June Quincentenary Ball in OUP Quad.

OUP Paper Mill at Wolvercote sold.

Dan Davin retires as Academic Publisher, succeeded by Robin Denniston.

VR retires as Printer in October, succeeded by Eric Buckley.

Special exhibition of VR's work held in Divinity School of the Bodleian Library.

1979 Resumes his private press work in earnest, using the Perpetua Press imprint for many books, notably those edited or written by Anne Ridler. The finest projects are printed letterpress in the garden 'printing house' at 14 Stanley Road, on a Cropper platen treadle press with text handset mostly in Bembo, and occasionally in Blado Italic or Arrighi Italic. In addition he continues to produce much printed ephemera and an annual Christmas card with a poem of AR's.

1980 26 March to 15 April Takes part as an extra in scenes filmed in Oxford for Mike Cimino's movie *Heaven's Gate*, and writes a vivid account of the experience.

Perpetua Press publishes exquisite small book of AR's poems of birth and infancy, *Dies Natalis*, handset in Bembo Italic and printed in 100 copies on mouldmade paper.

Sir John Brown resigns from OUP.

1983 Publishes most ambitious volume, *The Poems of William Austin*, edited by AR, handset in 18pt Bembo in an edition of 150 copies. Accolades in the press.

1984 *Mutiny on the Bembo*, by John Bell, handset in Bembo, 200 copies.

Hugo Brunner, then of The Hogarth Press, brings *Christmas Poems*, by George Mackay Brown, to the Perpetua Press, beginning a fruitful partnership with VR. It is published with wood engravings by John Lawrence, handset in Bembo, in a quarto edition of 100 copies, plus octavo edition of 750 copies.

1985 *Christmas Stories*, by George Mackay Brown, with wood engravings by John Lawrence, handset in Bembo, quarto edition of 150 copies, octavo 500 copies.

1986 *Selected Poems*, by Charles Williams (influential OUP editor between the wars), handset in Bembo, 130 copies printed for the Charles Williams Society.

1987 *Cosi Fan Tutte*, by Mozart, English singing version by AR, typewriter-set, 100 copies. Followed in 1991 by Mozart, *The Marriage of Figaro*, English singing version by AR, typeset by Neil Scott.

Magnus' Saga: The Life of St Magnus, translated by Hermann Palsson and Paul Edwards, with wood engravings by Kathleen Lindsley, 120 copies.

1988   Perpetua Press publishes six books, including:

Songs for St Magnus Day, by George Mackay Brown, with wood engravings by John Lawrence, handset in Bembo, 150 copies.

A Victorian Family Postbag, by AR, an account of her Bradby ancestors, set in Trump Medieval, issued to celebrate A & V's golden wedding.

Saint Frideswide, Patron of Oxford, by John Blair, filmset in Baskerville, 150 copies, with many paperback reprints.

The Poems of John Bampfylde, edited by Roger Lonsdale, set in Trump Medieval, 300 copies.

1988   Roger Elliott succeeds George Richardson as Secretary and Chief Executive of OUP.

1989   Closure of OUP Printing House.

The Guest from the Future, by Jon Stallworthy, a poem presented to Sir Isaiah Berlin on the occasion of his 80th birthday, handset in Bembo, printed on mouldmade paper and published by the Perpetua Press in an edition of 120 copies.

1990   *Shadows in the Water*, by Thomas Traherne, handset in Arrighi Italic, 100 copies printed on mouldmade paper: one of VR's most beautiful productions.

1991   *A Measure of English Poetry*, a short book of three essays by AR, composed in Palatino by Neil and Kate Scott.

1992   *The College Graces of Oxford and Cambridge*, compiled by Reginald H. Adams, composed in Palatino by Neil Scott: a bestseller for the Perpetua Press, with many reprints.

Brodgar Poems, by George Mackay Brown, with wood engravings by Paul Kershaw, handset in Bembo and Arrighi Italic, 125 copies printed on mouldmade paper.

1993   *The Graven Image*, by Clare and Robert Gittings, composed in Palatino by Neil Scott.

Exhibition of VR's work held in October at the Ruskin School of Drawing and Fine Art, Oxford, organized by Richard Wilson.

James Arnold-Baker succeeds Roger Elliott as Secretary and Chief Executive of OUP.

1994   *After Silent Centuries*, poems by Rowan Williams, composed in Palatino by Neil Scott, 500 copies.

         Latin in Oxford, compiled by Reginald Adams, composed in Palatino by Neil Scott, 750 copies.

         Exhibition of VR's work held in October at the Brynmor Jones Library, Hull, organized by Richard Wilson.

1995   *The Lord Lieutenants and High Sheriffs of Oxfordshire* by Christine Peters, with drawings by Sarah Blair, composed by Neil Scott.

1996   *Memorial Inscriptions in St John's College Oxford*, edited by Reginald H Adams, composed by Neil Scott.

1997   *Portraits in Verse*, chosen by Paul Gittins, composed in Palatino by Neil Scott.

         Monumental Inscriptions in All Souls College Oxford, second edition with translations and additions by M A Screech. First edition transcribed by F E Hutchinson, prepared for publication by Sir Edmund Craster, both editions composed by Neil Scott.

1998   Henry Reece succeeds James Arnold-Baker as Secretary and Chief Executive of OUP. Retires in 2009.

2001   AR appointed OBE; dies on 15 October at 14 Stanley Road, Oxford, aged 89, and is buried in Holywell Cemetery, marked by a stone inscribed with her words, 'Nothing is Lost, for All in Love Survive', lettering carved by Brenda Berman.

2004   Perpetua Press publishes *Memoirs*, by Anne Ridler, composed in Garamond by Neil Scott, 300 copies.

2008   To mark VR's 95th birthday, an exhibition is held at the Bodleian Library in December, displaying the many Christmas cards he and AR had received over the years from fellow printers and artists.

2009   11 January VR dies at 14 Stanley Road, Oxford, aged 95; his ashes are buried beside those of AR in Holywell Cemetery.

Further Reading

Nicolas Barker, *The Oxford University Press and the Spread of Learning 1478-1978* (Oxford at the Clarendon Press 1978)

Mick Belson, *On the Press: Through the Eyes of the Craftsmen of Oxford University Press* (Robert Boyd Publications 2003)

David Bland, 'The Perpetua Press', *The Private Library*, Vol. 3 No. 2 (Summer 1970), pp. 78-90

The Bodleian Library, *The John Johnson Collection: Catalogue of an Exhibition* (1971)

Harry Carter, *A History of the Oxford University Press* (to 1780) (Oxford at the Clarendon Press 1975)

Brooke Crutchley, *To be a Printer* (The Bodley Head 1980)

Roger Louis, Ed., *The History of Oxford University Press*, Vol. III 1896-1970 (Oxford University Press 2013)

Ruari McLean, *True to Type: A Typographical Autobiography* (Oak Knoll Press/ Werner Shaw 2000)

Stanley Morison, with the assistance of Harry Carter, *John Fell: The University Press and the Fell Types* (Oxford at the Clarendon Press 1967)

Anne Ridler, *Memoirs* (The Perpetua Press 2004)

Keith Robbins, Ed., *The History of Oxford University Press*, Vol. IV 1970-2004 (Oxford University Press 2013)

John Ryder, *Printing for Pleasure*, Rev. Edn. (The Bodley Head 1976)

Peter Sutcliffe, *The Oxford University Press: An Informal History* (Oxford at the Clarendon Press 1978)

University of Oxford, *Report of the Committee on the University Press*, Supplement No. 7 to the University Gazette, Vol. c (May 1970) (the 'Waldock Report')

Souces of Illustrations

The Editor is grateful to Sebastian Carter, Phil Cleaver, Anna and Ed Crutchley and OUP Archivist Martin Maw for considerable help in sourcing photographs. © Poppy Gaye, photo Bertl Gaye (courtesy of Anna and Ed Crutchley) plate 15; © Dona Haycraft (courtesy of Sebastian Carter) plate 14; OUP Archive, reprinted by permission of the Secretary to the Delegates of Oxford University Press *frontispiece*, plates 1, 4-12, 16 (© Brian Seed), 17-25; Ridler family archive plates 2, 3, 5, 26-31; © Deborah Wolpe (courtesy of Phil Cleaver) plate 13.

Index

in the Mesial...
...te again, and met...
Machine rooms, which...
...machine removal men were...
Front in to go through the auditors.
...period FC meeting with the auditors,
...one room at 2.30 was well attended by
...ugue represented the new auditors,
...) Cooper Bros. They did not knock their
...gh Chorley said that The arrangement
...us difficult to understand. He passed
...showing a new plan: This is certainly simpler
...ut, and was adopted without dissent. Coopers
Chorley was anxious to bring our presentation
to line with the Companies Act. He seems a
...smooth than his predecessor, which is something
...ition is rather hesitant and not always lucid.
...luting the chairman, tend to confess ignorance at
...nse of this. The V.C. was helpful in relating the
needs of Congregation. He is very much a political

...Playhouse meeting at 5.15.
...inner at St. John's, organised by CCMR to say farewell to
...ters who now go off the Delegacy under the new Waldock Pro...
...sided, and those present included Helen Gardner and Pro...
...next to me, with Hart on the other side. Bowra gave a...
...funny farewell speech, saying how skilfully and t...
...had been carried out. None of this pleased t...
...and made no comment later. The se...
...said a few sensible and unmea...
...and gave his usual teas...
...the heart when fer...
...ss and the ex...
...us, I fe...

At...
He...
62...
f...